consumer revenge

CONSUMER REVENGE

Christopher Gilson, Linda Cawley,
& Rick Schmidt

A Perigee Book

Perigee Books
are published by
The Putnam Publishing Group
200 Madison Avenue
New York, New York 10016

Library of Congress Cataloging in Publication Data

Gilson, Christopher C.
  Consumer revenge.

  Originally published: New York : Putnam, c1981.
  Includes index.
  1. Consumer complaints.   I. Cawley, Linda C.
II. Schmidt, Rick.   III. Title.
[HF5415.5.G54   1983]   381'.33   82-19066
ISBN 0-399-50709-4

First Perigee printing, 1983
Printed in the United States of America
1   2   3   4   5   6   7   8   9

acknowledgments

We'd like to express our appreciation to many people for their hard work and valuable insights. For making it happen, we're grateful to our agent, Peter Skolnik, and to our editor, Sam Mitnick, who labored mightily and effectively over the project. Thanks also to Paul Heacock, Ann Everds, Judy Linden, Rina Cascone, Phyllis E. Grann and Peter Israel at Putnam's for their contributions.

For creative inspiration, we'd like to thank Rosemary Samuels; Chris and Elda Nell Gilson; Gene Powers; Noel Frankel; Susan Eastham; Marjorie and Jennifer Samuels; Paul Donnelly; Gail Considine; Greg Oviatt; Mike Brown; Leon Schiffman; Alan Burstein; Lynn Michaels; Ted and Maureen Devlet; Don and Janice Turner; Faye and Randy Elkins; Randy and Jackie Fisher; Bob Petrocelli; Sol Stein; Scott Davison; Judy McMullen; Richard Rubin; Ellen Kingsley; Helen and Joseph Petes; Lee and Bill Schmidt; Cindy Presson; Andy Sandler; Sandy Cook; Danny Gauger; Noel Fales; Mark Hughes; Doug Hilbert; Mike Hash; and Glynn Owens. With special thanks to Cherie Miller of Type & Copy, New York City.

                                              Chris Gilson
                                              Linda Cawley
                                              Rick Schmidt

To Rosemary
CG

To my niece, Melissa, for her
fourth birthday (it's cheaper than
a pony) and to Scott, a vengeful
consumer, for his love and support.
LC

To my (poco) godson, Will Young
RS

contents

PART I

Have a
Nicer Day

1
consumer revenge

The Greatest Satisfaction You Can Have with Your Clothes On

We'll admit it here and now: Seeking revenge isn't one of the virtues most of us weaned on the Golden Rule have been brought up to admire, let alone follow as a systematic course of action. That's why the vast majority of consumer handbooks you'll find today either:

1. Catalog objective product and service information or help you avoid being taken in the first place, or

2. Outline strategies that may, after you've exhausted a litany of telephone calls, carefully worded complaint letters, and possibly drawn-out court appearances, afford you the "redress" of getting back what you lost in the first place. So after dedicating weeks or months to doing battle, you're rewarded with the princely sum of $39.50 to buy another toaster. That's redress. And for some people, it may be worth the effort.

This isn't a guide to the kind of shrewd homework you should do before venturing into the marketplace. Experience suggests that most of us don't really think about consumer frustrations until they happen and we need corrective remedies. And this certainly isn't a white-gloved text for pursuing simple redress. We feel that being granted a replacement product or your money back only satisfies when it comes after one indignant letter or phone call, accompanied by a heartfelt apology from those responsible for your troubles.

Unfortunately, the current state of human affairs isn't always amenable to fast and easy solutions. Your problem will most likely be shunted through a bureaucratic labyrinth of buck passing, broken promises, and generally debilitating indifference.

Don't Get Mad.
Get Even.

We believe that those nasty or negligent souls who drive lingering bats into your belfry should be made to suffer true retribution. And, judging by recent court decisions, so do some of the authorities charged with upholding your rights. For instance:

> After taking a vacation's worth of home movies, you drop off the film at a developing lab. They promptly lose your precious memories and, to express their sorrow, offer you a new roll of film as their standard compensation. Would you grudgingly accept the film and chalk up your experience to show biz? A Washington family didn't. They sued the lab for $7,500 damages and won. The Supreme Court of that state upheld their award, finding the lab's policy of limiting its liability to a new roll of film "unconscionable."

> You've hired a contractor to build a new house. But when you move into your happy home, it starts to behave like the Amityville Horror. Water drips mysteriously on your guests' heads. When you accidentally hit a light fixture with a broom handle, part of the ceiling falls down. To remedy the problems, construction workers move in and mill around like unwanted relatives. Would you consider yourself lucky to have the defects repaired at all? A Texas family tormented in this fashion wanted more. They sued the contractor and received three times the actual cost of $15,000 to put their house in order—plus a $5,000 award for "mental anguish" to settle their jangled nerves.

> You clutch your heart one day when a letter arrives stating that you've been turned down for auto insurance. Pursuing this undeserved rejection, you find that the insurer decided you'd be a careless driver on the basis of a credit report. So you undergo a steady diet of insomnia, anxiety, and time off from your job trying to persuade the reporting agency to disclose their information, which turns out to be neighborly gossip submitted as gospel by an investigator. Do you let the agency get away with a retraction? A Missouri man who was determined to share his sleepless nights with the credit reporters went to court and recovered $15,000 in compensatory and punitive damages for his troubles.

If you identify with those who've taken revenge on callous adversaries, you're not alone. Opinion polls reveal that most Americans today feel a deep and gnawing frustration. Among other sore points, they're tired of flimsier products that cost more, rude service people, tax-supported bureaucrats who sneer at their problems, and the like. But most unsettling of all, they feel powerless to do anything about them.

What did we ever do to deserve such angst?

The Roots of Our Discontent

Certain hassles have always plagued consumers. Problems with your landlord? Consider the harsher grievances that prompted organized tenant movements like the French Revolution. Your money doesn't buy what it used to at the supermarket? At least you're not trading wheelbarrows of it for a loaf of bread and hunk of sausage like the burghers of Weimar Republic Germany.

But let's confine ourselves to the past fifteen years or so: about the time people began noticing that things just didn't function as well as they used to.

Historian William Manchester traces the first rumblings of dissatisfaction:

> At some point in the 1960s, a man who had never run a stop sign did it. He was careful, nothing was coming; it was a silly statute, he reasoned; only robots obeyed it. . . . Though he overlooked the connection, he was annoyed because the attendant at his favorite filling station no longer checked his oil and cleaned his windshield unless asked. . . . At about the same time a door in his new car developed a hideous rattle; he dismantled it and found that some anonymous worker on a Detroit assembly line had left a Coke bottle in it. . . . Everybody had his horror story about the mails. Waitresses brought you somebody else's order. Your evening paper wasn't delivered. The druggist filled the wrong prescription . . . . Airliners were late taking off; because they didn't reach your destination on time you had to wait, stacked over it, and when you did land you discovered that your baggage had gone on to another airport. . . . Repairmen and sales-clerks were as bad, or worse. The fault was difficult to pin down, but it was everywhere. People didn't seem to care whether things worked any more. The discipline that knits a society together was weakening and at some points giving way altogether.

What had happened to American can-do? A number of forces conspired to bog down the machinery.

First came prosperity and egalitarianism, which meant that more people could enjoy middle-class status. Even plumbers and assembly-line workers bought pleasure boats and Chivas Regal. Unfortunately, our sights rose to the point that fewer people wanted unglamorous service jobs. If they had to take them, they didn't perform them in the traditional sense.

The twin cheerleaders of this new affluence were advertising and mass merchandising. As a greater volume of more affordable products was churned out, though, quality declined. Once-responsive companies multiplied into conglomerates and cared little about their customers. Government agencies mushroomed into the nation's number-one growth industry and cared even less about their taxpayers.

Then the seventies brought painful new twists—Watergate, South American–style inflation, and five A.M. vigils on gas-station lines. No wonder Tom Wolfe called it the Me Decade. We didn't just accept selfishness with a guilty conscience—we made it downright upright. If society had reduced our existence to a set of computer cards (programmed with varying degrees of carelessness) and everybody else was trying to exploit us, why shouldn't we devote our energies to looking out for number one?

Nasty Corporate Habits

The business-as-usual, institutionalized variety of self-interest today costs you plenty, whether it is practiced by business, professionals, or the public sector. John F. Kennedy's famous statement "All businessmen are S.O.B.s" isn't entirely true. For one, he forgot to include businesswomen. And second, the great majority of businesspeople aren't villains at all.

Decisions for the "corporate good" are often made in the anonymous, peer-pressured environment of committees that march to a different set of ethics than the same participants would follow as individuals. So good old Bob, the next-door neighbor who'd give you the shirt off his back, could turn around and indirectly pick your pocket as a corporate officer who helps approve a deceptive advertising campaign or shoddy product design.

To gauge how widespread unsavory business practices really are, ponder how many of our largest blue chip corporations have been caught in misdeeds. Of 1043 major companies traced in a recent *Fortune* magazine study, 117 or 11 percent were involved in serious domestic offenses over the past decade alone— such as price fixing, fraud, and antitrust violations.

Among those corporate delinquents are household names like Gulf Oil, Greyhound, 3M, Mattell, Seagrams, Uniroyal and U.S. Steel. (As one ironic note, Frito-Lay was charged with fixing the price of their snack foods, giving new meaning to those ads of a few years ago featuring the Frito Bandito.) And those are *reputable* companies, not the fly-by-night outfits that survive on unscrupulous practices.

The Tyranny of the Experts

Another source of mischief in an age of complexity is the army of specialists we need to keep our lives in working order. Most of us don't know how to fix our own cars or coffee machines. We certainly can't perform appendectomies on ourselves. And we're even reluctant to write our own wills without consulting a lawyer, for fear we'll omit some legal password and doom our children to become wards of the state.

Auto repairpcoplc and coffee-machine specialists adhere to commercial standards of ethics, a fact that unfortunately speaks for itself. But learned professionals like doctors and lawyers are supposed to follow rigid codes of ethical conduct enforced by their governing associations. In practice, medical and bar associations have established a much better track record for protecting their members' rights to coin money than for purging incompetents or watching out for consumers.

Most doctors' practices today are very successful, high-volume businesses. In 1978, doctors' average earnings ranged from a low of $140,200 per year for incorporated physicians in private practice to a high of $153,250 for surgeons. Now, there's nothing wrong with skilled healers turning a hefty profit—until you find out how some of them squeeze extra dollars to pay their country-club dues. Ralph Nader's Health Research Group sets the number of *unnecessary* operations performed every year in the United States at 3.2 million, costing consumers and insurance companies $6 billion. Figure another $1.4 billion for unneeded X-rays.

Even a greedy doctor might envy an avaricious lawyer, whose local bar association could, until recently, fix minimum and exorbitant prices for members' services. These bar associations also lobbied for laws that mandate redundant but profitable busywork like the legal piñata of probate, which exists mainly to ensure that lawyers can grab off a sizable portion of your estate before your heirs get to see it. (In private, attorneys rationalize this practice because your heirs didn't have to work to earn their share, either.)

We'll have much more to say about our learned professionals later.

PUBLIC ENEMIES

But before you conclude that individuals in the private sector enjoy a monopoloy on self-interest, don't forget the public servants who are supposed to be watching out for your interests. We're not just talking about legislators who take bribes from phony Arab sheiks or vote their academic friends massive grants to study the sex life of horned toads.

In an era of institutional selfishness, you can't even count on paid consumer watchdogs. Sometimes they take their own bite out of your wallet—like some of the investigators from New York's Consumer Affairs Department who were recently indicted for accepting payoffs from store managers while checking meats at food stores.

J.R. AS ROLE MODEL?

Some cynics argue that in the face of such rampant greed, negligence, and incompetence, we're fresh out of national heroes. But anybody who follows the popular "Dallas" series on TV knows better.

Will Rogers apparently never met a man named J.R. Ewing. Not even J.R.'s own thick-skinned family can stomach his meanness. Yet at a time when many Americans feel helpless to deal with daily frustrations, J.R. seems to draw a sneaking admiration from "Dallas" fans for having his way with just about everyone. We'd bet there isn't an auto mechanic in the state of Texas who'd dare to give J.R.'s Mercedes shoddy service. And woe betide the salesperson who doesn't snap to attention when he breezes through Neiman-Marcus to return a dozen gold watches.

Most of us lack the family fortune and armadillo hide to throw our weight around like J.R. That's why most of us could use some powerful strategies for righting wrongs to our satisfaction. And that's where this book comes in.

Although we've been stabbing our fingers at some of America's ugly warts here, we don't think that our system is corrupt, unworkable, or on its last legs. Nor do we think that anyone should arbitrarily adopt a fangs-out approach to life.

We believe in the system. But we also believe it could work a lot better if people were held accountable for providing the products and services they're supposed to and for treating one another with greater consideration. That also holds true for the neighbor who blasts her rock records through your living-room wall or the friend who borrows money from you and "forgets" to pay you back.

LIVING WELL IS STILL THE BEST REVENGE

So the purpose of this book isn't limited to exacting revenge for the thrill of it (although, to be honest, it can feel terrific to rest your foot squarely on the neck of someone who's made life difficult for you).

EXHIBIT 1-A

A STREET-WISE BUYING SAMPLER

We recommend these sources to help you make informed buying decisions and dramatically reduce your risk of getting into trouble.

Start with a subscription to *Consumer Reports*, published by a nonprofit organization that coldly evaluates products and services, rates them for you, and alerts you to problems. (Write to Consumers Union, 256 Washington Street, Mt. Vernon, N.Y. 10550.)

To find out what products to buy, arranged by category, refer to the *Consumer Reports Buying Guide* (published annually by Consumers Union).

To find out where to buy them at the best price, consult *The Guide to Discount Buying* (Consumers Digest, 5705 N. Lincoln Avenue, Chicago, Ill. 60659).

And for overall strategic advice, see John Stossel's *Shopping Smart: The Only Consumer Guide You'll Ever Need* (G. P. Putnam's Sons, 200 Madison Avenue, New York, N.Y. 10016) and the *Consumer's Marketplace Encyclopedia* (American Consumer Publications, Inc., 310 East 46 Street, New York, N.Y. 10017).

These guides are all available in paperback and can be ordered through any bookstore.

Our objective is to help you diffuse everyday problems as quickly as possible with a swift, surefooted response that lets people know it's in their best interest to make sure you get satisfaction. And when you confront adversaries who seriously want to take advantage of you, to impress upon them that they'd be better off picking on somebody less capable of a good offense.

You don't have to be an overly assertive ogre to use the strategies introduced in the following chapters. Most of them just involve following step-by-step instructions on what to say and what to do and taking advantage of special knowledge you'll possess that will give your adversaries pause. All the necessary forms are included in the Revenge Kits at the end of each chapter, as well as addresses and telephone numbers of the right people to contact when you need extra help.

So prepare your revenge arsenal carefully and start going after retribution instead of halfhearted redress. Then you can spend more of your time and money enjoying life. And that is the best revenge of all.

2
your revenge repertoire

What to Say and What to Do

Basically, the strategies you'll find throughout this book fall into four categories: (1) Coercive Tactics, (2) Preemptive First Strikes, (3) Righteous Whistle Blowing, and (4) Crafty Legal Maneuvers which you can usually perform without spending money on a lawyer. We'll also discuss some scruffy guerrilla tactics, and let your conscience be your guide to applying them.

Each type of strategy has its time and place. Some adversaries may cave in after a few well-chosen words. But many people who feel it's in their interest to foil you are accustomed to brushing off indignant consumers. And they'll treat your polite complaints and now-listen-here letters with yawning disinterest.

Most of the larger, organized adversaries who give you problems have also been in court before. Car dealers or appliance-store managers won't cry for mercy just because you threaten to sue them for your money back. They have little to lose in the normal course of redress. After you've worn yourself into a frazzle fighting them, the worst they can expect is a court order to give you what they were supposed to in the first place.

So the remedies here draw on creative, unexpected revenge strategies as well as purely legal maneuvers, which emphasize placing the responsibility for hassling on your adversaries. For each category of frustration, we'll recommend a sequence of attack to help you reach your objectives by the most direct, least energy consuming route.

COERCIVE TACTICS

These ploys are useful because they undermine a major source of resistance to getting satisfaction. People maintain psychological defense mechanisms to protect themselves from coming to terms with their own unreasonable behavior. Adversaries tend to rationalize whatever selfish or obstructive act they're committing by truly believing that you're wrong and they're right. That's why, after you've tried to reason with unhelpful salespeople, they roll their eyes and tell their colleagues about the "obnoxious" customer they had to deal with.

Coercive maneuvers avoid this problem by skirting the issue of right and wrong. Instead, they force adversaries to make choices that usually result in you getting your way. Sometimes you'll leave them no choice at all. Two simple examples are:

Forcing Collateral. Say that one of your neighbors borrowed fifty dollars from you several weeks ago and, despite a few hints you've dropped, hasn't broached the subject of paying you back. Now, many people who won't repay that kind of debt are spendaholics and permanent residents of Tap City—although they'd like to pay you back, they're forced to juggle your due against the utility bill and car payment. And since they know you can't shut off their lights, they'll probably just pay their other bills first and hope to get to you next week.

So instead of asking for your money back and embarrassing both of you, seize collateral more valuable than the debt in a neighborly way. Tell him, for instance, that you want to make guacamole and would like to borrow his two-hundred-dollar Cuisinart food processor "over the weekend." He's hardly in a position to refuse or to ask for it back until his debt is paid. In the meantime, hold the Cuisinart and experiment with gourmet treats.

The Greater Evil. Maybe you've run into a situation where some person of limited authority (and imagination) quotes "company policy" or "regulations" to thwart you. For instance, you've come late in the day to a distant branch of your bank that stays open on Friday evening to cash a check for the weekend. Sorry, the teller says. They can't cash it because your signature card isn't on file. Next customer, please.

So you see one of the bank officers, who recites the same policy about no checks cashed without a signature card, "for our customers' protection." In response to this doggerel, point to your checkbook that clearly shows you're a customer of the bank, no matter what branch, and produce the personal identification that says you're you.

Then announce that your closing out your account, since you refuse to do business with a bank that won't provide the branch services it advertises. Nor will you leave the bank until you receive the cash balance in your account. This is your legal prerogative. The officer knows it. She grasps The Greater Evil. It is far less painful for her to cash a hundred-dollar check than to grapple with the legal and public-relations tar baby you've created: first, her denying a customer the right to close an account, and second, the possibility of having to call the police to remove you from the bank. Those aren't the kind of scenarios that solid banking careers are built on, and you're now almost certain to get your check approved.

PREEMPTIVE FIRST STRIKES

There are more rough-and-tumble methods of dealing with real problem individuals, such as contractors who make promises they'll never keep or people who try to absolve themselves of any responsibility for shoddy products and services they sell you. These are the winning personalities who leave you choking with frustration, because once you've been wronged, you seem to have little or no opportunity for recourse.

The secret here is to outflank their best efforts by striking first. For instance, let's look at two different responses to a typical consumer problem—one a self-defeating nonstrategy with a predictably disappointing outcome, and the other a preemptive strategy that forces the desired results.

Marianne just picked up a month-old white suit from a dry cleaner she had found convenient but not exactly noteworthy for impeccable or polite service. When she got the suit home and unwrapped it, she noticed dark stains on the pocket that weren't there before. So back she went.

MARIANNE: I just discovered these stains on my jacket . . .

DRY CLEANER: What stains?

MARIANNE: *These* here. They weren't here when I brought the suit in.

DRY CLEANER: We sure didn't put them there, lady. They look like the jacket was on the bottom of a dirty suitcase or something.

MARIANNE: [Frustrated] Well, could you just get them out, please?

DRY CLEANER: We'll try.

So far, Marianne has committed several tactical errors. She started with the assumption that the cleaner would be honest, own up to his own negligence, and resolve the problem to keep her business. She failed to establish definitively that it was the cleaner's fault. In fact, she let the cleaner as much as call her a liar when she told him the stains were brand new. And she left the suit in the cleaner's hands, which said, in effect, that she accepted his version of events.

The next day she returned for the jacket.

DRY CLEANER: We couldn't get that dirt out, lady.

MARIANNE: Oh, no, That's a two-hundred-dollar suit and I've only had it a month. Besides, I told you it must have gotten soiled when it was here for cleaning . . .

DRY CLEANER: How could it get dirty in our cleaning machines? Anyway, you should have put in a claim yesterday if you thought it was our fault.

Now Marianne has placed herself at the mercy of the cleaner and, at best, she will be compensated only to the "maximum liability" presented on the customer's ticket—usually ten times the cleaning charge, or thirty-five to fifty dollars. Meanwhile, her new two-hundred-dollar suit is ruined.

Now say that Marianne had applied a first-strike approach to the problem. Based on her previous experience with this dry cleaner, she should have started with the assumption that he would disclaim any responsibility and try to reduce his liability to the absolute minimum if she insisted on pursuing it.

First, she would have taken the suit to a second cleaner for an analysis of the dirt, which could probably turn out to be "redeposition" caused by the cleaner's failure to scrub his own machines thoroughly. She would have the second cleaner sign a statement to that effect, then copy it along with her original bill for the suit and the first dry cleaner's receipt. Next she would go downtown to the local small-claims court and fill out the papers necessary to bring action against the dry cleaner. (More about this shortly.) But she wouldn't file them quite yet. Then she would return to the cleaners with (1) her packet of documentation, (2) the court papers ready to file, (3) the jacket, which she's photographed to clearly show the dirt on the back as it came back the first time—and slap them all down on the counter.

DRY CLEANER: What's this?

MARIANNE: My new suit was soiled by redeposition from your machines when it was in early this week. Here's the jacket, the analysis, and the receipts. If you can't get the dirt completely out so the suit is good as new, I'm going to file this action against you for two hundred dollars. That's the replacement cost of my suit.

DRY CLEANER: Well . . . uh . . . we'll try to get this out. But we're not liable for more than ten times the cleaning charge anyway. It says so right on the back of your ticket.

MARIANNE: The "exculpatory waiver" on the back of the ticket doesn't protect you against claims for negligence in this state. And you were negligent in failing to clean your machines properly, which caused the redeposition. I have plenty of time to spend in court until I get justice in this matter.

Now it's the dry cleaner who's at Marianne's mercy. She's already proven, with documents likely to stand up in small-claims court, that the cleaner was at fault. She knows that the "limited liability" waiver on the back of the ticket probably won't absolve the cleaner's liability in this case. And she's obviously the kind of dedicated zealot who'll make trouble for him until she gets justice. So the cheapest way the dry cleaner can extricate himself from this mess will probably be to settle with Marianne for all, or most, of the replacement cost of the suit.

RIGHTEOUS WHISTLE BLOWING

Sometimes one consumer, no matter how feisty, fails to strike terror into an adversary's heart. Maybe a company knows there are enough meek customers around to keep them in business. Or the cost of giving you real satisfaction may be "prohibitive." (For instance, there are an estimated 10,000 incorrigible lemons ground out by American automobile manufacturers every year. If they replaced every thoroughly sour car the way other companies replace cheaper defective products, it would cost about $50 million per year.)

In such cases, it pays to know which regulatory or action groups you can call on for help. For instance, there's probably nothing more satisfying than leading a cavalry charge of the local TV news crew into some health club that's bilked you, with lights flashing and a stern reporter cornering your tormentor for an explanation. This is the stuff that vengeful fantasies are made of. On a less dramatic level, it's gratifying to receive a truculent phone call from some moving company that's only succeeded in moving you to tears offering a settlement because you've called the wrath of the Interstate Commerce Commission down on their shoddy practices.

But before you dwell too long on these glowing prospects, consider a few realities. First of all, most organizations set up to help you enforce your rights won't jump in until you've exhausted all the normal courses of redress—letters, phone calls, and so on. And they expect to see documented proof of your efforts to resolve the problem on your own. Second, even helpful organizations have special interests. The media crusaders like stories that make for exciting TV coverage or newspaper copy. The "coldlord" who shuts off your building's heat when the temperature's below freezing will usually incite reporters to saddle up before they'll investigate your inert popcorn popper. Finally, many federal and state agencies are losing some of their old-time aggression thanks to budget cuts and deregulatory trends—a trade-off between taxpayer revenge and consumer revenge. Even the mighty US Office of Consumer Affairs has moved away from handling individual complaints. Instead, they now publish a book you should get (for free), which directs you to other sources of help.*

This doesn't mean you shouldn't seek champions for your cause wherever

---

* The *Consumer Resource Handbook* is available by writing the Consumer Information Center, Dept. 532G, Pueblo, Colo. 81009. It's short on revenge but long on useful listings of whom to contact for help with most consumer problems.

you can find them. But you shouldn't leave it up to government agencies or private resources, many of whom are choked with complaints, to wrestle your opponents to the ground. You should use those helpmates judiciously and creatively to bring pressures to bear that you couldn't muster on your own.

Self-Regulators. To keep their wayward colleagues in line (and often to avoid government regulation), industries have established their own complaint-handling organizations.

First is the *Council of Better Business Bureaus* (CBBB), which includes member bureaus across the country. The council studies complaints within each industry to see how successfully they're resolved. The individual bureaus process written complaints against local businesses via a form you fill out called the Consumer Experience Report. Then they wait for the company to answer. What happens if nobody answers? Well, maybe nothing—it depends on how assertive your local office is, since the BBB has no legal authority. But it does include your complaint in "profiles" of individual companies' performance. Since careful consumers ask BBBs about these profiles before they buy, local businesses often want to keep their files as clean as possible. Some BBBs have recently ventured into the arbitration field, setting up panels to resolve complaints to mutual satisfaction. If you're a reasonable sort who wants to give your adversary every opportunity to behave, you can call your local BBB to see if they offer this service and whether the company you're fighting with is one of the twenty thousand that's agreed to be bound by BBB arbitration.

Some of the industries drawing the most complaints from consumers have established *Consumer Action Panels* (CAPs) for mediating them. Two of the major CAP programs are AUTOCAP for the automobile industry and MACAP for major appliances. UnCAPed industries also support their own watchdogs, from the National Advertising Review Board to the Photo Marketing Association's Consumer Affairs Department. (See Appendix I for a complete list.)

Media Avengers. Journalists can be formidable allies in making your adversaries squirm. What guilty businessperson or arrogant bureaucrat wants Mike Wallace of "60 Minutes" raising his accusatory eyebrows at them? And one journalist, Jessica Mitford, was single-handedly responsible for bringing the multimillion-dollar Famous Writers School to ruin after one consumer complaint, through an elegant dissection of its more lucrative than literary practices. Local reporters can be just as relentless when it comes to exposing and correcting injustice, but, as we said, you'll be most likely to intrigue them with a story that will rivet viewers, listeners, or readers. The broadcast-news business is, after all, show business.

But many local TV and radio stations maintain "action lines" to handle mundane complaints. And local newspapers often have columnists who tackle consumer problems and write up the results. Call the local Consumer Affairs office (listed in your White Pages under city or state government) and ask for the names of consumer reporters who've worked with them before.

Table 1.
The Golden Lemon Awards

The Most Complaints
(in descending order of frequency of complaints to Better Business
Bureaus)
1. Automobiles
2. Radio and Television Appliances
3. Other Major Appliances
4. Mail Order
5. Clothing
6. Telephone
7. Food
8. Household Items

For Settling Complaints

(The Best)	(The Worst)
1. Department Stores	1. Pseudo "Market Research" Companies
2. Banks	
3. Telephone Companies	2. "Work-at-Home" Companies
4. Insurance Companies	
5. Chain Food Stores	3. "Business Opportunities"
6. Credit Card Firms	4. Paving Contractors
7. Hearing Aid Companies	5. Electrical Contractors
8. Utilities	6. Franchise Selling Companies
9. Savings and Loans	
10. Encyclopedia Firms	7. Reupholstering Shops
11. Small Loan Companies	8. Legal Services
12. Drug Stores	9. Home Maintenance Companies
	10. Roofing Contractors
	11. Dentists
	12. Funeral Services

SOURCE: Council of Better Business Bureaus, 1980.

Consumer Cops. Your most reliable allies are likely to be the federal, state, and local consumer-protection agencies that can bring police powers to your cause.

Within the federal government, they range from the well-known Federal Trade Commission (FTC), which effectively spanks advertisers for making, say, cold-cure claims about mouthwashes, to such little-known regulators as the Commodity Futures Trading Commission (CFTC), which can penalize the broker who swindles you on hog-belly futures. (See Appendix III for a listing of the Federal Information Center nearest you.)

Federal agencies tend to be more concerned with mass-market consumer protection and thus focus on complaints that will affect the most people. In the final analysis, your individual problem will probably receive the most enthusiastic attention at a source close to home—state and local government agencies for consumer protection or a local attorney general's office. (See the White Pages of your phone book under city or state government, or Appendix II for Federal Information Services.)

Then there's the ultimate whistle blowing tactic—reporting a particularly nasty adversary who you suspect is hiding some income source to the Internal Revenue Service. You can even receive a bounty for your trouble. We'll discuss the particulars later, for cases in which you've bartered goods, paid someone under the table, or otherwise have reason to believe they're not paying Uncle his full due.

When and How to Blow the Whistle. Lest we dismiss the effectiveness of outside agencies too casually, here are two situations in which you'll almost always want to call on the regulators.

1. *Problem with a mail-order firm.* When you've been bilked through the mails, it can be frustrating to try to get your money back. True, most mail-order advertisers put in some guarantee of "full money back if you're not satisfied," or "postdate your check for thirty days and, if you're not delighted *in every way,* return the merchandise and we will return your check uncashed." The truth is that such promises are a staple of mail order advertising. Some companies will give you your money without a struggle. Others assume that you'll be too timid to request it.

    For example, the get-rich-quick schemes you see advertised in national magazines are usually predicated on the notion that you won't return the book or whatever and ask for a refund. The advertisers assume you'll conclude that if you can't figure out how to get rich from the book when so many people who lent their testimonials to the ad obviously did, there must be something wrong with you. Thus you'll keep the book out of embarrassment, and they'll keep your check out of astute greed.

    If a mail-order company fails to send you what you've ordered within thirty days, or at least a notice within that time limit that tells you the product is temporarily out of stock and offers you the opportunity to cancel, you have a valid legal complaint. You also have a case if you've requested a refund and received no answer or a complicated shell game. (Some advertisers send you a tedious form to fill out before they'll consider your refund request.)

    But mail-order marketers, especially the slippery ones, know their real enemy—the US Postal Service. You might wonder why the same agency that takes a week to get your letter across town will intimidate a slick mail order marketer. The answer is that the post office seems to take stopping fraudulent mail schemes more seriously than delivering ordinary letters. When you have a problem with a mail-order seller, forget the usual complaint letter and write a terse note that says:

This is to advise you that I have waited more than thirty (30) days for my merchandise (or refund). If you do not contact me by mail or telephone within five (5) working days with an explanation, I will report this statutory violation of Title 39, Section 3005 of the US Code to the postal inspector of your zip-code region for immediate action.

All direct-mail marketers know about Section 3005. It's the federal law that empowers the postal inspector to stop their mail if they are suspected of fraud. Since stopping their mail will also stop their income, the sellers will be highly motivated to resolve your problem, unless they have long since absconded to Venezuela. The extra impetus is that you know enough about the mail (or at least mail fraud) business to file your complaint in the region closest to their home. Most rights-conscious consumers wielding empty threats would say they're writing to the postmaster general in Washington or give some other indication that their complaint can be tucked away with all the rest.

2.   *Problems with a utility.* Most people aren't too fond of utilities, perhaps because they can't generally shop elsewhere for better service. This monopoly status, and the fact that utilities supply a necessary service for anyone who needs heat, light, and a telephone, brings them under the authority of a state Public Service Commission listed under the state government in your White Pages.

Complaining directly to a utility will put you at the mercy of whoever picks up the phone at the other end, and those employees can vary in their ability and desire to help. But complaining directly to the Public Service Commission gives your problem top-priority status with every utility we've ever investigated.

Call the Public Service Commission as soon as trouble develops. This places your complaint at the top of the pile destined for the fastest resolution you're likely to see in dealing with your utility.

CRAFTY LEGAL MANEUVERS

But, in the spirit of self-reliance, we think you'll find it easier and more profitable to pursue justice on your own. And, contrary to popular belief, you don't have to spend a fortune on legal fees to do so.

The best approach for a shrewd middle-income legal consumer is to visit one of the legal clinics or law offices that offer a "free consultation" in their Yellow Pages, newspaper, or TV advertising. The competition for clients today is fierce, and most firms that handle consumer problems will offer a free half-hour or so to hear your problem and tell you pretty much what your options are. In many cases, this will also tell you what you need to know to pursue the case on your own. (See Chapter 15 on Lawyers and Doctors for full details on choosing a free-consultation lawyer.)

The Lawyer's Letterhead Gambit. If you've ever received one, we think you'll admit it. Virtually anything sounds more threatening when it's said on an attorney's stationery. A lawyer's letter by itself won't break hardened adversaries who always find several in the morning mail. But if you've been diddled by a small business or an individual, the very appearance of the envelope in the mailbox is likely to sting. Contrast two letters describing the same problem—one an individual wrote and one she had a lawyer write for her—in Exhibits A and B.

EXHIBIT A

Tenant's Letter

Dear Mr. Gruel,

I am writing this as I sit here shivering because of our heat problem. This apartment is so cold, I have even considered wearing gloves and earmuffs to bed!

As you know, my leaking faucet is still not fixed. And my son has a chronic runny nose which the doctor says is from lack of heat. My son's bedroom is like an igloo!

I have asked you nicely to fix the heat problem many times before and you have ignored me. WHY?? I always pay my rent on time.

I'm very upset that you haven't fixed the problems in my apartment as you promised in the lease, which I can't seem to find. Can you please send me a copy?

You said if I complained any more you'd evict me. Well, if you don't respond as soon as possible, I'll have to move to protect my family's health. If I have to move, I need the security deposit back which you said I forfeited.

But if you fix the heat, I'm sure we can work out a compromise.

Sincerely yours,

Ms. Tennent

EXHIBIT B

Lawyer's Letter
(on law firm's letterhead)

Mr. Sebastian Gruel
Country Club Lane

Dear Mr. Gruel,
Please be advised that this office has been retained by Ms. Rosalynn Tennent in regard to the apartment she leased from you at 123 Tinderbox Drive, which violates the State Housing Code Section _____.

I have advised my client to withhold any future payment of rent and to establish an escrow fund for that purpose until the heat problem is fully abated.

Moreover, for purposes of retroactive rent abatement, I am today filing with the district court an affirmative damage action based on your breach of the implied warrant of habitability, as codified in Section _____ of the State Annotated Code.

Should the heating not be fixed within ten days of the date hereof, I will advise my client to move, and you will be held for all expenses incidental thereto; in addition to all other claims which she has currently pending.

I am also enclosing all medical bills incurred by Ms. Tennent's son as the proximate result of lack of heat, and she will expect your check in full payment thereof within ten days.

Should you carry through with your threat to evict my client because of her legitimate complaints, we will sue you for an illegal retaliatory eviction and petition the court to award her punitive damages based on the inference of malice implicit in your willful and deliberate evasion of statutory duties to provide decent and safe housing.
I will make one further point explicit. In the event that my client is forced to move, we will expect a prompt refund of the security deposit, together with simple interest earned at the statutory rate. If you should refuse to return this deposit, we will amend our suit to include an additional claim for three times the amount wrongfully withheld and an award for reasonable attorney's fees.

Should you have any questions, feel free to call me or have your attorney or insurance carrier do so.

Very truly yours,

Attorney

The typical lawyer's letter shouldn't cost more than twenty-five dollars or so if you have your facts marshaled and see the right attorney. We feel that the added credibility of an attorney's letterhead and a message tailored to the occasion is worth the price, since you can often get a settlement for extra "damages" that you couldn't otherwise.

Do-It-Yourself Lawsuits. You can experience the thrill of bringing adversaries to justice completely on your own in small-claims court. This is the perfect arena in which to extract retribution for most consumer problems, since you don't need a lawyer. Small claims is the only court in which the judge will base his or her findings solely on principles of fairness rather than the mysterious twists and turns that lawyers use to obscure basic issues. In fact, the judge will probably discourage any lawyerly smoke screens from your adversaries to get at the truth of the matter.

The maximum amount you can sue for covers most problems—from three hundred to a thousand dollars, according to your state's limit. But with a little imagination, you can "divide" a larger claim into two or more separate lawsuits. If, for instance, you were charged six hundred dollars and seven hundred dollars on two separate occasions for car repairs that proved faulty, you could enter one action for each amount, even though the maximum in your state might be a thousand dollars. Furthermore, you can add consequential and incidental damages to what you're claiming, for all the trouble that getting satisfaction is costing you.

Most cases brought by consumers—about two-thirds—are settled in their favor. You do have to document the fact that you tried to settle the matter on your own. A "demand" letter, which spells out the situation and describes what you want from your adversary, is sufficient to prove your efforts.

Once you're awarded a judgment, you're empowered by the court to use all legal collection procedures to enforce the judgment if your adversary doesn't cough up what he or she owes on time. You can garnishee a percentage of the person's wages, attach bank accounts or property, or even show up at the place of business with a marshal at the end of the day and literally empty the cash register into your pockets.

We advise confining your legal maneuvers to small-claims court whenever possible. First, check Table 2 to see what the basic requirements are in your state. Then call or visit the clerk of that court to determine:

1.   Whether you can definitely sue the party in your local court. (You may have to sue where he or she does business.)

2.   What you have to do to file your action.

3.   How you can subpoena your adversary and whatever witnesses you need.

4.   What time period you have to file your claim—i.e., the statute of limitation.

We'll discuss specific small claims strategies, where they apply, throughout the book.

Civil Courts for More Rewarding Lawsuits. District and circuit courts dictate that you must have an attorney. This drives up the cost of admission, since your lawyer will want to take a hefty sum if you win (a contingency fee) or if you lose (flat fee). And it's not crafty at all to attempt suing in civil court without a lawyer. If your adversary's lawyer is even half-awake, you'll probably never get to open your mouth because the lawyer will bar all your logical arguments with rules of evidence and other hocus-pocus, and the judge will have to decide the case on legal issues. You will probably lose.

The time to use district and circuit courts to your advantage is when you're plotting a strategy with a lawyer that could award you up to five thousand dollars, which is the usual limit for district court, or even higher, which will take you to circuit court. We'll stress again that these forays into courts of higher earnings do not have to cost you a fortune in lawyer's fees. A careful reading of this book should give you a clear indication of when to visit an attorney to discuss a suit that could bring you special damages.

If you have a good case, the right lawyer will take it on a contingency basis. Many times when you're up against a powerful adversary, the chances are good that they'll have to pay you "punitive" damages and even pick up your lawyer's fee if you win. You can see now why a lawyer might want to talk with you, even on a free-consultation basis.

In fact, if you have a good case, it shouldn't even get to court. Most often, holding out the prospect of a higher-stakes suit will prod your adversary into offering a money settlement that you'll find much more rewarding than simple redress.

A Word About Guerrilla Tactics

Now let's take a brisk departure from legal strategies you can apply with society's blessings to explore more imaginative activities.

Maybe you've seen the movie *Animal House*, the story of gleeful revenge exacted by a fun-loving fraternity against the corrupt college administration and straight-arrow fraternity types who've conspired to remove our slobby friends from campus. Their retribution is the cleverly orchestrated demolition of Homecoming Parade and the entire campus town.

Some *Animal House* tactics are just good clean fun and clever besides. One sly gentleman we're acquainted with hated fishing his daily newspaper from a puddle outside his door where the delivery person always threw it, even though it was thoughtfully wrapped in a plastic bag. So he just as thoughtfully sent his weekly checks for newspaper delivery on time, but floating in a plastic bag full of water. They got the point, and he got dry papers.

Some methods are more drastic. Another acquaintance has a unique habit of punishing banks he's grown to dislike beyond normal bank-loathing. When he's been subjected to poor service a bank won't correct, he rents a safe-deposit box and locks a frozen mackerel inside. When the ice thaws, employees and customers can sense one person's evaluation of the bank's service performance.

We'll include these jocular tactics from time to time for their entertainment value, and leave the more drastic versions to your own imagination. They may just inspire you to come up with even more inventive strategies that you can tailor to a particular problem.

After all, in a society as diverse as ours, one person's unspeakable acts may be another's sweet revenge.

TABLE 2
SUING IN SMALL CLAIMS COURTS

State	Type of Court	Maximum Claim	Minimum Age	Lawyers: Permitted/or Required	Appeals Permitted by Plaintiff	Appeals Permitted by Defendant	Typical Filing and Service Costs
Alabama	Small Claims	$500	21	Permitted	yes	yes	$10-$15
Alaska	Small Claims	1000	18	Corps: Required / Others: Permitted	yes	yes	7-15
Arizona	Justice Court	999	21	Corps: Required / Others: Permitted	yes	yes	3-6
Arkansas	Municipal Court	100-300	[12]	Permitted	yes	yes	3-10
California	Small Claims	750	[13]	Not permitted	no	yes	2-5
Colorado	Small Claims	500	18	Not permitted	yes	yes	7-10
Connecticut	Common Pleas	750	21	Permitted	no	no	6-15
Delaware	Justice of Peace	1500	19	Permitted	yes	yes	10
District of Columbia	Small Claims	750	21	Permitted[1]	yes	yes	2-10
Florida	Small Claims	1500-2500[14]	21	Permitted	yes	yes	5-10
Georgia	Small Claims or Justice of Peace	200-300	18	Permitted	[2]	[2]	2-15
Hawaii	Small Claims	300	21	Permitted[3]	no	no	7
Idaho	Small Claims	500	21	Not Permitted	yes	yes	5-10
Illinois	Small Claims (State)	1000	18	Corps: Required / Others: Permitted	yes	yes	7-11
	Cook County[4]	300					
Indiana	Small Claims	3000	21	Corps: Required / Others: Permitted	yes	yes	6-10
Iowa	District Court	1000	19	Permitted	yes	yes	3-5
Kansas	Small Claims	300	18	Not permitted	yes	yes	10
Kentucky	Small Claims[5]	500	18	Permitted	yes	yes	6.50
Louisiana	City Courts	25	21	Permitted	no	no	10-20
	Justice of Peace	300					
Maine	Small Claims	800	21	Permitted	yes	yes	5
Maryland	District Court	500	21	Permitted	yes	yes	5-10
Massachusetts	Small Claims	400	21	Permitted	no	yes	2-3
Michigan	Small Claims	300	21	Not Permitted	no	no	7-12
Minnesota	Conciliation Court	500-1000	21	Not permitted[9]	yes	yes	3
Mississippi	Justice of Peace	500	None	Permitted	yes	yes	6

State	Court	Amount	Min. Age	Lawyers			
Missouri	Small Claims	500	21	Permitted	yes	yes	9-11
Montana	District Court	1500	19	Permitted	yes	yes	2.50
Nebraska	Small Claims	500	19	Not permitted	yes	yes	4
Nevada	Small Claims	300	[12]	Permitted	yes	yes	5-7
New Hampshire	Small Claims	500	21	Permitted	yes	yes	3
New Jersey	Small Claims	500	21	Permitted	yes	yes	3-5
New Mexico[6]	Small Claims[6]	2000	18	Permitted	yes	yes	6-14
New York	Small Claims	1000	21	Permitted[7]	yes	yes	3-4
North Carolina	Small Claims	500	18	Permitted	yes	yes	7-12
North Dakota	Small Claims	200-500	18	Permitted	no	no	3
Ohio	Small Claims	300	21	Permitted	yes	yes	2.75
Oklahoma	Small Claims	600	[12]	Permitted	yes	yes	5-10
Oregon	Small Claims	500	21	Not permitted[8]	no	no	15
Pennsylvania	Small Claims	1000	None	Permitted	yes	yes	6-12
Rhode Island	Small Claims	300	21	Corps: Required Others: Permitted	no	no	2
South Carolina	Magistrate Court	200-3000	21	Permitted	yes	yes	varies
South Dakota	Magistrate Court	1000	18	Permitted	no	no	2-4
Tennessee	Justice of Peace	3000	18	Permitted	yes	yes	25 bond
Texas	Small Claims	150-200	18	Permitted	yes[10]	yes[10]	5-8
Utah	Small Claims	200	[12]	Permitted	no	no	5-7
Vermont	Small Claims	250	18	Permitted	yes	yes	3-6
Virginia	District Court	5000	None	Permitted	[10]	[10]	3-5
Washington	Small Claims	300	18	Not permitted	no	[11]	3-5
West Virginia	Magistrate Court	1500	18	Permitted	yes	yes	7.50
Wisconsin	Small Claims	500	21	Permitted	yes	yes	5-7
Wyoming	Justice of Peace	200	21	Permitted	yes	yes	2-6

SOURCE: Arthur E. Rowse, ed., Help: 1981 (Washington, DC: Consumer News, Inc., 1981), pp. 130–31. Reprinted with permission.

[1] Law students allowed to represent parties; [2] Appeals allowed only for amounts over $50; [3] Lawyers not permitted in security deposit cases; [4] Lawyers not permitted in Cook Co. Pro Se Court. Corporations, partnerships and associations not permitted to use court; [5] In Jefferson Co., Consumer Court, for consumer plaintiffs only; [6] Small Claims Court in Albuquerque only; [7] Corporations, assignees, partnerships, associations and insurers not permitted as plaintiffs; [8] Lawyers may appear only with consent of judge; [9] Lawyer permitted in Minneapolis and St. Paul only; [10] Appeals allowed only for amounts over $20; [11] Appeals allowed only for amounts over $100. [12] Minimum age is 18 for females, 21 for males. [13] Minimum age 18 for married individuals, 21 for single individuals; [14] Lawyer required for claim over $1,500. Source: Dept. of Policy Research, Yegge, Hall & Evans, Denver, CO, 80202.

PART II

Caveat Vendor

3
advertising

Finding the Jugular Vein on Madison Avenue or Main Street

The ads are by far the best part of any magazine or book. Ads are news. What is wrong with them is that they are always good news.

—MARSHALL MCLUHAN

It's only fair to assume that the people who fooled Mother Nature might try to fool you, too. Just watch TV with an analytical eye for an hour or so, and you'll ferret out appeals that play on your emotions en route to your wallet, puffed-up claims you can explode with a pinprick of logic, and assorted tricky selling messages such as:

"Sergio Valente. Jeans for the way you live and love." A sexy notion when you see all those firm derrieres bobbing around. But does it make any sense unless you only like to "love" with your jeans on?

"New *softer* Charmin bathroom tissue." Ever wonder how they make it softer? By reducing each roll by a hefty number of sheets and fluffing out the remainder with thin air. So Mr. Whipple can fondle packaged rolls of tissue on TV and pronounce it even more irresistible. But does that say much about "softness" for its intended use? You could argue that it's the customer who gets squeezed by this ad.

"Anacin contains *twice* as much of the pain reliever doctors recommend most." Morphine? No, just aspirin. And even dedicated aspirin fans who need "twice as much" would do better to buy inexpensive generic aspirin for less than half the price of Anacin.

Funny how well those ads work, though, for a simple reason. The people who plan and create ads know a lot about your deepest needs and anxieties from spending millions on "psychographic" studies to probe your attitudes and lifestyle; and "focus groups" of customers discussing how they use the products, unaware that researchers are studying them carefully from behind a one-way mirror; and "physiological tests" hooking consumers up to lie detectors, or machines that measure eye-pupil size, to see what features of ads give them sweaty palms or make then wide-eyed.

Now it's time to turn the tables and discover the advertisers' little secrets, so you'll know where to strike when you've been victimized by a roguish marketer's fraudulent ads. But what constitutes fraudulent advertising? Some products are true innovations, but most companies feel safer imitating their successful competitors by offering "me too" products. We feel that advertising people should be allowed some creative license to say why one particular brand meets your needs better than all those other look-alike products crying out for you to take them home.

What galls us—and should whet your own appetite for revenge—is the cold, calculated effort to mislead or deceive you into buying products that haven't a prayer of living up to their advertised claims. The Federal Trade Commission (FTC), which regulates advertising, considers ads deceptive when there are:

> false or misleading statements or comparisons with other products

> important facts about the product concealed or omitted, like a tendency for some brand of hair remover to remove a layer of skin as well

> misleading impressions created even though what's actually stated may be true

Let's look at some wretched excesses in two different kinds of advertising— national and local.

When National Advertisers Mislead You

Most advertising you see in prime-time TV and in major magazines is national, placed by big-budget companies. Here the truth can be stretched in several ingenious directions.

Puffery. This has been interpreted by the FTC to mean the garden variety of hype that isn't intended to fool anybody. One example comes out of the files of the National Advertising Division of the Council of Better Business Bureaus, the self-regulatory group which receives complaints and attempts to scold troublesome advertisers into mending their ways:

> Do people believe there are mermaids who recommend tuna fish?
> Yes, whined a complainant from outside NAD. [The NAD hides the names of complainants in their files.] The jingle for Chicken of the Sea

tuna sang, "Ask any mermaid you happen to see, 'What's the best tuna?' Chicken of the Sea." The complainant tested viewers' comprehension of this spiel and argued that people thought the "best tuna" claim was a statement of fact. But NAD laughed at the test design, and called the mermaids' advice "puffery" and therefore "not subject to the test of truth and accuracy. . . ." So the idea of puffery opens a loophole large enough for a mermaid to swim through.[1]

No problem here. You know there isn't really a Green Giant who grows corn or a Man from Glad who'll fly in to wrap your leftovers.

Dubious Claims. A "claim" is what an ad says about the product to give a convincing reason why you should buy it. If a saving bank says "We pay you 2% higher interest rates on your savings than the East Bank of the Mississippi next door," that's probably a factual claim or the bank would be in hot water. The problem is that they can't say that. Interest rates, as of this writing, anyway, are regulated. All savings banks have to pay the same. So they *imply* that they pay more by saying something like "We pay the highest interest rates the law allows" or "We pay the highest interest rates in town."

Most advertisers are in the same predicament. Their products aren't unique, so they have to come up with a creative way to convince you they are. Hence the variety of claims sampled in Table 3.

TABLE 3
ADVERTISING CLAIMS COURT

(Six kinds of claims that mean little or nothing)

1. The question claim, which forces the listener to respond in a way that supplies an answer that could not otherwise be stated—as with "Protein 21 Hair Spray. What could be more natural?"

2. The preemptive claim, which tells you something about the product that is common to all products in its category but says it first, as in: "Sears House Paint, for great American homes, like yours."

3. The implied claim, which attempts to have the listener come to the proper conclusion without stating any facts, as in: "Imagine what Derma Fresh can do for your hands."

4. The assertive claim, which states nonfact in terms so positive as to convey the impression of real fact, as in: "Dodge. Depend on it."

5. The exclusivity claim, which coins a phrase or term that represents a common fact in an exclusive way, as in: "7-Up the Uncola."

6.   The noncomparative comparative claim, which compares the product to something nonexistent by using a superlative or inventing a generic term, such as: "Shick Styling Dryer—the one with the extra drying power."[2]

Lies. Sometimes product claims are so grossly deceptive that the FTC will force the advertiser to stop running the ads or, in the case of Warner-Lambert, to run "corrective" advertising to dispel any lingering ideas consumers might have from seeing the ad over a period of years. Warner-Lambert had claimed since 1921 that its Listerine mouthwash could help prevent sore throats and colds. The FTC determined in the 1970s that Listerine was no more effective against colds than gargling with warm water and forced the company to include a corrective statement (to the effect that the product was of no value in cold and sore-throat prevention) in the next $10 million worth of Listerine advertising.

When advertisers can't think of anything else to say about a product, they'll pay some well-known personality to endorse it, hoping that some of the celebrity's good name will rub off. But celebrities can lie, too. For instance, clean-cut former astronaut Gordon Cooper was named in an FTC consent settlement involving ads for an automotive valve that supposedly let drivers "convert air into energy . . . explode it like fuel . . . and get up to 7 more miles per gallon." The FTC said that Cooper represented himself as an expert in automotive engineering when he endorsed the valve, but, in fact, "had no such experience, misrepresented test data and consumer-use results, and failed to disclose he had a financial interest in sales of the product."[3]

As powerful and committed to their own style of chicanery as companies that spend $50 to $100-million a year on advertising might seem, most of them are actually very touchy about what people think of their ads. The more responsible companies see advertising as their public image and are concerned when someone tells them they're fouling that image with objectionable ads.

Virtually all companies are insecure about their advertising in another way. Years ago, John Wanamaker complained that "half my advertising dollars are wasted, but I don't know which half." Because advertising effectiveness is still very hard to measure, most marketers don't really know how it contributes to or kills off their product's sales. The executive most frightened of criticism is the advertising manager or product manager responsible for approving an ad campaign. And when things go wrong, an ad manager invariably blames the advertising agency hired to create and place the advertising. Thus your two most likely revenge targets are—and rightfully so—the advertising agency that created the bad ads and the advertising manager who commissioned and approved them.

WHAT TO DO ABOUT OBNOXIOUS ADS

If you're sufficiently annoyed at a TV commercial that tweaks you with a misleading claim—even if you'd never use the product—you can pay the advertiser back for your displeasure. Write a letter to the TV station that ran the ad, demanding substantiation. Stations that subscribe to the Television Code Authority of the National Association of Broadcasters (and most do) are required to have such documentation on file. Your letter should read something like:

> On Wednesday, January 28, at 8 P.M. I saw a commercial on your station for Flash Fire, which claimed to be "the shampoo for redheads." Please send me documentation to support the validity of that claim, in compliance with the Television Code. Thank you.

It could well be that Flash Fire is the same shampoo that advertiser sells to blonds and brunets under a different name and different claim. The documentation, or lack of it, will bear this out.

If so, go to your local library and refer to the *Standard Directory of Advertisers*. Look in the *Product Name Index* and you'll find the names of the president and advertising manager of the company that markets that brand. Write to the advertising manager, with a copy to the president, and say, for example:

> I recently saw a commerical for your product Flash Fire and wondered, as a redhead, why it would be better for my hair than another shampoo. I wrote to the TV station and asked for the documentation of your claim. When I read it, I couldn't see how you could make that claim—it seems just like any other shampoo.
>
> Frankly, I feel that calling Flash Fire the shampoo for redheads is misleading. I think you are selling your product under false pretenses.
>
> Would you please explain to me what product differences from other shampoos you use to base your claim?
>
> I'm looking forward to hearing from you before I pursue the matter further.
>
> cc: (president's name)

You'll have good reason to assume that the ad manager and the agency people responsible for the campaign are agonizing over your letter. The duplicate copy to the company president will also grate on their nerves. You might get a case of Flash Fire for your trouble or a nice long letter that reflects the general angst you've caused.

When You've Bought a Disappointing Product

When a commercial has actually persuaded you to buy a product, it doesn't live up to its advertising claims, and you can't get satisfaction from the retailer because the product isn't exactly defective, there's a coercive tactic you can use.

Susan has a problem with a waffle iron which doesn't turn out very appetizing waffles—contrary to the ad claims. She brings it back to the retailer, who says that every unit of that product is the same. He can't give her a full refund because she's already used it a few times, and it's coated with batter.

So she goes to her library and finds the *Standard Directory of Advertisers* and writes down the name of the president of the company, the advertising manager, and the marketing director. But she also notes the name of the advertising agency listed underneath. Now she refers to the companion volume, *The Standard Directory of Advertising Agencies*, to write down the names of the ad agency's senior executives. Since it's a small agency, she takes the name and phone number of the president.

The name of the ad agency is Grovel, Flummox and Hyde, and the president is Gordon Grovel. So she starts with a phone call:

GROVELS'S SECRETARY: Mr. Grovel's office.

SUSAN: I'd like to speak to him, please, This is Susan Eastham.

SECRETARY: He's in conference now.

SUSAN: Please tell him I'm preparing a complaint to the Federal Trade Commission regarding your commercial for the Madame Waffle, but I'd like to speak with him first.

SECRETARY: Just a minute.

GROVEL: Yes, Ms. Eastham. How can I help you?

SUSAN: I saw your commercial for the Madame Waffle waffle iron and bought one. But my waffles definitely didn't come out the way they did in your commercial. In fact, they're always over-cooked and they stick to the bottom of Madame Waffle's pan.

GROVEL: Did you ask the merchant for your money back?

Susan: He wasn't very helpful, Mr. Grovel. He said all your units were like that. The point is, I feel that the commercial misled me since it clearly states that you can make a perfect waffle every time. And mine are far from perfect.

Grovel: Well. I'm sure we can work something out with our client.

Chances are good that Grovel will figure out some way to wring a refund for Susan fast rather than allow her to proceed with her case. But if Grovel is uncooperative, she can call the advertising manager at the offending company and repeat the same story. The ad manager won't want a formal FTC complaint against the ads that he or she bought from the agency. This is the kind of embarrassment that causes management to fire ad managers.

If both agency and ad manager piously disavow any wrongdoing or—even worse—refer you to the company's lawyers, go over their heads. Call the vice-president in charge of marketing or the marketing director of the company. Say that you're filing a complaint with (1) the National Advertising Review Board and (2) the Federal Trade Commission if your problem isn't resolved within five business days.

Make sure you point out that you've brought your problem first to the attention of Mr. Quaver, the ad manager, and Mr. Grovel at the ad agency, but neither one has been interested in helping you resolve the problem. This won't sit well with the vp of marketing, who will probably wonder why they didn't cut off your complaint first.

Even if they come through with a full refund for the product and your phone calls, you'll probably want to avenge yourself and file complaints against them anyway. Use the forms in the Revenge Kit at the end of this chapter.

Suing for Damages Based on Misleading Advertising

If an advertiser makes some claim about a product's worthiness and you suffer damages because you "relied" on that claim, you have a good chance of suing the advertiser and collecting.

The most dramatic legal precedent featured an ad campaign for the Uniroyal tire which used the glib line, "If it only saves your life once, it's a bargain." One trusting consumer who bought Uniroyal relying on defect-free performance died after his car went out of control. It seems the "lifesaving" tire blew out. So his estate sued the tire company, and the New Jersey Supreme Court decided that Uniroyal's generous policy of replacing the tire under those conditions was unconscionable.[4]

And you might note that the "if it only saves your life once . . ." claim is fairly typical of the *assertive* variety advertisers use all the time. (see p. 43). So take the advertiser to task if a product you've bought because of glowing ad claims gives you trouble under either or both of these criteria:

> Incidental damages. This means money you've spent dragging, say, a faulty lawn mower back to the shop for repairs, renting a replacement, and writing or telephoning for help—all because you relied on ad claims about "dependability."
>
> Consequential damages. If that same treacherous lawn mower was advertised as "safe to use" but one day the rotary blade sends a rock flying up to strike you between the eyes, you could sue for your medical costs, time off from work, and other related expenses. As in the Uniroyal case, such personal damage is a consequence of your relying on assertions made in the ads.

Depending on the dollar amount of your claim and whether the advertiser is located in your area, you can sue in small-claims court for convenience or district court for greater awards. Don't be stingy with yourself in adding up your damages. Just keep excellent records to document your case. Some states, like California, let you sue for three times the actual damages. Before you bring suit, though, you should write either a demand letter for small-claims court (see the sample at the end of this chapter) or, if you're looking toward district court, send a lawyer's letter to the advertisers with copies of your documentation attached, and see if they make an offer. They may balk at the possibility of becoming another Uniroyal and settle with you before you ever have to go to court.

Outwitting Deceptive Local Advertisers

Most local retail advertisers can't afford the imaginative deceptions that national advertisers buy from their ad agencies. Deceptive hometown advertisers usually confine themselves to pedestrian, time-tested retail frauds. These often involve some variation of:

> "Bait and switch." You see an ad for "special sale" color TVs at $200. But when you arrive at 9:01 A.M. on sale day, sorry, they're already "sold out" and the salespeople are pushing $600 models.
>
> Phantom list prices. Some item is "marked down" from a "manufacturer's list price." But the price quoted as list is actually higher than prevailing retail prices for the same item in your area.

The warehouse that isn't. If you see an ad for a "warehouse sale" and find it's held in a retail store, that's already deceptive. A legitimate warehouse sale, curiously enough, has to be held in a warehouse. And an advertised "factory outlet sale" is only permitted by law when the seller really owns or controls the factory.

The "up to" claim. If sale prices are advertised as "up to," say, one-third off, at least 10% of the sale items have to be sold at that price.

Going out of business. Some retailers are permanently breathing their last gasp, so they can continue selling cheap merchandise at "sale" prices. If you buy a faulty product from one of these distressed merchants, you can return it even though they may have a sign proclaiming All Sales Final, unless the product is clearly marked "as is."

All of these loathsome practices are clearly illegal under federal or generally adopted state laws, so you shouldn't feel guilty about playing hardball with the uninspired merchants who rely on them.

"*And They'll Tell Two Friends.*" Far and away the greatest source of complaints about retail advertisers is the sale item that's "out of stock." But there's a coercive solution to this problem.

Gene sees an ad in the local paper for Serge's Stereo Asylum which offers a one-day sale item—a $400 Teac tape deck for only $250. So he rips out the ad and heads for the store.

SERGE: Hey, how ya doin'?

GENE: Hey. (Points to ad.) I'd like this Teac tape deck.

SERGE: Sorry, friend, all sold out. I've got 'em on order, so we'll get more in about six weeks. But check out this Pioneer deck. Only $399.

GENE: I'll take it for $250, since you're out of the Teac at your sale price.

SERGE: Oh, can't do that. Store policy.

GENE: Can I use your phone there for a quick local call?

SERGE: Sure thing.

GENE: (Talking into the phone so Serge can hear) Hi, Artie. Do me a favor. Come down to Serge's stereo and ask for the Teac deck on sale for $250. But call up Diana and Stephanie first and tell them to do the same thing. And ask each of them to call two friends . . .

SERGE: Whoa there, partner, what are you doing?

GENE: I think you're using bait-and-switch tactics and I want to file a complaint with the attorney general's office. I'd like to see you turn away a few more people, too.

SERGE: Well, hold on there. Maybe I could get you *one* Teac from another dealer this afternoon.

GENE: Why not give me a rain check now and sign it.

SERGE: I guess so.

Blowing the Whistle. If you can't persuade a merchant who uses dishonest advertising to do right by you, don't hesitate to state that you're going to report her or him to the state attorney general or the local consumer affairs office.

First establish your street wisdom by asking key questions. "Do you own the factory that you're getting your merchandise from for this factory sale?" Or, "This manufacturer's list price is higher than I've seen advertised at other stores. Where in this area is your 'list' the prevailing price?" Or, "Your ad said up to 50 percent off, but I don't see any merchandise for more than 20 percent off. Where are you keeping the stuff at the sale price you've advertised?" If you're dealing with a salesclerk who seems dense about the legal implications of what you're asking, speak to the manager. If the manager is "out," find out who owns the store and ask to call that person on the store phone. Then follow through on your threat. At least call either of the two offices mentioned above, tell them what you went through, and ask them to investigate.

And for a finishing touch, call the local TV consumer reporter and tell him or her what's going on, to see if the station will bring the cameras around. This is the kind of human drama that viewers relish—stammering salesclerks disavowing responsibility, and a confrontation with the owner who comes out of hiding to sweat like a cornered weasel.

Revenge Kit for Advertising

LETTER TO NATIONAL ADVERTISING REVIEW BOARD

To: Complaint Board
     National Advertising Division
     Council of Better Business Bureaus
     845 Third Avenue
     New York, NY 10020

Date:

  Re: Complaint against (advertiser) regarding a commercial/print advertisement for (product) which appeared (broadcast station or publication and date).

I believe that this advertisement was misleading and deceptive in that (state the slippery claim, ludicrous product comparison, or whatever you feel is deceptive. If you asked for and received some substantiation of the claim from the local station and you feel the substantiation is phony, attach that document.).

I understand that the NAD will evaluate this complaint and ask (advertiser) for substantiation. If the NAD does not accept (advertiser's) documentation, please keep me advised as to whether a National Advertising Review Board panel will be convened and, if so, what action may be taken against the advertiser.

Please note that I contacted (name of ad manager) at (advertiser) and (name) at (advertising agency) prior to filing this complaint, but received no timely response to my request for further substantiation.

Very truly yours,

cc: (president of advertiser
    company)

FEDERAL TRADE COMMISSION COMPLAINT

Name of Company
Complaint is Against_____

Address_____
　　　　　Street　　　　　City　　　　　State　　　　Zip Code

Telephone_____ Date of first complaint
　　　　　　　　　　to Company or Firm_____

<u>TYPE OF COMPLAINT</u> (Please check one)

Mail Order_____ Franchise_____ Credit Denial_____
Warranty_____ Debt Collection____ OTHER_____
Automotive_____ Credit Billing_____ _____
Advertising_____ Credit Reporting__ _____

Describe the events fully, in the order in which they occurred. Please include related dates such as warranty or purchase dates. Use additional sheets when necessary. Include copies of all related material. Do not send originals.

_____

_____

_____

_____

_____

_____

_____

_____

_____

Your Name_____
　　　　　First Name　　　Middle Initial　　　Last Name

Home Address_____
　　　　　　　　Street　　　　City　　　　State　　　Zip code

Telephone_____(Home) _____(Work)

Do you wish this complaint to be forwarded to company or firm named herein?

YES_____

NO_____

SAMPLE DEMAND LETTER FOR DAMAGES

NOTE: This is only appropriate for a small-claims-court action. A letter alleging more costly damages should be sent by a lawyer.

Mr. Arden Tinker
President
The Lawn Order Power Mower Company
Address
Date

Re: Suit for damages due to misleading advertising.

Dear Mr. Tinker,

This is to inform you that unless I hear from you within five (5) working days, I will bring action against your company for recovery of costs and damages arising from use of your Lawn Order Catch 22 Power Mower, Serial #12345678, purchased new at Jack Sprat's Hardware Store, (address), on June 5, 198____, to wit:

1. That I relied on a substantive claim made in your advertisement (attached) that clearly states: "The Catch 22 is so safe, even a 10-year-old can use it."

2. That the power lawn mower, while operated by the undersigned 35-year-old adult in normal and responsible manner, threw a small stone that hit me in the forehead.

3. That, while I lay unconscious, the lawn mower proceeded on its own power toward my house, where it mowed down a two-by-four-foot patch of prizewinning roses in my garden.

Pursuant to Collins v. Uniroyal, Inc., 126 N.J. Super. 401, 315A. 2d, 30, I will seek incidental and consequential damages amounting to $588.50, itemized as follows:

1. A full refund of the purchase price of the Catch 22 Power Mower, in the amount of $129.50.

2. Medical expenses in the amount of $186.00.

3. Time taken off from my work @ $25 per hour, in the amount of $225.00.

4. Replacement cost of 48 roses @ $4 in the amount of $48.00

Documentation of each expense is attached.

I am retaining the Catch 22 Power Mower in my possession to be used as evidence against you, but will release the machine to you upon your payment in full of the above-cited costs and damages.

If I do not hear from you within the time I have specified, the action will be filed as attached and I will notify the appropriate media.

In addition, I will subpoena all executives of your corporation who I may reasonably conclude approved the advertisement including, but not limited to, yourself, your marketing director, and your advertising manager. I will also subpoena those engineering and manufacturing employees who are responsible for the product design and manufacture of the Catch 22 model.

Very truly yours,

Certified Letter

(Enclose the filing papers for small-claims court and copies of your documentation.)

4
stores

A Crafty Customer Is Always Right

It takes objectivity to play devil's advocate when you find you're in the devil's clutches, and today a number of retail stores seem to belong to the same satanic conglomerate. But if you really wonder what happened to those nicer stores of your childhood, it helps to recognize some of the retailers' problems. Most have to operate on slight profit margins which make them, in a word, cheap. That's reflected in their frustrating refund policies when you're stuck with their shoddy merchandise; once they've latched onto your dollar, they're very reluctant to let it go. Add to their meager profits the apparent mass flight of competent salespeople, and it's a wonder that many stores can operate at all.

Before you start feeling too sorry for retailers, though, adopt the attitude of the contemporary salesclerk and remind yourself, "It's not my problem." If you suffer shabby treatment at the hands of rude salespeople or can't get satisfaction when you've bought a bad product or the furniture you've ordered with six-week-guaranteed delivery hasn't arrived after two months, you have a right to protect your own interests.

The Lone Deranger. It only takes one salesperson with the right combination of supercilious attitude and marginal job skills to drive you up a wall. We're not talking about normal people having a bad day. Salespeople in department stores have to deal with nasty people themselves, and the strain can show. We're referring to the misanthrope who would be happier as a prison guard or the haughty princess who expects you to wait until she's finished chatting with friends. These are the demonic types who can wring all the joy out of spending your money and turn your shopping experience into a debilitating ordeal.

For instance, you might be in a department store to buy a sweater and want nothing more than to pick out one you like, hand over your credit card, and leave. But once at the sweater counter, you're ignored by a dreamy-eyed salesclerk who's chattering away on the telephone. From what you can overhear, she's telling somebody about a long, involved hassle with her boyfriend. "So I go to Bobby, I go, 'Look, just 'cause Johnny said that doesn't mean it's true, y'know?' So he goes . . ." And so on through a verbatim accounting that would tax Miss Rona.

Rather than waiting for the end of this saga, you should leave quietly, find the store's personnel department, and ask to speak to a personnel officer on an "urgent matter." Be calm, polite, and specific.

> PERSONNEL OFFICER: Yes, can I help you?
>
> CUSTOMER: I'm sorry to bother you, but I'm quite bothered myself. Could you tell me who's the supervisor of your sweater department?
>
> PERSONNEL OFFICER: That would be the (department buyer/floor manager). But what's the trouble?
>
> CUSTOMER: I spent a good four or five minutes waiting for the salesperson, who for all I know is still talking on the phone about her boyfriend Bobby. I'm not trying to get anyone in trouble, but I am trying to buy a sweater and I can't get any help.
>
> Five minutes may not seem like such a long wait, but it is when you're as pressed for time as I am today. I would certainly appreciate it if you could just help me get my sweater so I can be on my way.
>
> PERSONNEL OFFICER: Yes, I certainly will. Let me come down with you.

If, as luck would have it, your clerk is now helping some other customer with gushing, bright-eyed enthusiasm, the officer's first order of business will still be to enlist another clerk to see that you get your sweater. There may also be a heated discussion with the clerk and her supervisor that you may or may not wish to witness. But you can be sure that someone will wait on you immediately. Remember, never waste time arguing with a belligerent salesclerk. Just prepare your case as you head upstairs. Marshaling someone in a position of authority will make the store work for you by letting someone else's angry energy deal with salespeople who are argumentative, who insult your taste, or just "serve" you with snaillike deliberation and disinterest.

Even if you return to the scene and a clerk's immediate colleagues lie on her behalf, your calm demeanor and simple desire to get your merchandise rather than punish the offender will convince most supervisors. They expect to find a certain amount of rudeness, laziness, and incompetence in their staff.

When a store doesn't have a personnel office, you should take your problem to the department *buyer*—generally a take-charge, highly pressured individual who won't recoil from bawling out an errant employee in front of you and anybody else within earshot.

Abuse As Store Policy. Nowadays clothing or specialty stores may acquire an image of fashion leadership based on their success in browbeating customers into believing that they're lucky to be admitted at all. Stores that use snob cachet to oppress prey upon their middle-class customers' dreams of upward mobility and the insecurities that go along with them.

One famous designer's shop in New York City used to be the quintessential example of a high-priced chamber of horrors. They closed for lunch every day during the only hours that most employed people could take time off to shop. They assembled an arrogant crew of frustrated Cinderellas and Lord Fauntleroys to insult customers. They even chased one well-dressed customer out into the street one day and dragged her back into the shop—not for alleged shoplifting but because she didn't complete a transaction to their liking. Bad word of mouth and harder economic times evidently caught up with this shop, which has since opened for lunch and otherwise tried to improve customer relations. But other stores that thrive on hating their customers abound.

This shouldn't imply that every fashion boutique is fair game for retribution. Most boutiques are in business to sell innovative designs you can't find elsewhere, offer highly personalized service, and charge higher prices accordingly. We do, however, resent high-handed treatment in "designer" shops that offer a line manufactured in Central American sweatshops, then marked up into the ionosphere—especially when their expensive buttons fall off two weeks later. When you're dealing with rabidly unhelpful salespeople in stores of this ilk, it makes no sense to complain to management, since they set the tone for their hirelings. But for sheer *chutzpah* in beating them at their own game, nobody does it better than our friend Lenore, a professional stylist who knows fashion merchandise.

Lenore has opened charge accounts by mail—presumably so she doesn't have to watch a credit application dropped on the floor in front of her when she requests it—in every high-priced, high-fashion shop in town. This protects her with first-strike capabilities when she wants to withhold payment on some item. (See Chapter 8, Credit, for the wealth of legal options you now enjoy for "stopping payment" on charge purchases.)

When Lenore enters overpriced fashion and specialty stores, she breezes in with the insouciance of a barefoot contessa and immediately begins putting the staff through their paces. First, she'll try on dozens of outfits without apology or even notice of the salesperson's spiteful ways.

SALESPERSON: (exasperated sigh) I just don't know what Madame could *possibly* be looking for.

LENORE: I saw some lovely things in your Paris store last month, but I can't seem to find anything comparable here. Is this *all* you have in suits?

When she finds a designer original for three hundred dollars or so that's up to her standards, she'll charge it and, often enough, take it to her own tailor to knock off a reasonable facsimile. Then she sends the original back to the store, well within the specified return period, with a note saying that her husband didn't care for it or pointing out a designer defect, for credit to her account.

If she buys expensive crystal or china at an arrogant department store, she'll try it out during a dinner party to see if guests ooh and ah. If not, it's through the dishwasher twice and back to the store for credit.

Or if the same store that's earned her disrespect offers free decorator services in their furniture department, she'll take full advantage of the decorator for ideas, then buy what she wants at another store that discounts the same merchandise.

OBTAINING A 40% DECORATOR'S DISCOUNT

Lenore also carries a professional card that lets her buy furniture, carpeting, fabrics, and wallpaper at substantial discounts from "closed" showrooms that aren't open to the public. You should be able to do the same. If you've always had a yen to be a decorator (or even if you haven't), you can order business cards printed with your name, address, phone number, and the magic words *Interior Design*.

This is all the identification that most professional showrooms ask from anyone who walks in, providing you also carry an air of assurance and either specify some items you want to buy or drop a few designer buzz words, both of which you can pick up from a department store's free decorator. It may even be worth your while to take an inexpensive basic course in interior design so you'll know the jargon. This will distinguish you, if you're a woman, from the amateurs who just want to look over some bargain furniture. (They're called bag ladies in the trade, after the unfortunates who live out of shopping bags on the streets of major cities.) If you're a man, they virtually never question you anyway—probably because most men haven't developed a keen interest in home decorating above the Barcalounger level and wouldn't bother with this theater approach to shrewd buying. But the rewards are definitely there, since you can save 40 percent on furniture and carpets, one-third on wallpaper and fabrics.

If you decide to order something, the question of credit will come up. Why don't you have an account with them? Because you'll identify yourself as soon as you walk in as a new designer just establishing your business. Be sure to tell them right away that you'll be buying "pro forma," meaning that you'll pay them up front. They'll be delighted to take your money, and you'll get better, more knowledgeable service than you could count on in most stores. You'll find the closed showrooms, by the way, listed under "Furniture Dealers—Showrooms" in your Yellow Pages.

WHEN STORES BREAK THEIR DELIVERY PROMISES

If buying with a decorator's business card doesn't appeal to you and you have to order furniture through a department store, never take their delivery dates seriously. Most furniture salespeople know that if they were totally honest about factory delivery schedules, you'd probably walk away and find another store that will gleefully tell you, "Four to six weeks." Because furniture manufacturers have their own problems, it can easily take longer. Sometimes a lot longer.

We hear many sad tales of "four- to six-week" deliveries that have straggled in after three or four months. And no amount of angry phone calls to the store salesperson or factory will help much. They assume, and reasonably so, that once you've been waiting seven or eight weeks already, you're not about to cancel the order and go through the same tiresome experience with another store and manufacturer.

So to make sure that you'll at least have furniture in your house while they assemble your new couch one feather at a time, arrange to charge your purchase to your credit account at the store. If you don't have one already, open one for the purpose. When the order you've signed states four to six weeks and it doesn't arrive on time, you can pick up your Yellow Pages and look under "Furniture Rentals." Arrange to have a rental company duplicate as closely as possible whatever it is you're supposed to have by this time—let's say it's a couch. Then keep the rental couch until your new one arrives. When you receive your statement from the store with the charge for the couch listed, deduct the amount you've paid for your rental and just pay the balance. Explain why you're contesting the charge. (See Chapter 8, Credit, for the fine points of contesting a charge.)

The store, of course, will be likely to launch horrified protests that it's "not their policy" to compensate customers for the inconvenience they cause with their Alice-in-Wonderland delivery dates. They'll say they can't be held responsible for the manufacturer. But you will adamantly refuse to pay, reminding them that the *store* promised you the delivery date, not the manufacturer, and telling them you'll be happy to go to court. (See letter in the Revenge Kit for a sample). The fact is that they've breached your contract, and a judge would probably find on your behalf, ordering the store to let you keep most or all of the disputed amount. So you'll undoubtedly be better off withholding the money and foisting the burden of collection off on the store rather than paying up and having to sue them.

Be sure to send your version of this letter to the store president, pointing out the store's culpability and professing your desire to drag this case through the courts if necessary. Most store presidents are, by virtue of training and experience, ready to weigh the value of (1) keeping a customer happy and (2) containing the matter before it gets out in the open and gives other people ideas. Most executives would decide in favor of closing their books on the matter *if* the expense of the couch rental is not too overwhelming—say $75 or less. But if you're deducting $692 for two months' worth of antiques you've leased, you should brace yourself for a serious courtroom battle. And see an attorney for a free consultation beforehand.

RETURNING SHODDY MERCHANDISE FOR PROFIT

Most of us can't confine all our shopping safaris to designer boutiques, decorator showrooms, and department stores with lofty images to uphold. When you need appliances and other mundane life machinery, you may have to cut through more squalid sectors of the retail jungle. For these trips, you need all your wits about you to deal with fast-buck discounters and other merchants who have no desire to give you your money back for the toaster that sends charred toast streaking toward the ceiling or the vacuum cleaner that strains to pick up a dustball.

Charge Everything. This advice flies in the face of what you hear from many consumer experts, who tell you to save money where possible by paying cash. That's all well and good for a world of worry-free products, but in our world, you stand a fair chance of receiving defective merchandise. And you probably want to avoid the frustration of stalking some retailer through the courts just to get your money back.

When you charge most purchases, you can make one good-faith effort to let the retailer repair your defective item, then summarily withhold payment until you get satisfaction. (See Chapter 8.) If you pay cash, you'll have to force the merchant into refunding your money or giving you a working product—but without the advantage of withheld payment. They can attempt to "repair" a defective tricycle again and again until your tot is off to college.

But we'll consider the likelihood that you've already paid for something that's gone wrong and you want not just redress but compensation for the trouble you've been caused. Fortunately, there are ways to accomplish that objective under federal regulations and state laws.

Revoking Acceptance Under Implied-Warranty Protection. There are two kinds of warranties that come with virtually any product you buy.

1. The Manufacturer's Express Warranty. This is the document you generally find when you pull apart the plastic bag that's packed into the box with your product. It's in there somewhere with the operating

instructions, the sales literature, and the identification card you're supposed to send back with your name, address, and your answers to a lot of nosy questions that the company can use as free market research. (Incidentally, many savvy buyers hold back on mailing these cards, since express warrantees generally have a limitation period. This way a buyer can "start" the warranty when a product develops some malfunction later in life and they feel the manufacturer should fix it free.)

The express warranty is always a *limited* warranty, in that it purposely restricts the seller's liability. For the buyer, it usually involves the tedious hassle of packing the product in a box and sending it back to the manufacturer for—at the manufacturer's discretion—repair or replacement on their own timetable. Exhibit A shows a typical warranty for a household appliance, in this case a food processor. What you'll notice most about this warranty, though, is the host of disclaimers about what it does *not* cover. By drafting their own warranty statement, manufacturers hope to skip around a body of law that gives you infinitely greater protection. And herein lies your more effective remedy . . .

2. The Implied Warranty of Merchantability. What's known as the Uniform Commercial Code (UCC) is federal law that has been adopted by every state but Louisiana. Section 2-719 of the code states that every product offered for sale—unless it's clearly sold "as is"—has to be suitable for its intended use in order to be considered "merchantable" or fit for sale. If you buy a product and it doesn't do what it's supposed to, like a tape player that won't play tapes, then the product is considered "substantially impaired." And if that's the case, you can *revoke acceptance* of that product after giving the seller a reasonable opportunity to set it right.

EXHIBIT A
A MANUFACTURER'S EXPRESS WARRANTY
(And Why You Should Forget It)

Destructo Food Processor

Limited Warranty

Destructo Corporation warrants this new Processor 1221B against defects in material or workmanship for a period of one year from the date of original purchase for use, and agrees to repair or, at our option, replace any defective unit without charge for either parts or labor.

DESTRUCTO IS NOT RESPONSIBLE FOR LOSS, INCONVE-
NIENCE OR DAMAGE WHETHER DIRECT, INCIDENTAL,
CONSEQUENTIAL OR OTHERWISE RESULTING FROM
BREACH OF ANY EXPRESS OR IMPLIED WARRANTY, OR
MERCHANTABILITY OR OTHERWISE WITH RESPECT TO
THE PROCESSOR, AND REPAIR OR REPLACEMENT WILL BE
DESTRUCTO'S SOLE OBLIGATION IN CASE OF SUCH
BREACH. NO ACTION FOR BREACH OF IMPLIED WAR-
RANTY, OF MERCHANTABILITY OR OTHERWISE, MAY BE
COMMENCED LATER THAN ONE (1) YEAR AFTER DATE OF
ORIGINAL RETAIL PURCHASE. Some states do not allow limita-
tions on how long an implied warranty lasts and some states do not
allow the exclusion or limitation of incidental or consequential
damages, so the above limitation or exclusion may not apply to you.

What this means, first of all, is that you should never buy a product marked
or sold "as is."

And, second, you can forget the manufacturer's limited warranty if you buy
an incorrigible product that, after you've had it back to the store once for
repairs, obviously can't be fixed. Now you should notify the store in writing that:

I am forthwith revoking acceptance of the (product description)
purchased at (store name) on (date) under Section 2-719 of the
Uniform Commercial Code. You may pick up the (product) at my
home on (date). I will expect a check in the amount of $
_____, representing a full refund of the purchase price plus
sales tax, within 10 business days.

It would be easier if you'd charged the purchase originally so you could
withhold payment, but let's say you didn't. Now the store will either take the
product back and refund your money, contest your revocation with some
peculiar argument of its own, or stonewall you to see if you can be stalled off
until after they sell the store. Since you obviously know your rights under the
UCC, they'll probably opt for delaying tactics, hoping to wear you down. In this
case, you should follow up with a demand note to the effect that:

On (date), I notified you that I had revoked acceptance of the
(product). You have not claimed the merchandise and refunded my
purchase price as of this date. Thus I must inform you that I am
preparing to sue you in small-claims court for additional incidental and
consequential damages as follows:

(list)

If I do not receive your check and you do not claim your merchandise within 48 hours, I will file the action as attached.

And you'll enclose a copy of the small-claims papers you've filled out but not filed as yet. As we described in Chapter 3, incidental and consequential damages are your best leverage now, since they keep piling up as long as the store withholds your refund. These can include (1) the cost of storing the product (say $5 per day), which now belongs—as far as you're concerned—to the store again; (2) your time off from work, and the time you spent writing letters and making telephone calls to resolve the problem; and (3) actual losses the product has caused you. Say you bought the Destructo Food Processor and it went berserk in your kitchen, hopping around and smashing expensive wineglasses on the counter. Now you sue for the replacement cost of these eight pieces of Bacarrat crystal (try to contain yourself to items that wouldn't cause a judge to laugh out loud at your claim) as well as any other breakage or injuries it might have caused. At this point, the store will perceive a point of diminishing returns in delaying a refund and probably be happy to get you off its back.

Be sure to revoke acceptance early in the game. If it appears that you've been using a product for a long time despite your claim of impairment, the store and a court may balk. The exception to this is when the store has cajoled you into bringing the product back several times for repairs, and this is what caused the delay. In practice, you can usually revoke acceptance within a year after you bought the product, but we can't imagine why you'd want to keep a nonfunctional product that long. And if we can't, the store probably couldn't either.

Other Exculpatory Waivers. Remember Marianne and her white suit the dry cleaner ruined in Chapter 2? When she brought it back, the manager tried to hide behind the waiver on the cleaning ticket that limited its liability to ten times the cost of cleaning. In many states, such an "exculpatory waiver" will not protect a seller from retaliation—it's just a ploy to try to gull the gullible. So call your local consumer-protection agency or civil-court clerk if a retailer tries to claim a similar waiver of responsibility, find out what the law is in your state, and cite the statute number in your demand letter.

If you press your claim aggressively enough and include your demand for damages, you can probably obtain a settlement that will give you not just redress, but some profit from defective merchandise. But you'll be in an even better position to do so if you can establish some *tort liability* on the part of the store's owners or employees. A "tort" is legalese for some wrong another person does you, for which he or she can be taken to court and punished by an order to pay you money damages. If you win.

Alleging Misrepresentation or Fraud. In building a case against a retailer that could gain you a bonus on top of the refund you should get anyway, it helps to review very carefully what you were told when you bought a product. If the owner or a salesperson made false representation to induce you to buy, he or she may be guilty of *tortious fraud.* And if that's the case, you have the right to sue for punitive damages that could be two or three times the purchase price plus attorney's fees in many states. All states have laws against fraud, of course, but in some you can't recover punitive damages beyond a refund.

So try to recall whether the owner or some employee of the store made statements of "fact" that you *relied on* in buying the product. If they were deceptive statements, you might have leverage. For example:

CUSTOMER: Is this watch waterproof?

SALESPERSON: Sure. It's a diver's watch, isn't it? (Deceptive if the watch is not waterproof and becomes waterlogged in the shower.)

CUSTOMER: Does it keep good time?

SALESPERSON: Accurate to a second a week. It's quartz y'know. (Deceptive if it's not a quartz watch, and loses a few minutes every week.)

CUSTOMER: Well, I like the watch, but frankly, I'd rather buy it at an authorized dealer so I can get it repaired more easily.

SALESPERSON: We're an authorized dealer. We're selling it, aren't we? (Deceptive if they are not, in fact, a dealer authorized by the manufacturer to service and repair its products.)

If you can't recall some verbal deception, review the advertising that brought you in to see if it violates any of the restrictions discussed in Chapter 3. If you think you have a case, see a free-consultation lawyer.

REVENGE KIT FOR STORES

SAMPLE LETTER ABOUT A DEFECTIVE PRODUCT

Torts Department Store
Shopping Mall Drive
Attn: President

Date:

Dear Mr./Ms. _____,

Last week I purchased a product manufactured under your store name labeled Tortious Shampoo (sales receipt attached).

While I was preparing to shampoo my daughter's hair, I attempted to twist the top off. Indeed the top twisted off; including the top of the bottle. The result was a long gash between my forefinger and thumb requiring stitches and three trips to the doctor.

Since I could not wet that hand, I was forced to have both my hair and my daughter's washed at the local beauty salon three times each last week (see invoice attached). I hereby make a demand for $92.30 for the doctor's visits, the beautician's bill, and the bottle of shampoo.

Your product was defective and was the proximate cause of a bodily injury. The nature and extent of my injury is clear. I enclose the doctor's statement concerning my treatment and prognosis. The bottle is presently in my custody.

Let me advise you that your negligent behavior as a supplier and my resulting injury is recoverable not only under the common laws of negligence but under statutory law for strict liability,* premised on the unreasonably dangerous nature of the product.

As well, you have fallen below the standards encompassed in an implied warranty of merchantability, which provides that the goods sold are fit for the ordinary purposes for

---

* The majority of U.S. courts have adopted such strict liability guidelines for defective products. ·

which they are used. Let me hasten to add there can be no abnormal use imputed to my handling of the bottle.

Please contact me within ten (10) business days to resolve this matter. You may consider this letter legal notification under the Uniform Commercial Code.

Yours truly,

cc: Insurance Company for Cavalier Department Store
Certified Letter

SAMPLE LETTER CONCERNING LATE FURNITURE DELIVERY

To: President
Torts Department Store
Address:

Date:

Re: Contested charge for breach of contract Charge Account
_____

Dear Mr./Ms. _____,

On April 30th, 198___, I visited your store to buy a bedroom set for my daughter. Since she had been away for a year at school, my husband and I believed this would be an appropriate welcome-home surprise.

Promised a delivery date for the week of May 20–27, I charged the $985 cost to my store account. Your promised delivery date came and went. As, might I add, did my little girl's feeling of welcome when she arrived home on June 5 to find her old belongings given to Goodwill Industries and nothing in their place.

On June 20, I decided my daughter could no longer sleep on the living room couch. I thus rented a bedroom set from Paradise Rentals. (See invoice attached hereto.)

On July 15, the furniture finally arrived. Simultaneous with its arrival came a statement from you (attached hereto). You will note that I have attempted to resolve this matter amicably by merely deducting from my bill the amount I paid for the rental furniture.

Your billing department finds this unacceptable. They tell me the manufacturer was late, not you. Let me remind you that I contracted with you for the furniture to be delivered in four weeks. I neither know nor care where you obtain it. I can no more imagine making that my concern than expecting my rental company to collect from you.

It is axiomatic in law that a contract is formed with an offer and acceptance based on *certain* terms. Please do not attempt to interpose your manufacturer into our contract. Your unilateral breach has been the proximate and foreseeable cause of my rental expenses. Correct your bill and send it to me by return mail. Failure to do so will result in my withdrawing my offer to pay anything for the furniture.

Then it will be incumbent on you to collect any money a court may decide that I owe.

Yours truly,

5
restaurants
Turning the Tables

There's a certain kind of "continental" restaurant—and most cities can claim at least one—whose closest tie to Europe is the ability to inflict punishment worthy of the marquis de Sade. In his book *American Fried*, Calvin Trillin notes that these sting parlors are usually called something like La Casa de la Maison House. Their school of culinary management follows a simple, cost-effective formula: Deliver fast-food quality at grand gourmet prices, and chill the patrons with icy arrogance.

Typically, you're greeted by a maitre d' whose French background could probably be traced to some bilingual Canadian border town. Your reservation is never honored promptly. "Zat table eez not ready yet," he sniffs. "M'sieur will please wait a few moments." Now you can join the other victims packed into the foyer, studying their shoelaces in humiliation. Or you can squeeze into the bar and order four-dollar martinis consisting of nine parts vermouth and a pile of olives. After three-quarters of an hour, you're hustled to a table right by the kitchen door and menus are shoved into your hands. Then the maitre d' rattles off a list of specials in his pidgin French—prices omitted—and disappears. Presently the wine steward arrives, with that oversize key or tasting cup bobbing around his neck, to sell you whatever wines are going bad. When your order arrives, your "fresh" seafood hasn't quite thawed out yet. And your companion's elderly duck is set on fire at the table with great fanfare to destroy the evidence of a poorly prepared sauce. Finally, if you linger over coffee for more than ten minutes, the whopping check is presented without your asking and you spot, if you're very sharp-eyed, a small-type notice of "20% service charge included." We can understand why.

It's one thing to put up with lackluster food and service at Rosie's Diner or even Howard Johnson's. But when you're paying a premium, you deserve top-shelf attention and should enforce that prerogative (although you'll find some tactics here you can use in the Howard Johnsons of the world, too).

If you really knew what those expensive cattle-car restaurants were like before you ventured in, you'd probably have your frozen dinners at home and save sixty dollars. But maybe you were betrayed by a food critic who wines and dines gratis at La Casa to rhapsodize about the place. Or a local hot spot has earned a reputation for worthwhile food, but success has gone to their heads and they think customers will keep crowding in no matter how they're treated. Whatever your reasons for suffering at La Casa or one of its steak- or seafood-house relatives, you've probably acquired a taste for retribution. Here's what you can do to satisfy that craving.

YOUR OWN "OVERBOOKING" POLICY

Even if you hold a reservation, you might have to wait a reasonable time for your table at any restaurant. Most likely the place is fully booked and the people holding your table are just staying longer than they should.

But to walk into a packed foyer that looks like a greedy doctor's waiting room is a dead giveaway that overbooking with a heavy hand is business as usual. This policy, of course, relies on sheepish customers who won't complain or strike back.

If you're kept waiting longer than twenty minutes or so for your reserved table, a certain pall tends to settle over your evening's enjoyment. You feel as if you're being treated like a steerage-class citizen. You're humbled in front of your dinner guests. What can you do besides telling the maitre d' you don't intend to wait any longer? In which case you'll have to walk out if he stonewalls you, just to preserve your self-respect. No great revenge there.

Well, you could check their Fire Department Occupancy Certificate that says something to the effect of "occupancy restricted to 50 persons," when they routinely crowd the place with over 100. This will be posted next to their restaurant and liquor licenses, probably near the cloakroom. Then ask to use the house phone so you can report them to the fire department and request an immediate inspection. But in some cities, they could be paying off the inspectors and giving the fire commissioner free meals besides so they can overcrowd the place with impunity. If that's the case, they'll just enjoy a hearty chuckle at your little gambit, and you'll have to slink away in worse shape than before.

Or, if the maitre d' claims that the party at your table is loitering over coffee and drinks, you can glance over and see if they're preparing to pitch a tent for the night. Then ask the maitre d' if he will offer to buy them an after-dinner drink at the bar so you can claim the table that's rightfully yours.

But chances are good that the maitre d' in a restaurant that thrives on overbooking will truly enjoy rebuffing your efforts to cajole or harangue him into giving you the table you were promised. And if you try to bribe him, he'll probably pocket your money with a solemn expression and keep you waiting just as long—maybe longer to remind you that his attention is priceless.

Generally, the most satisfying approach you can take is to return to your group, apologize for bringing them to such a hateful place, and pass the time by enlisting their help in a little revenge game that will be fun for everyone except the restaurant.

To turn the tables, you, the rest of your group, and other helpmates you bring in should each devote a few minutes the next day to a coordinated strategy: Each person calls to make a reservation for the most popular seating on the same evening under a different name. The more the merrier. Applying creativity, you can even program your calls to make an anagram that will show up on the maitre d's reservations book as:

8:00 P.M. Seating

Name	Party Of
Nelson	4
Ornstein	4
Bilodeux	6
Owens	4
Delahanty	2
Yellins	4
Schwartz	4
Copacino	8
Offenhouser	6
Maxwell	4
Ingraham	4
Nordstrom	2
Gibbons	2

Need we say that none of these parties will actually show up.

On the appointed evening, at about 8:20, the maitre d' will be wondering what curse has been visited on his restaurant as the occupied tables dwindle to a meager few and the usually overcrowded bar and foyer have emptied out completely. This would be an opportune time to drop in, with a few of your fellow gamesters, take the best seat in the house, and enjoy a leisurely dinner with plenty of staff to serve you.

You might even want to send a note to your local papers—anonymously, of course—letting them in on the community's distaste for that restaurant's unconscionable overbooking policy, explaining what you've done to show them up, and mention that you're all ready to strike again if they don't adopt a more considerate attitude toward their customers. If the reporter's interested, he or she will undoubtedly call the restaurant to verify the story, and the management will realize how insidiously the restaurant's victims can retaliate. Because the beauty of this gambit is that they'll never know when it's going to happen again. They might even try to confirm each reservation for a while, but as soon as they decide it was a one-shot aberration and slack off, you can all gang up to repeat the game and hit them with a new anagram like IT'S US AGAIN.

DISCIPLINING A HAUGHTY OR DIFFICULT STAFF

If you don't care for the supercilious attitude you encounter at La Casa, you can always apply some savvy-consumer techniques to keep the maitre d' and his henchmen on the defensive.

First of all, when the captain runs through his machine-gun litany of specials, stop him midway and say, "One moment. We'd like to know the prices of all the specials, too. If you'd start at the beginning, please." Monsieur will have to accommodate you, and you'll probably find that they're significantly more expensive than the regular fare on the menu.

Enforcing Truth in Menu. Next on the agenda is a perusal of the menu and what it claims. If you spot descriptions like "fresh shrimp" or "Maine lobster," that's not harmless puffery to be winked at but representations that the shrimp is really fresh, not frozen, and that the lobster truly hails from Maine waters and not California. A restaurant that plays fast and loose with the veracity of its own menu may be guilty of fraud if your city or state has adopted "Truth-in-Menu" legislation. It pays, if you go to restaurants very often, to check with your local district-court clerk or prosecutor's office to find out whether such laws exist in your community and, if so, exactly what they say.

Then if a restaurant tries to dupe you with a tough piece of mutton disguised as tender young lamb or an icebound red snapper touted as fresh, you can get just as tough and fresh with the management. Confirm your worst suspicions before you even order:

CUSTOMER: Is this fish really fresh?

MAITRE D': (offended) Of course, m'sieur!

CUSTOMER: Would you be good enough to bring it out for me please.

The maitre d' scowls his usual displeasure but trots off to the kitchen and returns with the suspect fish for your expert inspection.

CUSTOMER: Looks a bit cloudy in the eye, wouldn't you say? (An indication that this catch is not fresh at all.)

MAITRE D': (nervous glance at nearby patrons, who are enjoying this unexpected dinner theater) I can assure you that we only serve fresh fish daily.

CUSTOMER: Perhaps you could show me today's invoice then? I'm rather particular about fresh seafood.

MAITRE D':   I could not *possibly* search our chef's files . . .

CUSTOMER: Yes, yes, I'm sure. I'll have a look at the beef for your steak au poivre then.

(Light applause from the adjoining tables.)

Wine Tasting and Sommelier Basting. When you're studying the wine list in La Casa and hear the jingle of an oversize key and chain, this signals a bout with the wine steward or *sommelier*. His job is to unload some exorbitantly priced bottle collecting dust in the cellar rather than the perfectly good, fairly priced selection you're looking for.

Today, California wines can be as expensive as French, although they may be better than the imports in the same price class. On the other hand, they may not. Since restaurants mark wine up 100 to 125 percent and sometimes more, it's a good idea to do your homework at a wine shop or get a good book on the subject and memorize a few reasonably priced wines to order. If you don't see one on La Casa's wine list, and you don't think the sommelier can be trusted, you might be better off with the house wine—usually a decent California brand you could buy in a supermarket—and save some money. But you shouldn't order it without deflating the sommelier first if he tries to shame you into a high-priced label.

SOMMELIER: This evening I recommend a special offering . . . the finest in our cellar . . . Chateau Lafite Rothschild. (Good stuff, to be sure, but even the Rothschilds would die laughing if they saw you paying what La Casa will try to extract.)

CUSTOMER: (knowing smile) No, that's a bit much for a Lafite. I don't see any petite chateau bordeaux on your list. Don't you have a Chateau La Becade or a Fonreaud in your cellar? (Both excellent choices any wine snob would appreciate, from the Medoc and Listrac regions respectively. They should be priced at about $12–15 a bottle.)

SOMMELIER: No, we do not have any *petit chateaux* at present. (Or ever.)

CUSTOMER: Well, what's the house selection?

SOMMELIER: Paul Masson burgundy.

CUSTOMER: I suppose we'll have a carafe of that, then.

If you do order a bottle of wine from the cellar that tastes at all sour or funny, reject it immediately.

CUSTOMER: This wine has turned.

SOMMELIER: (tasting) M'sieur must be mistaken.

CUSTOMER: I've tasted quite a bit of wine in my time, and in my judgment, this wine has turned. It's not acceptable.

Now the sommelier and maitre d' may try to gang up on you by insinuating that your cheapskate selection isn't much to speak of and you got what you paid for. But there's an answer for that twisted logic.

MAITRE D':   (condescendingly) M'sieur must be aware that this label is low-priced and not one of our finer selections.

CUSTOMER: With all the perfectly good wines in this class, why would you deliberately try to sell me a bad one?

The only explanations are that they think their customers either won't know any better or would rather force down the worst swill than admit they made a mistake. Or the house just doesn't know how to buy wine. But the maitre d' isn't likely to admit either of those explanations. You should point out that you relied on their expertise to offer acceptable wines in each class. You can't be expected to police every single label that arrives on our shores to know what's fit for consumption and what isn't.

The Graduated-Tip Scale. We don't subscribe to the "stiff the waiter/waitress" method of getting even for anything that goes wrong in a restaurant. It's not the staff's fault that the management overcharges or the chef is an alcoholic who stuffs your guest's roast beef instead of your cornish hen.

But waiters and waitresses are obligated to give you courteous service. In fact, courts have upheld a customer's legal right to same. One case involved a Florida man whose waitress called him a "black son of a bitch" during an argument over a seafood platter. He sued for mental distress, and the court awarded him $2500 in damages. This kind of opportunity doesn't present itself often, and you shouldn't try to provoke hostilities every time you dine out in the hope of collecting thousands. But if a waiter or waitress or other employee is actually abusive, you can go home and send the restaurant owners the letter in the Revenge Kit at the end of this chapter to see if they'd like to settle with you before you take them to court and stir up some local publicity.

What you might consider is a firm policy of tipping on a sliding scale to reward or punish waiters or waitresses according to how well they really perform for you.

We know what you're probably thinking now. And we empathize with your desire to walk out of a restaurant psychologically unscathed by disgusted stares and sarcastic "thanks a *lot*" epithets hurled at your back because you didn't leave a standard tip. Those intimidating tactics, which most experienced waiters and waitresses have perfected over the years, can literally haunt you for days if you care at all what people think about you. Everybody knows that waiters and waitresses make virtually all their money on tips, and it can seem churlish or bullying to deprive them of their livelihood.

But look at it another way. Salespeople don't get paid commissions if they can't deliver their customers' orders on time. You wouldn't tip a cab driver who takes you out of your way and becomes obnoxious when you try to correct him. So why give a waiter or waitress special dispensation to be sluggish, surly, or incompetent and still command a standard 15 percent gratuity?

Instead, here's how to use a waiter's attempts to intimidate you against him, playing reasonable and respectful "adult" to his whiny and sarcastic "child." Say your party of four has been virtually ignored all evening, and you leave a five-dollar tip on a hundred-dollar check.

WAITER: (sneering) *Do* come again.

CUSTOMER: (looking him square in the eye) Sir, I'm sure you'll agree that we were *both* under par this evening. But I'm also sure that we'll both make up for it next time.

At the very least, you'll be a model of steely-nerved integrity to your dinner guests, who would probably sneak off if they stiffed the waiter themselves. At best, the waiter will respect you for facing up to him and actually give you premium service the next time if you greet him with a pleasant, let-bygones-be-bygones attitude.

BOLTING THE CHECK LEGALLY

Some people are of a temperament to keep their complaints about food and service to themselves. For instance, this account appeared in a British magazine:

There is a story of a kindly man who suffered a dinner and would have departed peaceably if the restaurant manager had not insisted on knowing what he thought of the meal. "If the soup had been as warm as the white wine," he said, "and the fish as fresh as the waitress, and the claret as old as the cheese, then it would have been adequate."[1]

We admire his restraint but wouldn't recommend such genteel resignation in most American restaurants. If you're dining out anywhere from a Bonanza Steak House to a haute cuisine palace, we think you should refuse to pay for food you can't eat and service you don't receive. Not that you should just bolt the restaurant without a by-your-leave, which is illegal and self-demeaning. But you should demand a final accounting in which you deduct as much as you feel proper.

First, audit the bill carefully and see if you've been overcharged. We don't have statistics on the incidence of bill padding, but we've found a lot of mistakes on our own bills over the years, particularly after we've had a few drinks. Sometimes the "error" amounts to ten or fifteen dollars on a hefty check—and never in our favor.

If you're with other people and two of you left most of their entrées untouched because the food was substandard (and couldn't be salvaged by a trip back to the kitchen), deduct the entrée charges from your bill. If the manager squawks, tell her to go ahead and call the police if she wants. You're happy to stay until they arrive, but you'll be damned if you're going to pay for an inedible meal. Point out, naturally, that you'll entertain a suit for false imprisonment if she does call the police. Most restaurateurs don't really want to run that risk and will probably accept what you give them.

If the house policy is "service included"—which implies that (1) a restaurant's service is so slovenly they can't expect customers to leave standard tips, or (2) they think their customers are deadbeats—you can contest this charge, too. If the service really was terrible, don't bother with the waiter. Just ask to speak to the manager. Explain to him that you have no intention of paying 15 percent for service you haven't received, and enumerate your points of contention: Your waiter ignored you for half an hour before taking your order, he didn't bring you another drink until you'd asked three times, and so on. Just build a good case— one small item isn't enough. If the manager balks at your reasoning, run through your "call the police" routine and he'll probably just let you go, although you might not be invited back.

If your meal is a complete disaster from beginning to end and the staff is so hopeless they don't even bring you your check for fifteen minutes after you've demanded it, leave a note and walk out. It should spell out your grievances along the lines of:

I waited 15 minutes to order, 35 minutes for an inedible lunch, and another 15 minutes for the check before leaving. If you expect me to pay for this kind of service—sue me. I would welcome an opportunity to see you in court.

> Name
> Address
> Phone Number

This pretty much fulfills your legal obligations. Your chances of being sued, unless your lunch "date" happened to be a party of twenty-five guests who swept out the door with you, are slim.

GUERRILLA DINING

No discussion of revenge etiquette for restaurants would be complete without a few particularly nasty tricks we've heard about.

Separate checks for the six of you. Not to be requested until you ask for the check. They'll rant and rave, but they'll have to oblige.

Appetizers for six at peak dining hours. Start by ordering just appetizers and linger a long while. When the waiter appears to take your dinner order, "Oh, we haven't time for *dinner* tonight. Why, it took you 45 minutes to bring our dinner Tuesday night when we were here!"

Send your steak back. Never for being too rare, which means they can just throw it back on the fire. Always for being too well done, so they'll have to throw it in the trash.

Bon appetit!

REVENGE KIT FOR RESTAURANTS

ANONYMOUS PRESS RELEASE FOR OVERBOOKING

To: (Newspaper or Station)
From: Les Enfants Terrible
Re: Vengeance on La Casa de la Maison House!

Last week we reserved a table for four at La Casa.

Forty-five minutes after our timely arrival, we were still waiting with over twenty other people victimized by this restaurant's cruel overbooking practices.

But this gave us ample time to devise a game which we call Restaurant Monopoly. Objective: To make sure we had a "monopoly" on their tables last night. Strategy: To book, in fictitious names, most of their tables with no-show reservations.

If you call La Casa to see how they enjoyed this turning of the tables, ask if the maitre d' noted the anagram we carefully made with the first letter of each fictitious party's name: N-O-B-O-D-Y-S- C-O-M-I-N-G.

We hope this will be a lesson to La Casa, since we will apply the concept of "linkage" to our future gaming.

If they keep us waiting again, we will strike again. Au revoir . . . until next time!

LETTER THREATENING SUIT FOR EMPLOYEE MISCONDUCT

January 13, 1981

A-1 Hotels
2 rue de La Street
Dumpville, USA
Attn: Manager
      Re: La Casa de la Maison House

Last Tuesday night I met a prospective client at your restaurant to discuss an important business venture. This became impossible as the maitre d' and waiter were extremely abusive. (List your grievances.)

I am sure you realize that under the common law of this state, a special relationship is recognized between your entity and its patrons. And your employees breached this relationship with their intentional infliction of emotional distress.

Further, I am sure your attorney can advise you that there is no need for me to prove actual damages. My prima facie case can be supported simply on evidence of my distress. I will, however, be seeking punitive damages as it is clear from your employees' behavior that they were motivated by malicious intent.

I will expect to hear from you or your attorney within ten (10) days, or I will file suit.

Yours truly,

6
health clubs

Giving Shady Operators a Workout

You're only as old as you feel. Keep telling yourself that as you self-induce whiplash in a vibrating hip belt or when you experience the first terrible pain that means a Nautilus machine is going to work on your behalf. At least the benefits of legitimate exercise are worth it. What may not be are the "benefits" you sign up for at some of the new health clubs. Like the people who run vocational schools and correspondence courses, health-club operators use a formula to calculate future profitability. That formula rests on their expectation that, like most buyers, you'll get tired of the whole idea within a couple of months and drop out. This way they can sell more memberships than they could ever begin to service.

Once operator of a popular health club chain tells us that roughly two-thirds of new members slack off dramatically or actually stop using the facilities after the first few months of membership. In fact, he counts on it. He would have to expand his facilities—at a great loss—if everyone with a contract showed up for the duration. That wouldn't be a bad revenge strategy in itself, but most people don't want a daily workout against their will just to get their money's worth. Most of us, in fact, join such clubs impetuously, or to slim down for summer so we don't have to lie on the sand feeling like beached whales, and our enthusiasm wanes as the warm weather does.

Whatever your reasons for joining, assume that if you sign up for a long-term club membership, you might one day want to cancel the balance of your contract and forget the whole thing. This, unfortunately, could play havoc with the club operators' profit formula. So the clubs tend to devise ironclad contracts that will not allow a member to be released on any grounds less compelling than the destruction of the universe. But why would you sign a contract like that in the first place?

Most health clubs are very clever when it comes to selling their memberships. They hire Susan Anton look-alikes to charm prospective male members and Arnold Schwartzenegger runners-up to bring women into the fold. These bronzed gods and goddesses take their charges for a fast tour of the facilities and concentrate on building rapport with the prospective members. They might promise you 15 pounds off in two weeks with a straight face, or purr irresistibly about a "special offer" you can qualify for if you sign up immediately. And through a skillful combination of flattery, empty promises, too much attention on your love handles, and high-pressure closing tricks, they'll seduce you into contract signatures.

EXERCISING CAUTION BEFORE YOU JOIN

The smartest way to join a health club is for the shortest time possible, without having to sign anything. If they insist you sign, ask a lot of questions. Find out how competent your trainers are, how individualized their instruction is, when you'll be able to use the club, and how busy it will be when you can drop by. The kind of response you get to these specifics will be a fairly accurate indication of what you're getting yourself into.

TRAINER: Hey, babe, good to see you!

MIDDLE-AGED SPREAD: Thank you. I'd like some information about your club.

TRAINER: No problem. I'd say you're about 15 pounds overweight. Let's get you started on our vibrating belt. Pound those pounds right off of you. You'll be a knockout. Ho, ho. (Back slap)

MIDDLE-AGED SPREAD: Your ad said you have personalized exercise programs, designed and overseen by qualified trainers . . .

TRAINER: Hey, you're looking at him. (Muscle flex)

MIDDLE-AGED SPREAD: Do you mind if I ask you what your background is?

TRAINER: What you see is what you get, babe. A couple of hours a week and I'll have you looking like a teenager.

MIDDLE-AGED SPREAD: My time's rather limited. What are your hours here? And what access do I have to the facilities on a daily basis?

TRAINER: Time? Listen, there's no time like the present to get started.

MIDDLE-AGED SPREAD: Well, why don't I take a contract home with me and look it over.

TRAINER: (chuckle) Reading isn't going to get you in shape, hon.

Even if a club and its trainers still look good after hard interrogation, resist signing the contract. Take a free workout if they offer one. Then question members about how the program works for them and if they've achieved results.

If the hours you plan to use the club coincide with the needs of everyone else who works from nine to five, the place will be overcrowded when you come to work out. Getting through an exercise program is grueling enough without people scowling at you to make you go away and let them use the equipment. So it helps to visit facilities during the same hours you'll actually use them. Make sure you get specific answers to your questions about the availability of facilities. One member took a trainers' vague mention of "weekend hours" at face value. She didn't find out until after she'd signed the contract that Sunday, her one free day to work out, was the club's day of rest. She also learned that her club rotated its more popular facilities on a male/female basis, which cut down her available time by half.

Bring a friend with you to help size up the club's blandishments. Two women we happen to know visited a club together for information. They were separated and taken on a tour by two different trainers, but given exactly the same exercise plan. One had come in with the objective of losing 30 pounds; the other just wanted to keep her trim, 110-pound frame toned up for tennis. So make sure your club's "personalized" plan consists of more than routine calisthenics assigned to everyone who walks through the front door.

You should also be aware of just how well "passive" exercise machines like vibrating belts really work. The consensus among experts is that as much as we might like to believe in high-tech solutions, no machine will do our exercising for us. The current state of the art seems to be the Nautilus method, which involves pushing lazy muscles to their limit in order to make them grow. We haven't tried it but hear from people who've gotten results that it can hurt as much as any exercise, even though it's worth it.

FLEXING REVENGE POWER

If you're already under contract to one of these health parlors and you're dissatisfied with the facilities, the hours, or the results you've been getting, what can you do? You've read over the agreement several times with a jeweler's eye for a flaw, a loophole of any kind, and find none. Unless your state has a cooling-off period of three to five days after signing a contract (you can determine this by calling your local consumer affairs office or court clerk), there's probably no direct way to get out of it. So we'll travel the indirect route to vindication.

Biological Warfare. Many clubs that practice hard-sell tactics to pull you in usually take a relaxed attitude to keeping their facilities hygienic. Take a look at the whirlpool bath and you might see what we mean. Many of them are so overcrowded and poorly maintained, they begin to look like a huge Petri dish. Bring a guest as your witness to verify what you're about to do. Wait for a moment when none of the employees is watching you. Then, one hand holding your nose, plunge the other in and take a sample of the whirlpool water for chemical analysis. The nearest university science department or government health department can tell you where to have your specimen tested. With any luck, your vial will contain elements sufficiently vile to run afoul of your state or city's health code. Make a copy of the lab report. Then, gas mask in place, visit your club manager and unleash a preemptive strike.

MEMBER: I slipped on that slimy stuff you let grow all around your whirlpool bath last week and swallowed some water. I've been on antibiotics ever since.

MANAGER: Sorry to hear that, but why tell me about it?

MEMBER: Because my doctor said I was infected by the bacteria you let accumulate. Here's a copy of the lab report analyzing the specimen my witness and I took from the bath—clearly, enough to account for my illness. And all in violation of section 123 of the health code. I also found out you can be fined up to $10,000 and closed down for a year for that violation. I can get an inspector in this afternoon and sue for my damages tomorrow. Or maybe you'd like to give me my money back instead.

If the whirlpool bath doesn't yield the right evidence, try the locker room. Anyone who's been in a high-school gym class can appreciate the possibilities there. Pay a biology student from a nearby university's biology department to come in as your "guest" and take a smear from the shower-stall floor to transfer onto a slide for testing. Then proceed as you would with the whirlpool scenario.

Refund in hand, there's no reason for a responsible citizen to quit. Complain to the health department, which will probably take action against a gross offender. And you can always alert the media to what you found with the letter in the Revenge Kit at the end of this chapter.

"Transferring" Your Membership. In the course of looking into health club–member vendettas, we found that some disgruntled members used a simple strategy which would not be legal in your jurisdiction, but we'll pass it

on to you as an example of what some people will do when driven by frustration.

Many clubs that overlook membership have multiple locations. One wily customer had a nontransferrable membership card in such a chain. By playing her card close to her chest, she "transferred"—all for practical purposes—her unassignable membership. Relying (accurately) on the premise that checking other identification is too much to ask from most club employees, she sold her card at a reduced rate to a friend, with one stipulation: that her buyer use a facility other than the one frequented by the original owner. Since her friend used the card at a different location, she was never found out. And for all we know, that buyer passed the membership along to someone else when she grew disenchanted with the club.

If your club does permit transfer of membership, you can sell your rights by running an ad in the classified section of your local paper. At a nominal discount, it's a bargain for anybody but the health club. And if your club turned out to be less than you bargained for anyway, you shouldn't feel guilty about making it give long-term value for its money.

Alleging Fraud. If you can establish that a club misrepresented facts about its facilities or what you could hope to lose, and you relied on these "facts" in signing your contract, you might be able to free yourself from your indentured status with some legal maneuvering.

Here it's important to have visited the club originally with a friend, who was present when they launched their Herculean sales effort and will attest to what you claim they said. Of course, shoddy health club operators are probably up on fraud statutes themselves and were careful to separate the two of you, thus avoiding the witness problem.

But if you were promised a certain weight loss or facilities that weren't made available to you, proceed on your own if necessary by sending them an adaptation of the demand letter in the Revenge Kit, with court papers filled out but not yet filed. Then call the club manager.

MEMBER: I trust you received my letter. I'll give you this opportunity to refund my money before I take all of you to court.

MANAGER.   What do you mean "all" of us, tubby? It's your word against my trainer's, and he knows he didn't tell you any of that stuff you claimed in your letter.

MEMBER: I was so sure you'd say that, my lawyer's going to subpoena your entire staff to testify. As well as all the members who joined up the same week I did.

MANAGER: Sez you. (click)

Now the manager will have to weigh the unpleasant prospect of coaching his entire staff in how to perjure themselves against refunding your money. As a businessperson, albeit an unethical one, he'll probably opt for the cheaper and less perilous course.

REVENGE KIT FOR HEALTH CLUBS

PRESS RELEASE TO SEND TO HEALTH CLUB OPERATOR AND LOCAL MEDIA

To: (Newspaper or Station)
From: (Your Name and Phone Number)
Re: The Terror at Strongarm Health Spa

If you have already reviewed films such as *The Creature from the Black Lagoon*, you may be interested in seeing what real-life creatures inhabit the Jacuzzi at Strongarm Health Spa.

I recently subjected a sample of water from that stagnant pool to independent laboratory analysis and found the percentages of three strains of harmful bacteria described in the attached lab report.

I am also reporting these violations to the health department, so better hurry. I don't think that anyone will be admitted during the Jacuzzi's last minutes of operation.

SAMPLE DEMAND LETTER TO CLUB OPERATOR

To: Manager
Strongarm Health Spa
Address

January 2, 198____

Dear Mr./Ms. _____,

I visited your health spa on October 30, 198____ to obtain some information. While I had no immediate intention of joining, your sales tactics coerced me into contracting for a membership. This pressure applied, in conjunction with actual misrepresentations, is the basis for my letter and position.

You told me at the time that if for any reason my doctor recommended I not participate in strenuous exercising, I could get a refund, pro rata, for the additional time under my contract. When I advised you last week that my doctor felt I should not at this point continue at the club, you stared at me blankly and said that was "my problem." And that there would be no refund.

During my introduction to the club, you also pressured me to join on the spot as membership costs were "going up on Monday." I have checked and they have not.

Be advised that unless I receive a complete refund within ten (10) days, I will file the attached papers in court alleging fraud and misrepresentation.

Under state law I shall prevail, as I was clearly induced to enter into a transaction by your fraud and misrepresentation upon which I reasonably and actually relied.

Litigation costs aside, consider the unseemly attention your behavior will elect from the media. You can count on it, as I will dedicate myself to seeing my experience brought to light.

Yours truly,

Certified Letter

7
automobiles
How the Suckers Can Get a Better-than-Even Break

We don't know when America's love affair with the automobile went sour, but virtually all of us have some automotive horror story these days. Maybe you bought a used car that died of massive valve failure after a few thousand miles. Or you accepted a factory-fresh model that shimmied all the way home and continued to shake your molars loose five months later, after spending most of its young life in the dealer's service department. You may have been overhauled by mechanics more often than you'd care to guess.

And for those of you who don't own a car, maybe you've rented one. Have you ever taken a $19.95-per-day bargain for a three-day weekend and found that, when they added all the little extras at check-in time, your final bill was twice what you expected?

When it comes to buying and repairing cars, the odds of being driven to desperation are roughly even. One dealer who prefers to remain anonymous tells us that about 50 percent of new cars from American manufacturers have defects, the majority of which can't be fixed. And a 1979 US Transportation Department study disclosed that 50 percent of the $50 billion we spend on car repairs every year pays for unnecessary work, courtesy of mechanics' incompetence or outright fraud.

So if you're buying a car or leaving one for service or repairs, it's only fair to expect problems. Be prepared with preemptive first-strike tactics to better your odds, or you might spend many frustrating hours seeking redress from the road gang, who have a lot of experience and even more at stake in blocking your efforts.

THE NEW CAR SHUFFLE

In all fairness, dealers don't make those troubled vehicles themselves. They inherit them from the manufacturer. The problem is that they can't give nine-thousand-dollar automobiles back for credit as if they were spoiled can goods. So they pass them on to customers along with the good ones, cross their fingers, and hope for the best.

Factory Follies. Starting back at the manufacturers', some entire model lines reveal quirky design defects that management considers too insignificant or expensive to correct with a general recall.

Sometimes they're safety hazards you don't hear about until it's too late. Some recent-model Ford cars had an erratic habit of slipping into reverse gear and rolling backward when they were supposed to be safely in "park." Some of them rolled right over their owners, stirring much controversy but no recall. Another Ford product, the Pinto, featured a rear-mounted gas tank that would explode when hit and envelop the car in flames. Although Ford successfully defended itself against lawsuits for wrongful death, the disclosure of a company financial analysis of potential problems from the gas-tank design spoke volumes. When projected costs for fixing the tank were weighed against estimated "social costs" (meaning lives lost and resulting litigation), Ford apparently chose to save the retooling costs instead.

A recent "60 Minutes" story on Jeep Corporation's popular CJ5 disclosed it as more of an "off-the-road" vehicle than some owners had imagined. An insurance testing institute found that the jaunty Jeep would flip over at a usually safe 22-mile-per-hour turn as well as during fairly commonplace evasive maneuvers. The Jeep Corporation responded with film showing a stunt driver taking the same turns at higher speeds. But when "60 Minutes" did a camera closeup, both right wheels were dangerously off the road in an attitude that most nonstunt drivers couldn't handle.

Lemons that Squeeze their Owners. If you have the misfortune to buy a problem car that just can't be fixed, you're likely to find little sympathy from the dealer when you want it replaced. They'd rather have you bring it back time and again and put in three new engines than own up to the car's incorrigibility.

As we mentioned in Chapter 2, the industry considers—for economic reasons—replacement of defective cars out of the question. When you insist that the car is a lemon, they're likely to tell you to go ahead and sue them, since they know full well that your attorney's fees will exceed the price of the car. (And you probably won't be able to recover lawyer's fees unless you can prove that the dealer defrauded you, which isn't easy.)

Saab Story. To these factory-origin difficulties, dealers have been known to add their own careless or greedy wrinkles. As a typical example, a friend of ours recently bought a fourteen-thousand-dollar Saab on a Monday. Because it had to go through the rigors of a five-day dealer prep, she gave the salesman his check and postdated it for Friday. But by Tuesday, the salesman was so anxious to cash the check and collect his commission, he had the service department speed up their work and called to tell her the car was ready that day. She picked up her Saab and drove toward a party that night 100 miles away. At the 90-mile point, the car ground to a halt and refused to budge. And when she finally got it towed to a gas station after much grief, the mechanic found that the hurried prep folks had neglected a few items that caused about three hundred dollars' worth of damage.

And such negligence doesn't begin to touch on the slippery tactics that some dealers use as standard policy, from bait and switch to the "aftersales" scam, in which an outside telephone salesman representing himself as the dealer's "service manager" calls up and tells you to bring your week-old car in for service. The real motive of such calls is to high-pressure sell you more options you didn't buy initially at prices now way above the factory list.

Dealing with an Uncooperative Dealer. When you buy a new car off the lot or on order, *plan not to accept the car* the day you're supposed to pick it up.

Most people go to the dealer fully intending to get rid of their tired old wreck and drive off in the shiny new one. Because their expectations make them impatient, they tend to slough off little problems because they assume they can bring the car back the following week to correct them. The salesman gladly agrees with unenforceable verbal assurances. They sign the final contract and roar off in a white cloud of euphoria tinted with the black smoke from a defective engine.

That's asking for trouble. Instead, go with the intent of leaving the car there a few more days and putting the dealer on the defensive. Bring along a sharp-eyed Mr. Goodwrench of your own and go over the car religiously, writing down anything you don't want to accept as permanent. Then, with your mechanic, take the car for a good hard test drive under different road conditions. Look out especially for the items that are virtually impossible to repair—a bad emission control system, shimmies, hesitation. Your mechanic should know. If you can't find a mechanic you can trust, take it to an independent electronic diagnostic center (listed in the Yellow Pages) and get a complete readout during the test drive.

Finally, take it back with a list of all the adjustments you want made and set a date to accept final delivery. When you return, repeat the whole procedure before you sign the contract. And, if necessary, leave it again. The dealer won't like this much, but you'll like the consequences even less if you don't, because your dealer's interest in satisfying your demands will plunge dramatically once you've given him your check.

Consider very carefully financing the car through the dealer. We know that this is exactly what most consumer guides tell you not to do, but there's a good reason. If your car develops real problems, it's much easier to withhold payment from the dealer's own organization than to involve a bank or credit union. And considering soaring bank interest rates, you probably won't pay much higher interest with the dealer's financing plan.

What if you've already accepted the car without those safeguards? Your warranty should give you some period of time to make "service adjustments"— usually sixty days. This covers what should have been done in the first place to make the car fit for sale. If you've had it in the shop once and the basic problems remain, you've given the dealer a chance to correct them. Realistically, if they can't be fixed the first time, they probably can't be fixed the third or fourth time either. But for the sake of demonstrating good faith to support your next measures, you should let the dealer's organization strike out at least twice before you proceed. Here's what to do.

1.   Document that after one service trip, the car is still faulty, by taking it to a diagnostic center and making a copy of the report.

2.   Ask to talk to the manufacturer's representative for your area. Show this person the problems and leave the car a second time.

3.   If they're still not corrected, send the dealer a demand letter outlining the problems and telling him you want a replacement or a refund. If . . . or rather when . . . he refuses and asks you to bring the car back in for service, submit your claim to an industry mediation or arbitration service if there's one in your area. These include: the manufacturer's own local consumer appeals board, which you should find listed in your owner's manual or through the dealer; AUTOCAP (Automobile Consumer Action Program), which is sponsored by the National Automobile Dealers Association); or the AUTOLINE complaint arbitration service sponsored by the Council of Better Business Bureaus. We would recommend AUTOLINE if you happen to live in one of the few cities in which you can find it. What's most important is that you choose a group whose decision will be binding on the dealer but not on you, in case you don't like their decision and want to go ahead on your own. Ask before you proceed. (See the Revenge Kit at the end of the chapter for a sample demand letter.)

    If you don't have access to any of these services, send a copy of your demand letter directly to the manufacturer with a cover note as shown in the Revenge Kit.

4.   Now you've gone as far as any sane person could to resolve your difficulties with the dealer amicably. If you still aren't satisfied with the outcome, it's time to get difficult yourself.

As you can see, getting stuck with a bad car may subject you to a lot more grueling redress procedures than we normally recommend. The problem is that there's more money at stake than in most consumer squabbles, and you're up against a hardened adversary. Also, you need a powerful backlog of documentation to show you've given the dealer ample opportunity to repair your lemon before you can hope to win in the courts. So, because you're forced to go through so much aggravation, let's up your ante for winning the battle.

Revoking Acceptance and Suing for Damages. For this tactic, you should get to a law office and take advantage of a free consultation to review your case, then pay for a lawyer's letter. What you're basically doing is refusing to accept the car and giving it back to the dealer, according to the principle that the car wasn't "merchantable" at the time of sale and the dealer hasn't been able to put it right. So the dealer is in breach of an *implied warranty* under the Uniform Commercial Code, which states that a product has to be suitable for its intended use.

Of course, the *express* warranty your car manufacturer provides is a bravura attempt to skip around the implied warranty by limiting liability to certain repairs within a short time period. So it's really designed to afford you less protection than you should be getting. However, you do have a case if you've had the car for less than a year and the only reason you've kept it this long is to exhaust the possibilities for redress within the dealer's system.

The revocation-of-acceptance letter from your lawyer is a clear signal that you mean business, and the dealer may try to offer you some alternative proposal. But it probably won't be satisfactory. To put teeth in your revocation, you should cancel the insurance and the registration on the car. And you should also send a letter to the bank or credit union, if you used one, that's financing the car and stop making payments. Now you can see why it helps to use dealer financing—to contain the whole matter in the dealer's and manufacturer's arena rather than having to deal with a third party.

At the same time that you revoke acceptance, you should also sue the dealer, through your lawyer, to recover your down payment and any monthly payments you've made to date. Then you should determine your damages and add these on, too. Damages would include your out-of-pocket expenses for rental cars, other alternate transportation, phone calls, time off from work, attorney's fees, and other costs you've incurred in your struggle with the dealer. The action, of course, will have to be taken in civil court.

Look for Misrepresentation or Fraud. It would be very helpful if you could determine that the dealer tried to defraud you in some way, such as representing the car as brand new if, in fact, it had already logged a few hundred miles when you bought it. One recent case brought by a Texas buyer involved a Lincoln he'd bought from a dealer as a brand-new car for $12,517. In fact, the car had 669 miles on it, but the dealer had asserted—from a very imaginative reading of the odometer—that it was only 66.9. (The buyer collected a rebate.) Or maybe the service department lied to you about some aspect of the repair work, which you could document with your records. Your attorney can help you determine if this is the case. And if the dealer misrepresented facts, you can sue for punitive as well as regular damages.

Advertise Your Displeasure. Another course you can follow, in lieu of or in addition to suing, is to publicize the dealer's shoddy performance—or at least threaten him convincingly.

Write an ad for your local newspaper that says in effect:

DID YOU BUY A LEMON FROM
(NAME OF DEALERSHIP)?

If you've bought a bad car or had service problems with (Dealership), call (your phone number) to discuss a class-action suit. Together, we can sue for substantial damages!

(Your name)

Before you place the ad, send a copy to the owner of the dealership and point out that it's going in the paper the next day unless you hear from him. He will probably call you up to find out what you're up to.

DEALER: What's this about a class-action suit? You don't really think you can gain anything by this do you?

BUYER: I sure do. And I'm going to ask the local TV news people if they can help me publicize it.

DEALER: Just what is it you want?

BUYER: My money back. Plus reimbursement for what I've spent letting you try to fix this lousy car.

DEALER: (Sigh) Well, why don't you come in and talk to me first and see what we can work out.

Or maybe the dealer will just call and tell you to stuff your ad. If so, place it in the paper and see what happens. And call up the local TV action reporter and tell her or him about it. Try to make it a TV station that the dealer doesn't use to run ads, so they won't have to worry about losing money. Chances are good that you'll get some calls from other people who've been stung by the dealer, as well as some free publicity.

In fact, you may catch a break if your local paper refuses to run the ad because (although they won't say so outright) the paper sells a lot of advertising space to the dealer and is timid about offending him. Then you can probably get a TV reporter to air your case just to get in a good shot at the local print media, who tend to sneer at TV journalists out of professional snobbery and envy.

Eventually the dealer should cave in if he sees a groundswell of support for your case and offer to buy you off with a settlement, which you should be happy to accept, unless you enjoy leading Quixotic crusades.

Guerrilla Tactics. You've undoubtedly heard about the people who paint lemons on their bad cars and park them in front of the dealer's lot. This might work. But then again, it might not. Most people may just assume you're some kind of nut and hurry past with a frightened glance in your direction as they go in to buy cars. However, it wouldn't hurt to pay a sign letterer twenty-five dollars or so to do two placards to hang on each side of your car that say:

I BOUGHT THIS LEMON AT *(DEALERSHIP)*.
ASK ME ABOUT IT!

This will get you some attention, expecially when you bring the car into the dealership on one of your regular repair missions. A Baltimore man had his wife and their friends—seven of them—picket a dealership daily from 9 A.M. till closing time. This started on a Monday. By Thursday, *nobody* was seen going into that dealership and, desperate for a reprieve from such dedicated vengeance, the owner finally came out and made a satisfactory settlement.

FEAR AND LOATHING IN THE USED-CAR MARKET

You have to be prepared for the same kinds of problems when you buy a late-model used car, whether it's from a dealer or a private party. Only now the warranty is even more limited and the redress situation even less satisfactory. So you should work faster to overcome a bad bargain.

If you buy from a dealer, get their financing for the same reason you would with a new car. If you experience problems that can't be cured by an exorcist, let alone the dealer's service people, take the car to an independent diagnostic center and see if the dealer misrepresented any facts about the car's condition.

Rollback Revenge. Your best bet is to determine whether the odometer has been rolled back to show lower mileage. On some used cars, the odometer is taken back so far, the figures may appear as Roman numerals. If you can prove that the dealer defrauded you, you can contact a lawyer and sue for consequential and punitive damages. For good measure, you can file a formal complaint with your state's department of motor vehicles, which is the regulatory agency for used-car dealers. If you have no hope of proving fraud, use the same publicity tactics discussed under new cars to force the dealer into refunding your money.

If you buy a car from a private party, remember that you have the same recourse as with a dealer if the seller knowingly misrepresented facts about the car's condition or mileage. If the person you buy from swears that the car has never been wrecked but you find after, say, a wheel falls off that it's a veteran of some major accident, you can sue for your money back. The problem is that an individual isn't a deep-pocket adversary like a car dealer. A dealer may not want to give your money back, but dealers usually have funds available in the event that they're ordered to pay up. Your private seller might already have spent it while celebrating the day he or she hung that automotive albatross around your neck.

But you can take a private seller to small-claims court to recover money you've spent repairing a condition he or she misrepresented. And if you win, you can garnish wages or bank accounts. (First send the demand letter at the end of the chapter.)

Shaming a Private Seller. One delightful *Guerrilla* tactic will only work if you bought your car from a socially established person who's sensitive about public embarrassment. If you bought it from a resident of Tobacco Road, nobody will care much about peer pressure and you may only get mugged for your trouble. But consider how an acquaintance of ours persuaded a private seller to take back a problem car and refund his money. When our friend, whom we'll call Dick, was twenty-two and his wife nineteen, he bought a used Thunderbird from a very buttoned up investment banker. This pillar of the community lied calmly and persuasively that the T-Bird had never been in an accident. But shortly after our young couple took the car away, some little eccentricities developed under certain road conditions. The T-Bird shook nervously and pulled compulsively to the right. A quick check at a gas station revealed that the car had indeed been in a collision and couldn't be fixed properly and was thus worth about one-third of the purchase price. Dick located the address of the banker's prestigious investment firm and, after a dress rehearsal, his wife embarked on an errand of vengeance.

You might be aware that an office reception room is generally considered a public place. (Unsavory bill collectors use this fact to their advantage by stalking delinquent debtors' waiting rooms dressed as skid-row bums, reeking of garlic, and demanding to see their victims "about some money.") So into the investment banker's plush reception area came a lovely but painfully distraught nineteen-year-old woman, who sobbed to the receptionist that she had to see "Mr. Vestment" immediately. The horrified banker appeared in an instant, to a gush of tears and recriminations about the "terrible car you sold us . . . and *you swore* it had never been in an accident."

"Look," she demanded, thrusting some Polaroid photos and a scrawled note at her red-faced prey, "that's the mechanic's report and pictures of the bent frame. Well, I'm not leaving until you give us our money back." To the guarded amusement of several secretaries peeking around the door, she was handed a signed letter in no time at all which permitted the couple to return the car and receive a check through the seller's attorney.

The moral of this story is to buy your used car from a solid citizen. Such a person may not be any more honest, but he or she will probably be a lot more vulnerable.

Fixing the Auto Mechanic

Auto mechanics, the knights of the road, have established an overall industry record documented in one recent Transportation Department survey: When typical used cars were brought to sixty-two repair shops in seven major cities, needless repair work was done on 78 percent of the engines, and repair work that should have been done was neglected on 89 percent.

You've probably heard all the sound advice you care to about getting a good repair shop and staying with it, about using only mechanics certified by the National Institute for Automotive Service Excellence (call them at 202-833-9646) or approved by the American Automobile Association.

If you've found a mechanic you can always trust, fine. If not, the odds are that you'll be taken for a ride at least some of the time, with you feeling the brunt of all the aggravation. You wind up paying the shop to get your car back, discover that the trouble wasn't fixed, and are then reduced to pleading with the mechanic to take it back and fix it properly without gouging you all over again. Alternatively, you could send demand letters, drag the repair people to small-claims court, and recover your damages, provided you've gone through all the usual tiresome redress procedures. The problem is that the burden of proof and frustration is always on you, never on the people who should be made to suffer for their incompetence or fraud. So consider an alternative strategy that puts the wrench in your hands for a change.

First Strike Option: The After-Hours Pickup. Service departments and garages always take your keys and leave them with your car's paperwork. They assume that you'll pay your bill before you take your car away. But one guerrilla type we know does it differently. He finds a shop that parks their cars in an outside lot and makes sure he keeps an extra set of keys. After they've worked on his car (twenty minutes' work and a few extra days' waiting time), they'll call him to bring $438 for the bill and pick up the car. When they call, he finds out what time they close. If it's six o'clock, he arrives at seven and leaves a note under the door that says in suitably vague terms:

> Arrived late to pick up car. Will come by in the A.M.
> Sandy Davis

Then he uses his extra keys to drive the car away and take it for a good test drive. If the car seems fine, he goes back in the morning and settles up, saying he came late but needed the car, so he took it. Since he's paying them, who cares?

But let's say it's still behaving badly or has even developed some new problem under the mechanic's skilled care. Now he takes it to another repair shop the next morning, finds out what's wrong, and leaves it to be fixed properly. He leaves the shop (so he can do the same to this new crew) and calls the first mechanic.

MECHANIC: Hi, Mr. Davis. Got your note. Car's all ready. Come and get it.

SANDY: I've got the car, and it wasn't all ready.

MECHANIC: Huh?

SANDY: I've just verified that it's still got the same problem. You can forget about collecting on that bill.

MECHANIC: Wait a minute, buddy. You owe me $438.

SANDY: So sue me. Just remember that I've got the documentation to prove you didn't do the work you charged me for. I'll be happy to go to court.

MECHANIC: Well don't ever come around here again, ya goddamn crook! (Slam)

And you'll never have to, because there are enough garages and dealers to "shop" after-hours until you find a reliable one. Before you try this tactic, though, check with your local consumer protection office by phone to see if there's a "mechanic's lien" law in your jurisdiction that would prohibit the after-hours pickup. If there is, don't do it.

Making a Car-Rental Company Try Harder

The most common complaints about car-rental agencies have to do with not having a car that you reserved or the outrageous bill they present after you return the car. There are several safeguards to protect you from these mishaps and a few strategies for retribution if the agencies still cause you problems.

When you rent a car, make sure to specify the type you want and confirm the rate, and make sure to ask for the reservation number so you can document that you did reserve it (many companies will provide you with a voucher through the mail if you reserve in advance). If they don't have a car when you arrive, ask them to find a car at another location and either drive the car to you or you to it. Don't let them think you'll pay the cab fare to pick up your in-city car at the out-of-city airport. If no car is available, tell them to get you a car from one of their competitors or from a local dealer.

If they won't give you satisfaction, take a cab to where you're going and then bill the agency for the difference between the estimated cost of the rental and the cost of the cab. Ask the cabbie to keep a record of your mileage and use the rental agency's rate to calculate the total. If the agency refuses to pay, take your claim to small-claims court and tell the judge that the agency breached their "contract" to give you the car when and where they had promised it, and bring documentation to prove it.

Curious Billing Practice. Agencies usually offer all sorts of package deals that give either free mileage or a weekly rate. You may find it to your advantage to reserve a car for a week at the special rate even if you'll only be using it four days, because the weekly rate-and-mileage allowance may be cheaper than the time-and-mileage charge. We recommend that if you need a car for four or more days and are driving long distances, you rent at a weekly rate and then, when you return the car, ask for a comparison of the time-and-mileage charge *vs.* the weekly package rate with unlimited mileage. Then pay the cheaper rate.

If the size of the final bill goes beyond the advertised rate, refuse to pay it. Since almost all rental agencies refuse cash, they'll use the credit-card imprint they took when you picked up the car and charge the bill to your account. (It's usually better to have a few charge accounts with the national car rental agencies, which will bill you directly. When you refuse to pay, they will settle disputes more quickly.) Send a copy of their ad or brochure, which advertised the rate, with a letter demanding that they explain what you believe to be an overcharge or an unfair rate. Offer to pay what *you* calculate the bill to be or nothing at all. And send a copy of the letter to the president of the company, alleging a pattern of overcharging. Eventually some executive may determine that the company is spending more in employee time than the amount you're disputing and reluctantly accept the reduced payment.

A note about those "corporate" discount rates: many companies have arrangements with national car rental agencies to give their employees a substantial discount on normal time-and-mileage rates. But when you ask for the discount, they may try to tell you that corporate discounts work only at "participating locations." If you make your discount eligibility clear when you make your reservation, and the employees at that particular location claim later that they don't participate, refuse to pay your bill until you get the discount. Unless they clearly post a sign saying that they do not participate in national discount rates, they must grant you the discount. Threaten to report their lack of compliance to your parent corporation, and lobby for a corporate boycott of the agency (if you really do work for that company).

REVENGE KIT FOR AUTOMOBILES

SAMPLE LEMON LETTER TO NEW CAR DEALER

To: Sales Manager
Automobile Dealer
Address:

Date:

Re: (Type of Car and I.D. #)
Date of Purchase: 3/18/8____

Dear Mr. _____,

It is clear that this car that I purchased from you is not fit for its ordinary use and breaches both express and implied warranties that govern and define the sale of this item.

A short synopsis of my experience is as follows:

On driving the car off the lot, I discovered that it did not have a gas cap. This minor immediate problem foretold later substantial problems and indicated a pattern of sloppy work that would characterize your attempts to fix and correct other difficulties as they appeared. Within the first one and one half weeks of ownership of the car, I had to bring it back for numerous repairs and adjustments, including, by way of illustration and not limitation, a loose rocker panel, no FM radio reception, a broken tuning knob on radio, air leaks in the windows, rust in axle region, a defective cigarette lighter, and a noisy rattle that resulted from improper installation of the dash. The most serious problem, however, relates to the car's transmission. I've had the car back to you several times to allow you a fair opportunity to fix the defective transmission, which, as you know, slips and idles too fast. I've had the car inspected by an independent mechanic, who indicates that the car is missing second gear and reverse gear is delayed.

In order to settle this matter, without prejudice to other remedies I may assert, I am willing at this point to give you one more opportunity to cure these problems. I will call you on Wednesday of this week to arrange for a mutually convenient time to have the car repaired. Of course, I will insist on a monetary settlement in the amount of $500.00 to compensate for the breach of your agreement, assuming that the car is once and for all properly repaired. In the event we are unable to reach a meeting of the minds on this point, I have been advised to revoke acceptance of this car under applicable provisions of the Uniform Commercial Code.

Very truly yours,

Certified Letter

LETTER TO USED CAR DEALER TO TAKE BACK YOUR LEMON

To Used Car Dealer
Name:
Address:
Date:

Re: Year and Model, I.D. #
and date of purchase

Dear Mr./Ms. _____,

Since I bought my car from you on (date), it has been in the repair shop four times: (list dates and repairs). I have seen a lawyer, and in an effort to avoid legal proceedings, he has suggested that I give you one chance to replace the car with a suitable substitute, or, if none is available, to give me a full refund of the purchase price. I will give you one week from today to decide on your course of action. If I don't hear from you within the prescribed time, I will be forced to sue for damages.

Very truly yours,

LETTER TO PRIVATE SELLER
(ATTACH MECHANIC'S REPORT)

To:
Address:
Date:

> Re: Year and Model, I.D. #
> and date of purchase

Dear Mr./Ms. _____:

 The car you sold me on (date) is not fit for use. It has been in the repair shop four times since last week, and I have documented the problems in the attached mechanic's report. You told me the car had no engine problems and was in "great shape." Thus unless you give me a full refund by _____, I will be forced to sue you for breach of contract and tortious fraud.

Very truly yours,

LETTER TO NEW CAR MANUFACTURER

To: (Consumer Affairs Director of Company—call the company's 800 number for his/her name)
Address:
Date:

> Re: Year and Model, I.D. #
> and date of purchase

Dear Mr./Ms. _____,

 I bought a new (Model) from (dealer) in (city) on (date). He is an authorized (manufacturer) dealer, and I am enclosing a copy of my contract for the record. Please use your influence to advise the dealer to comply with the contract and give me a car that meets basic warranty requirements. If I do not receive a replacememt car or a refund within 10 working days of this date, I am planning to revoke acceptance of the car, as it's not fit for its ordinary and foreseeable use, and I have been advised by my attorney to sue you as manufacturer along with the dealer to recover my losses.

Thank you for your cooperation.

Very truly yours,

LETTER TO DEALER
REVOKING ACCEPTANCE

To: Dealer
Name:
Address:
Date:

Re: <u>Year and Model, I.D. #</u>
<u>and date of purchase</u>

Dear Mr./Ms. _____,

As you know, I bought a new (make) from you on (date), and it has now been in the repair shop five times since that date: (list dates and supposed repairs). This car is not fit for its ordinary use and is in breach of the warranty of merchantability that is implied by our state law. I am enclosing a copy of the diagnostic report I got on the car that itemizes the various problems I have faced in attempting to get the car to work as promised. The car still does not meet basic warranty requirements.

In light of the foregoing, this letter will operate as legal notice that I am today revoking acceptance of the car and am demanding that you promptly refund all money held on account and compensate me for consequential damages in the amount of $_____. The car may be picked up at my house. If you don't pick it up within 5 working days, I will charge you storage at the rate of $_____ per day* until reclaimed. If you have any questions, please

---

* Use the same amount the dealer's service department charges you for storage after you've been notified to pick it up.

contact my lawyer: (name), whose telephone number is
_____.

Very truly yours,

LETTER TO RENTAL AGENCY

Car Rental Agency
Address:
Date:
           Re: Car rental date _____

Dear Sir:

I rented a car from you on (date) (see the enclosed copy of
contract). I used your company because I relied on representations made in your advertisement appearing in (name
of publication) (a copy of the ad is enclosed). This ad stated
that your daily rental rate was _____and that the
first 100 miles was included in the rental rate, and that
thereafter _____cents per mile is charged over
basic rental rate. The bill I received when I returned the car
did not reflect your advertised rate, and I feel defrauded. The
overcharge comes to _____, which I refuse to pay. I
am enclosing payment based on your advertised rate. If you
do not rescind the overcharge immediately and notify the
credit-card company of the same, I will refer this matter to
the (state or local) Consumer Protection Agency and seek
criminal sanctions based on the inference of fraud implicit
in your use of illegal bait-and-switch tactics.

Very truly yours,

LETTER TO AUTOCAP
REQUESTING ARBITRATION

AUTOCAP
8400 West Park Drive
McLean, Va. 22102
Date:

> Re: (Your name) vs. (Dealer)

Gentlemen:

Please send me the forms necessary to initiate mediation of the problem I am having with a local (manufacturer) dealer. I understand that a panel will be convened that is made up of 50 percent consumers and 50 percent dealers, and they will render a decision that is binding on the dealer but not on me, once both of us have had an opportunity to be heard.

Thank you for your cooperation. I will look forward to receiving the forms in a short time so I can begin the mediation process.

> Very truly yours,

PART III

It Isn't the Money

8
credit

Avenger's Paradise

It's ironic that the same system of justice that once confined poor-but-honest citizens to debtors' prison has turned credit into a kind of Disneyland for vengeful consumers. Of course, there are still instances of abuse on the part of credit bureaus, collection agencies, and other members of the credit establishment. But these excesses pale by comparison with the blanket protection you're now afforded from billing errors, creditors who insult you with defective products and poor service, obnoxious bill collectors, and most other consumer frustrations. This protection is guaranteed by both federal and state laws.

By using credit, you can also wield a heavy club over not just creditors but third parties from whom you decide to withhold payment. In the old days, a disreputable merchant could sell you a defective TV set on time payments, then stroll next door and sell your credit contract to a "holder in due course"— usually a finance company—and be home free. Even if you returned the TV, you'd still have to pay the finance company, because the finance company wasn't responsible for the merchandise. The slippery merchant got all the money by selling your contract. The finance company got your legal obligation to pay the debt. All that a customer got was a burned-out television and the dubious prospect of taking the merchant to court. Today you can refuse to pay credit charges for most shoddy goods, no matter who holds the contract, until your complaints are resolved. Thus using credit when you buy products and services is a first-strike strategy in itself, provided you follow certain guidelines.

THE COSTS/BENEFITS OF CREDIT GAMING

Some credit buffs have developed nimble evasive techniques—routinely withholding payments for ninety days or more, bluffing bill collectors, playing tricks when creditors take them to court—all with the objective of holding onto their money longer.[1] Even though these techniques may mean you'll lose some charge accounts, if you juggle payments to your creditors carefully, you can keep some of your cards even though others will be taken away. You'll never go to jail; the worst that can happen is that you'll spend a lot of time in civil court. But you risk winding up with a very bad credit rating indeed, since many creditors, like Mastercard and Visa, regularly report late payments to TRW Credit Data, the major credit bureau. In addition, virtually all creditors report accounts turned over to collection agencies (called, not surprisingly, collection accounts) and accounts they've given up hope of collecting ("charge-offs"). You can be sure that a procession of bill collectors will enter your life, and you will be certain to find an assortment of demand notices in your mailbox every week. Believe us, this can be debilitating for even the most thick-skinned credit gamester. And as heavy gamblers and drinkers find out, it's hard to balance yourself on the brink forever.

But if all this doesn't put you off and you feel that the whole credit system cries out for revenge, you'll find some points here on how to get even with shameless merchants and nasty creditors.

ASSEMBLING THE RIGHT CREDIT PORTFOLIO

To use credit as a weapon, you need plenty of it and the right kind. Today most individuals who earn twelve to fifteen thousand dollars a year can qualify for most credit cards. Start by gathering charge cards for all the department and specialty stores at which you shop. Then obtain some extra store cards for traveling. Better department store cards from the likes of Bloomingdale's and Neiman-Marcus are always useful. Tiffany's in New York City is a nice addition because it's an easy account to get and they're very courtly about not pressing you too hard for payment, let alone reporting a slow-paying customer to TRW.

Next obtain a good number of oil company and airline cards. Pick up both Mastercard and Visa. Then apply for the three so-called executive cards— American Express, Diners Club, and Carte Blanche.

Backup Strategy. Why do you need so many cards? You really don't, but you want to have charge privileges everywhere you'll do business, so you can choose not to pay a bill if necessary. You won't use most of them, or you'll just use them very occasionally. But you may someday lose your job or suffer some other financial reverses and find yourself in hot water with creditors because you can't meet their payments. And if worse comes to worst—they cancel your cards or you're forced to declare bankruptcy—you'll be delighted that you had the foresight to obtain *backup* cards that you've always kept fully paid. For example, say you only had American Express (Amex), which is the most useful T&E (travel and entertainment) card. It's almost universally accepted, you don't pay interest, you can get travelers' checks with it, and they don't become really nasty until you're about ninety days behind in your payments. The problem is that if you have real financial difficulties and can't pay them anything for an extended period, like four or five months, American Express may very well get nasty and cancel your card for good. (They might tell you when they're trying to collect their money afterward that "they just want to help you get a new card," but you shouldn't count on that forgive-and-forget policy from any creditor.)

On the other hand, if you used Diners Club or Carte Blanche as your regular T&E card and saved Amex for distant ports and other emergencies, you would have covered yourself. Even though you might lose your Diners Club card through a financial crisis, you'll have kept the most useful card unblemished and be ready to charge away when you're back on your feet. The same principle serves for oil-company, department-store, and airline cards. Remember that as long as you keep an account in good standing, the creditor has no reason to recheck your current credit profile and revoke your card because you defaulted on its competitors.

Using Local Credit. Wherever possible, it's smart to establish charge accounts at local service stores in order to hold out payment when you have a problem. The dry cleaner who loses your shirt will be much more responsive to giving you a decent settlement if you owe him for a month's worth of cleaning bills and he'll have to take *you* to court to settle the claim.

Most small businesspeople don't like to go to court, even small-claims court, since it means time away from the store—especially if you add to their grief by subpoenaing other workers in the shop and all business records for the month in question, then phone in to the court clerk at the last minute for a postponement if, say, you're legitimately too sick to show up. The store owner and crew, of course, will have wasted half the day to no avail.

Here we must advise you, though, to pay your local creditors promptly unless you have a real complaint. Otherwise you could be branded a local deadbeat. You should scrupulously keep a good credit record in your community in case you ever run into hard times financially and need to charge your life-support purchases for a while. Save your nasty tricks, if you must use them, for anonymous national creditors, who can only bad-mouth you on a TRW report.

Cleaning Up a Bad Credit Profile

What can you do about a bad credit rating? Actually, consumer credit bureaus don't give individuals a "rating" at all. What they do is assemble as much information as their members (credit-granting companies) care to provide on your borrowing and payment history with them. An individual credit-granting company reviewing your application decides on the basis of the profile, plus internal company guidelines, whether to give you a credit line. A history of frequent, very late payments or a charge-off on your profile will prompt a rejection by most creditors.

There are two reasons you could have those blemishes on your profile: Either the credit bureau made a mistake (which may actually be the fault of the creditors who reported to them) or you have a couple of skeletons rattling around in your credit history, and you'll have to try to banish them. We'll examine both possibilities.

Looking into Your File. First, check the rejection letter you received from the creditor who declined your application. If the company made the decision on the basis of a credit bureau's report, the federal Fair Credit Reporting Act (FCRA) of 1971 requires that the creditor tell you the name and address of the credit bureau that issued the report. You will have to either visit or write that reporting agency and assert your rights under the FCRA to find out what's in your file.

If it's a local credit bureau, you should make an appointment to visit it. The law says these bureaus have to tell you the "nature, substance and sources" of the data in your file. They don't have to show you the file itself, but they might anyway. Ask pointed questions about *negative* information—What is it? Who reported it? What do those abbreviations and code words mean? Is there more?—until you've exhausted all the negatives. Then see what *positive* information they have. Take careful notes if you can't take a copy of the report home with you. (There's no charge for this visit if you contact them within 30 days of the creditor's rejection.)

If you were turned down by a major creditor, chances are the report came from TRW Credit Data—the General Motors of credit bureaus, with over twenty-six thousand credit-granting members who receive "TRW Updated Profiles" on you and other credit applicants. Contrary to most people's expectations, TRW is responsive, even friendly, when it comes to complying with this aspect of the FCRA. Just write to the FCRA at the address on your rejection letter, and they'll send back a copy of your current Updated Profile with a careful explanation of what every coded item means. Even if you weren't rejected recently, send for a copy of your TRW Update and see what it says. It can make the difference between a life of blissful acceptance or stern rejection in your credit dealings. Use Letter A at the end of the chapter and enclose a check for $8.

Correcting Errors. Let's say you find some erroneous information. Here's what to do: (1) If there's an item about a late payment or whatever that was actually a contested bill, or an item that obviously belongs on some other person's file, send a letter demanding a reinvestigation to correct it (Letter B in the Revenge Kit). (2) Write a hundred-word-or-less explanation of any contested bill, which must by law be entered on your file. (3) Be sure to include in the letter your demand that all creditors who've received the report in the last six months be sent the corrected version. (4) Wait twenty days and reapply to the creditor who turned you down, to make sure they received the corrected copy.

Dealing With Truly Negative Information. If you've been cavalier about paying off some major creditors in the past, your TRW file will probably reflect it. If it doesn't, consider that an undeserved blessing. But if you discover one or more items that you know reinvestigation won't correct, you can take these steps in filling out Letter B:

(1) Demand, under the FCRA, that all negative information seven years old or more be deleted. (Bankruptcy, unfortunately, must stay on your record for 14

years.) (2) If you have a more recent problem, say a late payment or chargeoff, write a hundred-word-or-less explanation. You might have been ill, out of the country, out of work, or have another reasonable excuse for not paying. If you still owe the creditors money, call them and offer to settle if you can afford it. Offer 50 cents on the dollar first and see if they'll accept your settlement. If not, pay up in full and enter in your explanation the fact that you've settled the account voluntarily. Most new creditors you're applying to will see this as a commendable act of good faith if it's coupled with a sound explanation for your past behavior. (3) If you've had excellent payment histories with other creditors that don't appear in the file, ask the credit bureau to investigate and add them to the report. They aren't legally required to comply with this request, but they probably will for a service fee. These new entries will help offset your negative items, if there aren't too many of them.

Now your profile should have a distinctly upbeat look, which will probably inspire creditors to overlook a negative item or two in favor of the glowing reports you've added.

It's very unusual for a credit bureau to stonewall you when you make these demands, since delinquent bureaus have been taken to court and slapped with hefty punitive damages for noncompliance. But if you sense some unnecessary delays or obstructive behavior, send Letter C, with an attached copy of an FTC complaint, and give them five business days to comply before you file it.

WHEN TO WITHHOLD PAYMENT

Once you have a full arsenal of charge cards, you're ready to enjoy one of the great rewards of all this labor, which is striking back at companies that do you wrong.

Refusing to Pay for Defective Merchandise. When you charge a purchase to a general credit card, you have the right to withhold payment for defective merchandise until the merchant resolves your problem to your satisfaction. This is guaranteed by the federal Fair Credit Billing Act of 1975, and applies to purchases you make with a bank or T&E card. You do have to meet these requirements, though:

1.   The purchase must be over $50.

2.   You must try to resolve the problem with the merchant first.

3.   You have to make the purchase in your home state or within 100 miles of where you live.

Notify the credit-card company with Letter E, and the company will deduct that amount from your bill until they're notified to the contrary. (But you're still obligated to pay the uncontested balance due the credit-card company.) This gives you a bold new negotiating power over the offending merchant. They don't get paid until you get satisfaction. And the credit-card company is not allowed to dun you, charge interest for the amount withheld, or report your nonpayment to a credit bureau.

If you charge a department-store item with the store's own card or a gas-station purchase with the oil company's card, the 100-mile restriction doesn't apply. So if you have problems with the suit you bought at Neiman-Marcus using your N-M credit card while you were in Dallas, Texas, you can withhold payment back home in St. Paul, Minnesota, until the store resolves it for you. If you bought new tires at an Exxon station 1000 miles from home and paid for the tires with Exxon's own card, you can "stop payment" for defects in the tires. This is true because the credit grantor is also the merchant, whether the store you patronized is directly owned by the creditor or franchised. The same rule restricting the creditor's right to collect from you applies here. So enter the appropriate information in Letter D and wait until they respond to your complaint. Time, for once, is clearly on your side.

You can also waltz around the "holder in due course" bear trap—the one that kept so many underhanded merchants and finance companies close friends— with another federal law called the FTC's Preservation of Consumer's Claims and Defenses Rule of 1976. If a merchant sells you a defective TV and sells your contract to a finance company, you can withhold further payments from the finance company if you decide to revoke acceptance, and sue both of them as co-defendants to recover any down payment or other payments you've already made. This rule also applies to a car you buy through the dealer's own financing organization, like GMAC (which is why we recommend dealer financing in Chapter 7). The only restrictions in this rule are that:

1.   It doesn't apply to purchases over $25,000, to real estate, or to business purchases.

2.   You can sue only the merchant for incidental and consequential damages you suffer because of a defective product. The finance company's liability is limited to the money you've already paid them.

So adopt Letter D to demand action on a problem with goods you've bought under these circumstances, and notify both parties that you're making no further payments.

Notice how just by taking advantage of credit purchasing, you've completely reversed the usual order of dealing with your adversaries. In each case, the total burden of responsibility lands squarely on their shoulders, because you control the payments. No longer will you have to spend time and effort chasing some wily merchant to get your money back.

Disputing Charges on Your Bill. A great source of consumer annoyance over the years has been the computerized bill that duns you for, say, $62.50 for a nonworking appliance you returned to a store several months ago that they did take back. Now the store's computer seems to be after you in some demented vengeance crusade of its own. You wrote back to it once, but it filed your letter in its inactive circuits and bombarded you with the store's collection-letter cycle. What do you do?

First of all, don't try to reason with the computer. Send Letter E disputing that item on your bill under the Fair Credit Billing Act, and wait for a human reply. Once they receive your letter, the store is obligated to acknowledge your complaint within thirty days and act upon it within ninety. In the meantime, you can't be dunned or charged interest for the disputed amount (although you're responsible for paying the undisputed balance), and they can't report your nonpayment to a credit bureau.

Need we say that there are any number of valid reasons to dispute a billing item. A department-store charge statement may not indicate clearly just what it is you bought (i.e., "38.40: Giftware"). Or a bank-card statement might come in with a "cancellation fee" for a hotel reservation you canceled with plenty of warning to that hotel. Or a T&E card may just list a charge with an establishment's account number rather than the name of the store, restaurant, or whatever.

Don't be bashful about challenging whatever charges you might dispute or just don't understand from the information given. Again, time is on your side, particularly when you consider that the bureaucratic sluggishness that normally drives you up a wall now grinds along to your advantage.

Punishing Creditors Who Run Afoul of Federal Laws. You may wonder at this point how closely creditors actually comply with these fascinating rules and regulations. By and large, commendably. They tend to assume, and rightfully so, that the consumer smart enough to invoke them in the first place will also figure out how to bring heat down on them if they don't. (Curiously enough, most consumers still don't take advantage of these rules, even though they're plastered, by law, over every contract and new-customer retail credit agreement they apply to.)

So if a creditor tries to pursue you for money you're withholding over a disputed bill, send the company Letter F. Remember that the creditor is required by law to investigate your claim and respond to it within ninety days. This means that you must receive a letter from them during that time period saying either:

1.   They've investigated your claim, decided that you were correct, and are wiping out the disputed balance.

2.   They concluded, upon investigation, that your claim lacked sufficient

merit and are holding you to the original charge. But they also have to give you a full explanation and supply you with documentary evidence if you demand it.

If they fail to respond properly, the creditor automatically forfeits collection of the disputed amount up to fifty dollars. Violations of the Fair Credit Billing Act also carry punitive damages, including your creditor's liability for paying your attorney's fees if you win. So a tough notice will usually be enough motivation to make your creditor comply.

Inflicting Paperwork Pain. Of course, there are independent actions you can take to enjoy a little smug satisfaction over a particularly troublesome creditor. You could, for instance, try some guerrilla correspondence.

The creditor has to respond to your requests for more information during a billing controversy or over a contested charge. There's no law that says you can't ask for more substantiation or introduce some new relevant question in the middle of their efforts to resolve your complaint. Once you've identified the people who process your correspondence, you can begin hitting them, at regular intervals, with new wrinkles on the original complaint, such as asking for duplicate statements and the like. Since time is clearly on your side, this won't work to your disadvantage. It will just stretch out the process of resolving your disputed or contested charge. You can't, however, accuse them of not responding quickly enough to your first inquiry and claim the fifty-dollar punitive writeoff if you choose to bombard them with additional correspondence.

DEALING WITH BILL COLLECTORS
AND COLLECTION LAWYERS

We can't stress too strongly that if you want to keep your credit profile respectable, you should prevent your accounts from falling into the heavy hands of bill collectors or, ultimately, lawyers who will take you to court and try to collect a judgment against you. Collection accounts and lawsuits will invariably show up on your credit file, and new lenders will disapprove mightily. If you feel yourself sinking into financial quicksand and know that you won't be able to make payments, you should contact all your creditors right away and ask them to either reduce your payments to an amount you can afford for a specified period of time or give you a grace period to get back on your feet, after which you can resume payments.

But let's say it's too late for that, and you're already the target of some relentless collection agency or lawyer. The main difference between the two is that bill collectors can't take you to court. All they can do is make a legally regulated effort to collect your debt (and their commission) before they have to throw up their hands at your obstinancy and pass your account along to an attorney for legal action—the last stage in the collection cycle.

The lawyer will probably send you at least one letter threatening a lawsuit. Then if you don't respond and the account is over $250 or so, the lawyer will start an action in civil court. You'll receive a summons that tells you to appear in court at a specified time and place. Now the lawyer is crossing his or her fingers and praying you won't show up, so he or she can obtain a "default judgment" against you and attach whatever assets you might own or income you might be receiving without battling you in court. Most debtors who've been terrorized this far along on the cycle don't show up when summoned. But you should, since this is your best opportunity to make a favorable settlement for, say, twenty-five to fifty cents on the dollar. Before you get to this point, though, you have ample opportunity to strike back at your tormentors if they step out of line.

Defanging the Bill Collector. It doesn't take much imagination to visualize the kind of adversary you'll be dealing with when a collection agency starts calling. The requirements of the job favor persistent, irritating personalities who try to intimidate you into paying your debt as quickly as possible. The idea is to make sending a check seem a lot more desirable than having to talk further with the collection agent. But after many years of running roughshod over debtors with every dirty and devious trick imaginable, bill collectors have recently been forced to curtail some of their vilest tactics by strong federal and state laws. Not that they won't try to browbeat you anyway if you let them, but most collection agencies that want to continue plying their trade are wary about baiting customers who know how to turn around and attack their methods.

Under the Fair Debt Collection Practices Act of 1978, which is enforced by the Federal Trade Commission, bill collectors are *not* allowed to:

> Contact friends, relatives, or your employer about your debt, except to ask for their help in locating you. And they cannot identify themselves as bill collectors in the process. Nor can they use any outside identification or correspondence that identifies the letter as a collection attempt (like a return address that says "The Thunderbolt Collection Agency").

> Although they're not allowed to tell your colleagues that they're collection agents, they can't misrepresent themselves as lawyers, government-agency or credit-bureau employees, either. Say somebody at your office gets a call claiming to offer you a free club membership and leaving a phone number. If you call back and it's a collection agency, you can use your co-worker's message to you as documentation in building a case against the agency.

Use abusive language, empty threats about lawsuits or criminal prosecution, or make phone calls at inconvenient hours. Bill collectors can't curse at you, call you a deadbeat, or say that they're going to sue you if they're not likely to follow through (if, for example, your bill is for $38, which wouldn't be worth pursuing in court).

Calling you before 8 A.M. or after 9 P.M. is unlawful, as is phoning you at your office if you've informed a bill collector that your employer doesn't permit you to take personal calls at the office.

Now that you've seen what bill collectors can and cannot legally do to you, this is what you can do to *them* if they overstep their prerogatives when they call you.

You can demand the name of the bill collector and the agency before you talk further. (But collectors tend to use phony names so debtors they've driven to insanity won't call them back at 4 A.M.)

You can demand a letter *verifying your debt* before discussing the unpaid account. When you request this on the phone, you'll have to send Letter G, too. As a result, the collector will be restricted from calling you again until the debt is verified, which takes time. You must exercise this right *within 5 days* after the collector first contacts you.

If you don't want to talk to a bill collector at all, you can tell her or him so on the phone, then send Letter G, which directs the collection agency to cease further communications under penalty of law. However, this will probably accelerate the collection cycle by getting your bill turned over to an attorney for legal action.

If a bill collector continues to pester you or otherwise violates the law, and you can prove it, you can sue him or her in federal court for violation of the Fair Debt Collection Practices Act and ask for $1,000 in punitive damages plus attorney's fees. You can also file a complaint against the collection agency with the FTC.

You can also threaten to file a complaint against a bill collector who "abuses or harasses" you over the telephone with your state's Public Service Commission. Abusive or harassing phone calls are a violation of the Federal Communications Commission regulatory "tariff," which requires your local telephone company to cut off the service of a subscriber who violates this tariff. The prospect of discontinued phone service tends to instill rare fear into collection agencies, which rely almost totally on telephone service to visit their charming ways on debtors.

You can threaten to sue the creditor for "intentional infliction of emotional distress," if you've been sufficiently harassed to need psychiatric care, and seek substantial punitive damages against the creditor. This is particularly useful when you come up against a creditor's own collection agents, who are *not* regulated by federal law—the FTC rules cited here apply only to outside collection agencies. And some major creditors like American Express have their own collection people on staff.

If you run across a particularly nasty collection agency, you can wield the ultimate threat of a *class-action suit* against the agency in federal court, which can result in damages of up to $500,000 or 1 percent of the creditor's net worth. Now you might apply the "newspaper ad" preemptive-strike gambit to show the creditor what you plan to do. Send the agency a copy of your proposed "ad" for the newspaper, which will read:

HAVE YOU BEEN UNLAWFULLY HARASSED BY THE THUNDERBOLT COLLECTION AGENCY? If so, contact me at (phone   ) to discuss a Class Action Suit for substantial damages.

This will produce a quick response from a collection agency, which would rather let up on your $182 debt than see a host of vengeful debtors crawl out of the past's woodwork to sue them for all their historic excesses.

But if you decide to sue a collection agency or creditor, you should see a free-consultation lawyer first, and make sure you can impress a judge with your "good faith" attempts to resolve the debt. Judges frown on debtors who use a vast repertoire of legal revenge strategies to weasel out of paying *legitimate* debts.

So when an overly aggressive collector tries to intimidate you, be ready to practice turnabout as fair play.

COLLECTOR: Edward Jones there?

JONES: This is he.

COLLECTOR: I'm just gonna give you one chance to pay the $383.80 you owe the Feral Appliance Company.

JONES: Whom am I speaking to and whom do you represent?

COLLECTOR: Who d'ya think?

JONES: Are you refusing to identify yourself and your agency?

COLLECTOR: I'm T. Smith and I'm with Thunderbolt Collections. Now when are you gonna send me a check?

JONES: First I want a letter verifying the debt, which I dispute.

COLLECTOR: Look, don't get cute with me, Jones. You owe the money and you're going to send me a check tomorrow or I'm going to sue you. You'll have to pay lawyer's fees on top of the bill you owe.

JONES: Are you representing yourself as an attorney?

COLLECTOR: Whad'ya mean?

JONES: You said you would sue me. Are you an attorney empowered by your client to bring a lawsuit against me?

COLLECTOR: Look, Jones, this smart stuff doesn't work with me. I want a check and I want it in my hand in 24 hours.

JONES: What your agency will receive in 24 hours is a copy of my complaint to the FTC citing your unlawful violations of the Fair Debt Collection Practices Act. I'm also reporting your abusive and harassing telephone tactics in a complaint to the Public Service Commission, to get your agency's telephone service suspended for violation of the FCC's tariff . . .

COLLECTOR: (Click)

Negotiating with a Creditor's Lawyer. A collection lawyer will probably send you at least one letter before suing you in civil court. At this point, you might want to negotiate a reduction of the size of your debt. By now your creditor has spent a lot of time and money in the collection effort and may well be willing to get any money out of you. Contact the lawyer and make an offer of paying 25 to 50 percent of your debt.

If the lawyer refuses the offer and follows through with his or her threat to sue you, be sure to show up in court on or before the appointed date and ask for an extension. If you have a disputed or contested bill, you should consult an inexpensive lawyer to help you prepare a case.

You may, for example, subpoena key executives in the creditor company and all the records related to the transaction. You can also ask for an extension from the judge on the first day you meet the creditor's people in court in order to find yourself a lawyer if you haven't hired one yet. When the creditor sees that you're likely to give them a protracted court battle by pulling out every lawful trick at your command, you're in a better position than ever to negotiate. Chances are good that the creditor's lawyer will try to take you aside on court day:

ATTORNEY: Look, you know this is a legitimate debt and you can't go on delaying a judgment forever.

DEBTOR: I know I'm entitled to make a legal defense against your action, since I believe the debt isn't valid (or) the creditor has dealt with me illegally.

ATTORNEY: Just what are you trying to accomplish?

DEBTOR: Complete and total vindication. I'm prepared to see you in court for as long as it takes. I would only consider settling now for one-third the disputed amount, and that's a take-it-or-leave-it offer.

ATTORNEY: (shaking his head) I couldn't advise my client to settle for so little, but I'm duty-bound to tell them your offer.

If you've treated them to a disturbing sample of your willingness to drag the creditor's whole army into court for several appearances, they may well decide to make a counteroffer and settle for 35 to 50 percent of the debt at this point.

BANKRUPTCY: THE ULTIMATE REVENGE

It's possible that you've already become so overextended that there's no hope of stalling or negotiating with your creditors. Now you may have to bite the bullet until your teeth turn to chalk and wipe out your debts by declaring bankruptcy. But you could also take advantage of another federal law.

The Bankruptcy of Your Choice. The latter option is known as Chapter XIII, or the Wage Owner Plan provided by the Federal Bankruptcy Act. Under this plan, you petition the court to consolidate and pay off your debts at a rate you can afford. But first you have to get the approval of your creditors, who will generally go along because they'll get more of their money back than if you declared plain old bankruptcy. Once they agree, you pay a hefty amount to the court every month, which is split up among your creditors and, after a fixed time period (usually three years), your remaining debts are discharged. Consult a lawyer before you file for this plan.

Maybe your debt is so monstrous and your prospects for paying so bleak that you'll want to file a *traditional bankruptcy*. This involves notifying your creditors beforehand and petitioning the court to divide up your meager assets among them. Once the court has declared you a bankrupt, the creditors you've named in your petition are prevented from further action against you. Again, you should consult a lawyer to decide whether it's your best bet. The advantages are:

If you live in a state like Texas that places a friendly and protective arm around its bankrupts' overburdened shoulders, you can keep some of your most valuable assets—your house, car, and personal belongings.

You'll have one simple black mark that says "bankrupt" on your credit file, rather than a long, dismal catalog of lawsuits that makes you look like a hardened deadbeat. It's more socially acceptable, in a way, to be a bankrupt than a deadbeat. And why devote the energy and money to paying off your debts when you'll just end up with a terrible credit profile anyway?

The major disadvantages are that you'll have the bankruptcy listing on your file for fourteen years, rather than the seven-year maximum for other negative information, and you won't be permitted to declare bankruptcy again for another six years.

Coming Out Ahead of the Game. But remember the advantages of having "backup" creditors you didn't list on your bankruptcy petition, who weren't represented in the proceedings and with whom you still have good credit because you kept your payments up to date. Bear in mind that it's *clearly illegal* to give some creditors preferential treatment over others by paying them before you go bankrupt and leaving the rest empty-handed. But if you haven't even used those backup cards for the past six months or so prior to declaring bankruptcy, you probably haven't given them preference while you sorted out your problems with the creditors. Ask your lawyer to be sure.

Remember that it's also illegal to hide assets from your creditors in a bankruptcy proceeding. Respect the judge's intelligence. Don't try to convince the court that you sold your house and furniture to your sister just last month. That's an obvious ruse to dispose of your property before it can fall into your creditors' clutches. But you might have sold certain of your belongings over the past year of so, even to close relatives, to cope with your deepening financial plight. Or you might have already registered some worldly goods in your sister's name long before it would ever become an issue of trying to defraud your creditors. Nobody says you can't give your sister a sailboat when you're in the money. And nobody would expect her to turn *her* boat over to *your* creditors later on when you're in bankruptcy court.

THE BORN-AGAIN DEBTOR

Now we'll assume that you didn't take the precaution of having backup cards and that your credit is ruined through bankruptcy or a string of lawsuits. What can you do to rebuild your desirability as a debtor?

If your profile reflects a whole closetful of fairly recent collection accounts and charge-offs, the kind of cosmetic surgery discussed earlier in this chapter won't help much to cure the basic impression that you're a bad risk. You can't even try to pawn yourself off as another John T. Smith, because your social-security number is the scarlet letter that identifies you as John Smith, deadbeat. It has to appear on every credit application, so it can be matched up with the number on your profile. And trying to obtain money or credit under false pretenses is fraud, with substantial criminal penalties. Sorry, but the credit system isn't set up to let dropouts wriggle back in easily. You'll just have to wait seven or fourteen years from your last misdeeds. Or you might try this approach:

If the negative items in your file fall within a particular period of time, you can go to a local banker and lay your hard-luck story on the table. For instance, maybe you went into a new business venture in the past year with a couple of partners who skinned you alive, and you were stuck personally for all the bad debts. Whatever happened, point out to the banker that you're arranging with your past creditors to settle old accounts, but you want to build your credit back up again. Now you'd like to take out a fully secured six-month loan for, say, $1,000 with your savings passbook as collateral. If you're sufficiently forthright about this and have a story that provokes sympathy for your plight, the banker may grant the loan. The bank can't lose, anyway.

Next, pay the loan back religiously every month, before the date agreed, and use the bank loan as a reference after a few months to get other credit in your community. Look for small concerns that won't check beyond your local reference. With a few paid-up accounts in hand, go back to the banker after six or nine months or so and ask to get a secured bank card—Mastercard or VISA—for "convenience." You always need credit cards for identification today, even to cash a check or rent a car. Your banker knows this. Again, you're willing to guarantee your entire $500 or $1,000 credit line with your passbook account as collateral. Again, the banker has little to lose and might agree.* If not, and you need a credit card for identification, ask for a *debit* card—Mastercard II or

---

* If your own bank won't do it, write to the Olympic Savings and Loan Association, 926 Taraval Street, San Francisco, Calif. 94116 and ask for an application for a VISA card. This bank currently issues a secured VISA card if you deposit a minimum of $1000, with a credit line equal to half the amount you have on deposit.

VISA. It looks like a credit card but just debits your checking account when you make a purchase. Hence no credit check.

Now you have local credit at a few stores, a bank credit card, and a bank reference for the loan. And all of your monthly payments are "as agreed." Have these positive items inserted on your credit profile as described earlier. And write a hundred-word-or-less explanation for your file that describes your bad business deal or other sob story. After eighteen months or so, you'll have a pretty convincing pattern of onetime credit suicide with a more recent rebirth that may persuade new creditors to take a chance with you. Everybody likes to see a hard-luck case rehabilitated. So you might even be able to start building up some backup cards and play the game more shrewdly this time around.

REVENGE KIT FOR CREDIT

LETTER A: FOR A COPY OF YOUR TRW PROFILE

TO: TRW Credit Data
PO Box 271
Parsippany, NJ 07054

Please send me a copy of my TRW Updated Profile:

Name:
Social Security #:
Current Address:
Previous Address:

I have been denied credit within the past 30 days as the result of a report from TRW. A copy of the statement of denial from the creditor is attached.

(or)

I am enclosing a check for $8.

Yours truly,

LETTER B: CLEANING UP YOUR CREDIT PROFILE

NOTE: This sample letter (1) corrects factual errors; (2) gives your side of events in 100 words or less, where negative information is recorded; and (3) directs the agency to contact creditors who would give you good references.

To: Credit Reporting Agency
Address:
Date:

Re: Incorrect data on credit
profile of _____(Your Full Name)
Social Security # _____

Please correct the errors cited on my credit profile and enter my explanation of "negative" entries as follows:

1. The item marked "Delinquent 180 Days" for Exxon Oil Company Account #1234567 is in error, in that the balance of $184.50 was withheld due to a billing error pursuant to the FCBA. Please investigate and delete.

2. The item marked "Charge-off" for Mastercard Account #000001 is incorrect, in that my Mastercard Account number is 000002. Please reinvestigate and delete.

3. The item marked "Judgment $1150" referring to the East Bank of the Mississippi Checking+ Account should be amended with this explanation: "In March of 1979, I received this credit line for $1000 and made payments as agreed for one year. Then I suffered serious business reverses. I notified the bank that I was temporarily unable to make further payments and asked for a grace period, which they declined. I am now working with my lawyer to pay off this judgment."

4. The item marked "Inquiry by Diners Club 4-8_____," without a further entry that they granted me credit, suggests that I was turned down by this creditor. Please amend it with the following explanation: "Although Diners Club offered me a credit card after considering my application, I subsequently decided to obtain a Carte Blanche card instead and declined Diners accordingly."

Please make these reinvestigations, corrections, and amendments, and send copies of the revised report to all creditors who have received this profile within the past six months, pursuant to the FCRA.

Please also investigate my excellent credit history with the following companies:

1. General Motors Acceptance Corp.
    Account #1001-2002

2. Carte Blanche
    Account #1234-8910

3. State Power and Light Company
    Account #667788

4. Regional Telephone Company
    Account #4778932

I will be happy to pay reasonable fees to cover investigation of these references and inclusion of your findings in my revised report.

Thank you for your cooperation. I will expect to hear from you within the next 30 days.

Very truly yours,

Certified Letter

LETTER C: THREATENING ACTION FOR CREDIT BUREAU'S NONCOMPLIANCE WITH FCRA

To: President
Credit Bureau
Address:
Date:

Re: _____ (Your Name)
v. _____ (Credit Bureau)

Unless I hear from you within five (5) working days, a

complaint will be filed with the FTC regarding your non-compliance with provisions of the FCRA:

(State your problems having the report corrected, in sequence. Document any dereliction on the part of the reporting agency. For example, "I notified the bureau for the second time by telephone on Feb. 16 and spoke with a Ms. Reddy. She assured me that the correction would be made within 48 hours, but subsequent checking determined that the correction had still not been made.")

Be advised that unless you contact me within the time period stated above, I will also file suit for money damages pursuant to Millstone v. O'Hanlon Reports, Inc.

Very truly yours,

Certified Letter

(Enclose prior letters and other documentation.)

LETTER D: CONTESTING CHARGE FOR DEFECTIVE MERCHANDISE

To: Billing Department
Greedcard, Inc.
Address:
Date:

Re: Contested charge purchase
Greedcard Account # _____.

This is to advise you that I am contesting the charge on my January 198____ Greedcard statement for two pairs of Buffalo designer jeans purchased at Surly's Boutique. (Copy of charge receipt enclosed.)

The two pairs of jeans split their seams under normal and reasonable use, thus were not merchantable at the time of sale. I have notified Surly's by mail of the contested charge and am holding the jeans pending their response.

Please investigage this matter. I am enclosing a check for the noncontested balance.

Very truly yours,

Chubby Chaser

Certified Letter

LETTER E: DISPUTING A BILLING ERROR (Must be sent within 60 days after you receive your statement.)

To: Billing Department
Mogul Oil Company
Address:
Date:

Re: Billing Error
Account # _____

This is to notify you of a billing error on my April 198____ Mogul Oil Card statement (copy attached).

Please note that the statement indicates a charge of $184.50 for two Mogul radial tires purchased on March 12, 198____. In fact, these tires were defective, and were returned to my local Mogul Oil Station at _____(address) on March 16, with the station manager's assurance that the charge would be deducted from my account.

Pursuant to the Fair Credit Billing Act, please credit my account accordingly and notify me as soon as the correction is made. I am enclosing a check for the undisputed balance of _____.

                         Name
                         Address

Certified Letter

LETTER F: THREATENING CREDITOR FOR DUNNING YOU OVER A DISPUTED BILL

To: Billing Department
Mogul Oil Company
Address:
Date:

> Re: Pending action for damages for violation of
> Fair Credit Billing Act
> Account # _____

This is to advise you that unless I hear from you within ten (10) working days, I will commence action against you in district court for violation of the Fair Credit Billing Act, to wit:

1. That despite my letter of _____(date) attached, notifying you that your statement of April 198____ assessed an improper charge in the amount of $184.50, I have been dunned for the disputed balance on three successive statements.

2. That I have been contacted by persons representing themselves as employees of the Thunderbolt Collection Agency with regard to nonpayment of the above-cited balance.

3. That I have suffered money damages and emotional distress from these violations and shall seek to recover my losses under the penalty provisions of the Truth-in-

Lending Act, plus all court costs and reasonable attorney's fees.

4. That I shall pursue, through contacting the appropriate media, a class-action suit for damages if it is determined that other persons holding Mogul Card accounts have suffered like damages through your willful disregard of the Fair Credit Billing Act.

I will also file a formal complaint with the Truth-in-Lending Division of the Federal Trade Commission citing your misconduct at that time.

I suggest that you contact me immediately to resolve this problem.

Very truly yours,

Certified Letter

LETTER G: DIRECTING A BILL COLLECTOR TO VERIFY YOUR DEBT/CEASE AND DESIST

To: President
Thunderbolt Collection Agency
Address:
Date:

Re: Verification of Debt
Mogul Oil Card # _____

Please be advised that this account referred to your agency reflects a disputed balance of $184.50, thus was referred to your company in error and unlawfully.

You are hereby directed to (verify this debt/cease and desist from contacting me) pursuant to the Fair Debt Collection Practices Act.

Very truly yours,

Certified Letter

9
banks

Making Them Appreciate the Value of Your Dollar

Most people become particularly unglued when their bank gives them second-rate service. It might have something to do with the fact that it's your money they make you wait in line for, or your money that's withheld because a branch office doesn't have your signature card on file. And it's downright insufferable when bank personnel ignore an error *they* made on your statement or fail to credit a deposit properly and then bounce your checks.

Everybody makes mistakes; and you do expect bankers to be prudent—even wary—about whom they give your money to. But you may still wonder how Bert Lance could write $100,000 worth of overdrafts while your $13.98 overage draws surcharge penalties. You may also be confused when huge financial institutions freely lend millions to virtually bankrupt foreign governments and then refuse to extend you $500 Checking Plus privileges because you fell two months behind in a credit-card payment.

The cruel truth is that "banking the way you want it to be," to coin one bank's solicitous ad slogan, is a rich man's game (with exceptions like New York City's First Women's Bank). Even though the world may go 'round more easily for the rich, there are a few tactics that can help encourage your bank to offer you some of the pleasantries enjoyed by their most-favored customers.

UNDERSTANDING THE BANKING MENTALITY

Getting more service for your money starts with recognizing the sensibilities of the people you're dealing with. Most employees working behind a counter are regular people with exacting jobs who have to follow a training manual to the letter or they'll find themselves in big trouble. Thus it makes little sense to argue with a bank teller who can and will do nothing that involves deviating from policy to help you out with your problem. Our first rule is to save your energy, stay calm, and go directly to a bank officer beforehand if you think your transaction will prove too troublesome for a teller. This has nothing to do with discourtesy or incompetence. In big cities especially, tellers reflect the strain of large, demanding crowds—especially during the peak lunch hours, when impatience runs high. But that's still no excuse for rudeness, which should immediately be reported to the chief teller or the branch manager.

If you find yourself waiting interminably on a long, long line for one of three active tellers when other employees are standing around doing nothing, be good to yourself. Ask the person behind you to save your place and request the chief teller to open up another station. If this reasonable request is smilingly ignored, see the manager. And if others in your line look annoyed about spending their lunch hour inching toward their money, don't be afraid to ask in a pleasant but frustrated tone: "Could anyone here help me persuade the manager to open up another teller station?"

Most customers don't like to be the first to complain but will gladly support your effort if they're as tired of the shuffling march as you are. And the manager who perceives a threat of mass insurrection among the bank's usually docile prisoners will generally send some officers to take up teller stations if nobody else is available.

The most farsighted and ambitious bankers usually aren't doling out consumer loans and approving checks. They are in back rooms figuring out how to improve the bank's daily cash position by directing funds from cocoa futures to oil. Most officers you deal with, unless you keep six-figure balances or do commercial business with that bank, are likely to be stolid, go-by-the-book types. If you find such an officer no help at all, you can ask to see other executives charged with keeping the bigger picture of customer satisfaction in mind.

Since the branch manager is the person who has the authority to make exceptions to rules, he or she is the one you should normally talk to as soon as you sense bureaucratic stonewalling. If the manager is "too busy" to see you, the *refusing to leave* gambit described in Chapter 2 is generally useful in banks, particularly if you can force a good show of willingness to stay there indefinitely until you're granted an audience. They can't leave you there overnight, and the prospect of ejecting a customer forcibly is too horrible to contemplate for most bankers. Generally speaking the manager will be the executive who least wants to offend.

The Marketing Director. If you're in the bank's main office, one corporate-level executive who might be willing to help you unravel your problem is the person in charge of marketing. Here's someone who goes beyond just not wanting to offend to actually viewing his or her mission as getting new customers and persuading them to use more of the bank's services. The ideal times to ask for a visit with a marketing director are (1) when you feel the bank is not living up to its advertising claims by offering all its services at all its branches (such as cashing your check), or (2) when you've been badly treated by an employee and get no satisfaction from the bank manager. Just remember to be as pleasant as you are firm, so you're not dismissed as a crank:

MARKETING DIRECTOR: What can I do to help you?

CUSTOMER: First of all, thank you for taking your time to see me, Mr. Groesbeck. It's not really my nature to complain about an employee's performance, but I don't believe that one of your officers is reflecting your bank's usual standards. Or at least not over a simple problem I'm having with my account.

MARKETING DIRECTOR: Oh? What seems to be the trouble?

CUSTOMER: Well, I asked your officer, Mr. Shirkwell, to resolve an error on my statement that's been showing up for several months. But he keeps telling me that there's a 15-day limit on reporting errors, after which the bank can't be held liable. Now, I know that's what it says on your statement, Mr. Groesbeck, but I'm sure you're aware that position isn't valid under state law.

MARKETING DIRECTOR: I'm afraid I'm not a lawyer, Ms. Considine. Heh, heh.

CUSTOMER: I'm sure the bank's lawyer is aware of it, but the reason I came to see you is more a customer-relations matter. I'm afraid I'll have to close my account today if this situation isn't resolved. And I'll certainly take my case to civil court. Besides, I have to believe that your officer has his facts wrong and this isn't a firm bank policy. It certainly isn't very good for customer relations.

MARKETING DIRECTOR: Well, if you'll wait just a few moments, I'll see if I can straighten it out.

The marketing director will probably try to bend the rules to keep you from making waves. This approach may prove more effective than seeing the bank lawyer, who will throw up a smoke screen of intimidating legalese, or the manager, who might envision an army of customers waving three-year-old statements if he opens the door with your case.

Common Banking Annoyances
and How to Handle Them

Most nagging problems with banks occur when they don't credit your account properly, when a check bounces, or when you're refused credit for reasons you consider arbitrary or discriminatory.

Improperly Credited Deposits. You've deposited $1000 in an automatic-teller machine on a Monday, but when you check your balance that Thursday, there's no record of it. So you call your branch, give the person you speak to the number on your deposit record, and demand to know what happened to your money.

> OFFICER: We have no record of receiving that deposit, but I'll start our investigative procedure.

> CUSTOMER: Please call me back this afternoon. I've already sent out checks written against that deposit.

> OFFICER: Sorry, our investigation procedure takes ten days.

> CUSTOMER: Ten days! I can't wait ten days!

> OFFICER: Sorry, that's how long it takes.

Now you should call the president's office and explain the problem, even if it's to the secretary, stating that the ten-day policy is unconscionable when you need immediate access to your money.

> SECRETARY: I'm afraid that's how long it takes. There's a lot of paperwork, you know.

> CUSTOMER: Then please give me the name of an executive who has authority to correct the error and report back to me by tomorrow morning.

> SECRETARY: I guess that would be Mr. Ogelthorpe, vice-president in charge of branch operations.

Next call your local civil court and ask for the name of a judge who will be on the bench the following day. Then call Ogelthorpe's office and tell his secretary you've been referred to him by the president's office for fast action on your problem. Explain that you can't be expected to wait for your money due to the bank's error, and that if you don't hear back from him by Friday noon you'll see Judge Sternheart to issue a show-cause order directing the bank to produce their records. And you will also hold the bank liable for all consequential damages you suffer from having issued checks against your valid deposit.

The hovering specter of both the bank president and Judge Sternheart will undoubtedly move Ogelthorpe to bump your case ahead of the troublesome depositors waiting to hear about their money. He will probably report to you by your deadline. In all likelihood, what happened was no great catastrophe. An employee taking deposits out of the automatic teller probably stamped your slip right over your account number, or some other simple problem they could resolve quickly if properly motivated. Deposits are seldom actually lost— bankers just give themselves leisurely schedules for problem solving.

Bounced Checks. If you bounce a check either through negligence or a temporary inability to cover it with funds, you'll just cause yourself embarrassment and spoil your perfect banking record. A clean record is a definite asset, especially when you need to impress upon a bank that your behavior is exemplary, thus it *must* be the bank's fault if you have a problem.

If you find you can't cover a check, you have good reason to phone the bank and stop payment. For example, you mailed a deposit but you see from looking at the balance that it hasn't arrived at the bank to be entered into your account. Make sure you call the payee to report that you had to stop payment because your mailed deposit hasn't been credited. Emphasize that you'll bring a new check the next day, after you've made a new deposit in person, and ask the person's indulgence to wait two days to enter it. That way it won't be returned for "funds on deposit but not yet collected."

If your checks bounce because the bank made an error, you should see an officer or the manager immediately. They have form letters they'll grudgingly send on request to cover that contingency, but we don't feel that this is good enough after they've blackened your good name. Instead, ask the manager to send a letter stating that the check was returned due to a bank error and insist that the wording include a phrase to the effect that "Ms. Considine has established an excellent banking history with us, with not a single case of checks returned due to her own negligence."

You can consider holding the bank liable for damages when you deposit a check you believe to be good and, relying on the validity of your deposit, you write checks against it. The bank originally credits the deposit but later hears from the clearinghouse that the check is no good and dishonors it. You, however, have scattered your own bad checks around town because your balance clearly showed those funds to cover them in your account. What you should do is send a letter telling the bank it's liable for making your bad checks good. (See Letter A at the end of the chapter.)

When You're Turned Down for Credit. If you believe that a bank's reasons for refusing you credit are discriminatory, you should ask which regulatory agency the bank reports to. There are several, depending on the kind of bank you're dealing with—commercial vs. savings and loan, nationally chartered vs. state chartered, and so on. Then you should put the manager and bank attorney on notice that you're filing a complaint. What you should do first is get a free consultation from a lawyer to see if you have a reasonable complaint and, if so, what you might stand to gain. A valid discrimination suit can produce a hefty award.

Guerrilla *Banking*. In all fairness, banks can be very good indeed about resolving your complaints (Note their high marks in the Better Business Bureau's survey in Chapter 2.) The reasons for this behavior are several—they're usually image conscious, they're competing against a lot of other banks for customers' money, and bankers themselves tend to be civilized people who may want to do right by you on a purely ethical basis. But some arrogant and quarrelsome people still slip in through the cracks, even at the higher strata of management.

So if a bank really does you wrong, you may feel as spiteful as customers who've responded by:

1. Keeping a purely convenience account in the problem bank. This means the customer deposits large amounts—preferably in quarters—at a convenient branch, then immediately writes a check to another bank on the other side of town that treats the customer well. The problem institution has all the hassles of sorting out deposits and sending monthly statements, without profiting from the use of the customer's money.

2. Using the problem bank as personal secretary. If the bank offers prearranged bill paying, a customer can deposit just enough money in an account on the first of the month to cover any number of bills, which the bank has been instructed to pay on the second, effectively draining the account for another thirty days.

3. Cashing exotic checks. Some banks won't even give you counter checks anymore if you run out of your printed ones. They expect you to buy money orders until you receive your new "standardized" checks in the mail. In fact, a check can legally be written on anything and still be negotiable, as long as you include all the information you'll find on your printed checks. A check could be written on the side of a cow (this has actually been done and "cashed"), a tablecloth, or a parachute!

4. The mackerel for safekeeping. You can keep anything in a bank safe deposit box. We happen to think this is a bit sophomoric. But we also

promised to report on the state of the art in guerrilla tactics, so let your conscience be your guide.

REVENGE KIT FOR BANKS

LETTER A, DEMANDING SATISFACTION OVER A BANK ERROR

Mr. Cecil Rothschild, President
East Bank of the Mississippi

Re: Acct. #76-0093-15
and #76-0093-16

Dear Mr. Rothschild:

I am the holder of two checking accounts at your bank, referenced above. The first account, herein referred to as 15, is my general operating account. The second account, herein referred to as 16, is money I hold for specific purposes.

Account 16 bears no authorized signatures other than my own, because I cannot afford any errors concerning it, and thus I hold myself solely responsible. Last Tuesday, January 25, 198_____, your bank debited account #16 instead of account #15 for a check correctly written on account #15. The result was an overdraft of $632.82 on the #16 account.

The first knowledge I had of the bank's unilateral error was notice that seven (7) checks had consequently been returned to my payees marked "insufficient funds." I immediately contacted the bank and demanded that the matter be rectified. Four days of frustration passed until my accounts were properly credited.

I do not consider this satisfaction. I now make the following demands. The first two are not negotiable. The third leaves room for negotiation within reasonable bounds.

First, that you will personally write a letter to the seven people to whom those checks were returned. You will explain that it was your bank and not I who was at fault.

This letter must also include a statement accurately reflecting my conscientious handling of my accounts with your bank since they were opened two years ago. Further, you will apologize for inconveniencing my payees and offer to pay all service fees, if any, charged by their banks.

Second, that you will credit my account appropriately for any fees accruing out of this error. You will not assess your monthly service charge against my account in recognition of the fact that your "services" rendered only served to damage my business and personal reputation.

Third, that you will remit to me the sum of $250.00. This sum represents a business opportunity I lost on the third day after your bank's error. (See attached documents substantiating this loss.) Had your bank decided to act expediently, you could have avoided this additional liability.

In the event I do not hear from you within five (5) working days, I will forward this letter to my attorney.

At that point, I assure you we will be looking for your adequate compensation and will assess punitive damages against your bank.

Very truly yours,

(NOTE: Banks are being held more accountable for their mistakes every day, through this type of creative litigation. And settlements are bringing the wronged customer considerably more than a proper credit on their statement. Evidence of the bank's malice is helpful, of course, but not a necessary prerequisite for bringing such a suit.)

LETTER B, COMPLAINT
ABOUT AN EMPLOYEE

Mr. Rothschild, President
East Bank of Mississippi

Re: Acct. #765-93-001

Dear Mr. Rothschild:

I have been a customer of your bank for over seven years.

Your service has always been more than satisfactory in terms of courteous customer-employee relations.

Yesterday an emergency occurred when my brother suddenly was hospitalized and needed to borrow $1,000 from me. I immediately went to the hospital and, shortly after, presented myself at the closest East Bank (I usually bank at the main branch). In the chaos, I had forgotten my checkbook. I asked the teller for an unencoded check to withdraw my funds. I had proper identification to document the transaction. Yet she refused to call the other branch to verify my account, stating that your computer had been down, that she was "too busy" to call it again, and advising me to come back later. I told her I had been a customer for seven years and she replied with a rude "I can't help that."

I trust that you care about the problems one unhelpful and rude employee can cause your customers. Unless I receive some satisfaction that this employee, namely Jane Sloth, teller ID #743, Westview Branch, is disciplined for this breach of her duty and, I presume your bank's standards of employee courtesy, I will be withdrawing my account. And, I might add, suggesting that my friends do the same.

I feel that an apology from Ms. Sloth and the bank are in order, as well as more tangible evidence that the bank values me as a customer. Precisely I refer you to the fact that I have casually in the past inquired about your Checking Plus and have been told it was not available to me as my current employment has been for too short a time.

Please check my banking record with you. After the many years without a single bounced check, I feel I am more than entitled to a reasonable credit line of $1,000.

Please advise as to both of these matters. I will expect to hear from you within two weeks.

Very truly yours,

THE LEGAL REQUIREMENTS OF A NEGOTIABLE CHECK

A check is a contract you enter into merely by signing your name. But a check is controlled by rules specifically designed to govern it and not by ordinary contract law. It must be:

in writing (printed, typed, or handwritten)

signed by the maker (an X will do)

contain an unconditional order (to give somebody a certain sum of money)

payable on demand (or at a definitive time)

written "pay to the order of" or "pay to the bearer of" and the payee's name (payable to "cash" means to the bearer)

Once you satisfy these requirements, it can be legally presented in virtually any form.

MAKING A FORMAL COMPLAINT TO A REGULATORY AGENCY

Many jurisdictions have an "informal" complaint mechanism. To put it into motion, with minor differences according to your state:

1.   Call the aggrieving bank.

2.   Demand that bank personnel tell you which regulatory agency they report to. It will probably be called something like _____ (State) Banking Commission.

3.   Call and ask for an examiner.

4.   Request a complaint form. If your jurisdiction has one, use it. If your state commission does not have one, they will handle your problem over the telephone 75 percent of the time. Otherwise, they request a letter explaining your position.

5.   We recommend a slight wrinkle in this procedure. Whether or not the commission wishes to handle the matter by friendly discussion, we suggest you document the grievance in writing. This will tend to assure faster handling and more serious consideration.

We suggest using as your model:

Examiner's Name
(State) Banking Commission

Re: East Bank of Mississippi

Dear Mr./Ms. _____,

As you'll recall, I spoke with you this morning about improprieties committed by the above bank. Although you suggest we can deal with this matter by phone, I would prefer that we reduce all our communications to writing. I would also ask for copies of any correspondence you send to the bank.

This is no reflection on the commission, of course, but rather a desire on my part for complete documentation of all dealings with the particular bank, as I have found them to be less than accurate about oral communications in the past.

Therefore, please send me a memo to the effect that the East Bank will be contacted by the end of this week as you indicated this morning.

Thank you again for your help.

Yours truly,

10
brokerage houses
The Wisdom of Pleading Ignorance

Playing the stock market can mean fearsome risks for anyone. But in the clubby sanctum of Wall Street, history suggests that it's a lot riskier to be a small investor than a large one. One former Merrill-Lynch sales trainee recounts what we might realistically expect: When push comes to shove, the small investor can wind up with whatever the big customer wants to get rid of: "Back when I was a trainee with the nation's largest brokerage firm, it was unloading Howard Hughes' TWA holdings . . . a line that the boys liked to use when calling their little clients was, 'I've saved some of Mr. Hughes' stock for you.'"[1]

So when your stockbroker calls with a friendly word that could make or break your future, you might do well to consider that the smartest brokers in your house are probably working the big accounts, while the ones who deal with smaller portfolios may be working you over. And if a commodities broker you've never heard of calls you up one evening with a carefully worded hot tip, you might do even better to hang up. Some of the major commodities frauds in diamonds, leveraged gold contracts, and other high-rollers' sports over the past decade have been committed with high-pressure telephone sales. But we're not dispensing advice about how to play the stock or commodities markets here. Rather, here's a bit of strategy that could help you recoup your losses if your broker turns out to be incompetent or worse.

What Brokers Get Paid to Do. Brokers don't analyze stocks—they rely on the brokerage house's analysts for that. The broker or account executive or whatever else he or she gets called around your brokerage house has a pretty carefully defined responsibility, which is to sell you stock. And the broker, like any salesperson who's charged with motivating you to spend your money, gets paid on commission. That doesn't mean the broker makes a killing with you when your stock goes up. Brokers make the same fixed commission for each transaction whether you win, lose, or draw, so their best interest lies in churning your account to keep you an active buyer and seller. You probably wouldn't buy a new car every month because your Chevy dealer called you up and explained why you should. But you might be tempted to keep your portfolio more active than necessary if your broker is particularly hungry.

The Socratic Approach

Socrates' much-touted wisdom extended to recognizing his own ignorance—a neglected philosophy in this age of aggressive self-hype. But it's a useful model to follow in your market dealings, for crafty legal reasons if not lofty philosophical ones. If a broker makes a mistake on your account or even makes a recommendation that you follow to your regret, you have several possibilities for striking back.

Correcting Minor Errors of Omission. An acquaintance of ours, Ted, once put in an oral sell order to his broker, who somehow didn't sell as he should have and later called up to tell Ted that he'd lost about seven hundred dollars when the stock plummeted. So, after an unproductive "Yes I did, no you didn't" conversation with the broker, Ted hung up and called his supervisor.

"You know," the supervisor admonished, "that a sell order has to be confirmed in writing to be valid."

"No, I didn't know that," Ted explained, "because nobody ever told me." Ultimately the house took the loss, because there was a good possibility that Ted hadn't been properly informed by his broker. And generally speaking, employees of a brokerage house will be intimidated at an ethical level when there's a chance that the customer is right.

What Ted did know was that the house maintained—as many do—a reserve fund in which he could keep his money at 15 percent interest until he bought something with it. So he reduced his risk to a degree unprecedented in the stock market by keeping his money there for over a year.

Avenging Gross Errors of Judgment. Sometimes a broker can give you truly catastrophic advice. If you lost your shirt by following such sterling counsel, remember that there's always a risk when you buy or sell stock.

But the question that would save your assets is, was it a *reasonable* risk?

The Securities and Exchange Commission (SEC), a federal agency which regulates brokerage houses, isn't in business to protect you from brokers' bad calls *unless* you can present a convincing case that the broker violated SEC regulations and you suffered accordingly, in which case you can threaten to sue the broker for malpractice. And if you have such a convincing case, the people at the brokerage house will probably see it in their self-interest to do without the harmful publicity you could cause them.

First of all, SEC law views a broker's responsibility to protect your interests in direct proportion to your sophistication about the market. In one California case, a physician sued a brokerage house for deflating his portfolio and won damages because even though he'd traded a lot of stock in his time, he wasn't sophisticated in the particular area of his traumatic loss. Thus he relied on his broker, whose advice was found to be less than competent. So you should always have—on record—some statement of your ignorance about the market in general. Then give your broker written instructions to "buy or sell at your own sound discretion." This tends to place the burden of responsibility more squarely on his or her shoulders.

Once you've established your blushing innocence, you can respond to losses you suffer courtesy of your broker's recommendations by:

1. Demanding to see the information on which he or she based his or her advice. Brokers can't just give you intuitive tips founded on little more than a hot desire to grab off a commission. They have to base each recommendation on solid financial information.

2. Buying on margin, so when the broker asks you to make your losses good, you can tell him or her to go ahead and sue you for the difference. But they'll be risking, of course, your immediate countersuit for malpractice.

If there's much money at stake—over the small-claims-court limit—you should find a lawyer who knows the labyrinthine passages of SEC law before going to civil court. Sizable damage suits involving stock trading can usually be handled on a contingency basis if the attorney likes the look of your case. (And, of course, you should ask for a free or reduced-fee preliminary consultation in any case to explain your problem and see if you stand a good chance of winning if you proceed on your own.)

The Arbitration Alternative. There's another possibility if you don't want to take the trouble to sue or be sued. For a small filing fee of twenty dollars or so, you can submit your case to arbitration by the National Association of Securities Dealers or the stock exchange where the transaction occurred. Before you do, though, consult a lawyer to determine how strong your case really is. Brokerage houses tend to come out ahead in arbitration as often as disgruntled investors.

Blowing the Whistle. You'll probably also want to tell the National Association of Securities Brokers and the Security and Exchange Commission what you think of your broker's competence and the house that supports him or her in formal complaints. See what other complaints have come before them concerning your broker and the house (which an investor should theoretically do in the first place, before trusting the house's judgment, but let's assume we're too late for that). If there's a growing rat's nest of complaints, the house may be more kindly disposed to resolving your problem with a settlement if you withdraw your charges.

REVENGE KIT FOR BROKERAGE HOUSES

GENERAL LETTER TO BROKER

Name:
Firm:
Address:
Date:

Dear Mr./Ms. _____:

Please buy (number of) shares of _____Co. for me.

Since I am a novice at buying stocks, I will have to rely on your advice. Therefore, I am giving you my written authority to sell any stock in my portfolio and use the proceeds to replace that stock with an appropriate substitute based on your sound discretion and the exercise of due diligence.

Thank you.

Very truly yours,

DEMAND LETTER FOR DAMAGES

Name:
Firm:
Address:
Date:

Re: _____Stock Transaction
Date _____

Dear Mr./Ms._____:

As you know, the stock you advised me to buy and did, in fact, buy in my name dropped 16 points in the first week of my ownership. This has resulted in my losing (amount). You have now advised me to sell this stock. I hereby authorize you to make that transaction. Inasmuch as this loss was directly related to your breach of your obligation to use sound discretion in the handling of my portfolio, by failing to observe reported significant changes in the company's performance, I am demanding that you immediately reimburse my account for the loss your lack of due diligence has caused. I would appreciate written confirmation of your acknowledgment of your firm's liability in this matter.

Very truly yours,

TO ARRANGE FOR ARBITRATION

Contact the director of arbitration at the organization nearest you:

- American Stock Exchange Inc.
  86 Trinity Place
  New York, New York 10006
  (212) 938-6000

- Boston Stock Exchange, Inc.
  53 State Street
  Boston, Massachusetts 02109
  (617) 723-9500

- Chicago Board Options Exchange, Inc.
  141 W. Jackson Boulevard
  Chicago, Illinois 60604
  (312) 431-5600

- The Cincinnati Stock Exchange
  205 Dixie Terminal Building
  Cincinnati, Ohio 45202
  (513) 621-1410

- Midwest Stock Exchange, Incorporated
  120 South LaSalle Street
  Chicago, Illinois 60603
  (312) 368-2222

- Municipal Securities Rulemaking Board
  1150 Connecticut Avenue, N.W.
  Suite 507
  Washington, DC 20036
  (202) 223-9347

- National Association of Securities Dealers, Inc.
  Two World Trade Center

New York, New York 10048
(212) 938-1177

• New York Stock Exchange, Inc.
11 Wall Street
New York, New York 10006
(212) 623-3000

• Pacific Stock Exchange Incorporated
618 South Spring Street
Los Angeles, California 90014
(213) 489-4800

• Philadelphia Stock Exchange, Inc.
17th Street and Stock Exchange Place
Philadelphia, Pennsylvania 19103
(215) 563-4700

SAMPLE ARBITRATION APPLICATION

UNIFORM SUBMISSION AGREEMENT

Print Name of Sponsoring Organization With Which Claim is to be Filed

In the Matter of the Arbitration Between

Name of Claimant(s)

and

Name of Respondent(s)

Please Print or Type

1. The undersigned parties hereby submit the present matter in controversy, as set forth in the attached statement of claim, answers and all related counterclaims and/or third party claims which may be asserted, to arbitration in accordance with the Constitution, By-Laws, Rules, Regulations and/or Code of Arbitration Procedure of the sponsoring organization.

2. The undersigned parties hereby state that they have read the procedures and rules of the sponsoring organization relating to arbitration.

3. The undersigned parties agree that in the event a hearing is necessary, such hearing shall be held at a time and place as may be designated by the Director of Arbitration or the arbitrator(s). The undersigned parties further agree and understand that the arbitration will be conducted in accordance with the Constitution, By-Laws, Rules, Regulations and/or Code of Arbitration Procedure of the sponsoring organization.

4. The undersigned parties further agree to abide by and perform any award(s) rendered pursuant to this Submission Agreement and further agree that a judgment and any interest due thereon, may be entered upon such award(s) and, for these purposes, the undersigned parties hereby voluntarily consent to submit to the jurisdiction of any court of competent jurisdiction which may properly enter such judgment.

5. IN WITNESS WHEREOF, the parties hereto have signed and acknowledged the foregoing Submission Agreement.

Claimant(s) Signature   Respondent(s) Signature

_____   _____

_____   _____

STATE OF   )

                              :   ss.:

COUNTY OF   )

On the _____ day of _____ , _____ ,
before me personally appeared _____
to me known and known to me to be the person(s) who
executed the foregoing instrument, and (__he__) acknowledged to me that (__he__) executed the same.

                          _____
                              Notary Public

* A corporate claimant is required to execute an acknowledgement in the form approved
by the state in which it has its principal office. If assistance is required, please contact the
Director of Arbitration.

11
barter

An Eye for an Eye

Barter remains one of the most satisfying and profitable forms of revenge. And it is a rare variety that both parties can enjoy.

First of all, people you barter goods and services with are more inclined to be honest and helpful than those who just expect you to hand them your money and go away. There's usually a spirit of camaraderie in simplifying the exchange process, which tends to humanize it, too. For instance, you stand a better chance of getting your car fixed correctly by a mechanic whose bookkeeping you're doing in exchange (partly, of course, because whatever damage he could inflict on your pistons pales by comparison to what you could do to his business with his own books). And it's easier to ask a plumber to repair your overflowing dishwasher on a Saturday if you're paying him or her in valuable old records, because she shares your soft spots for Knuckles O'Toole or the Andrews Sisters. In short, barterers treat each other like cohorts instead of soulless and irritating customers.

Second, barter eliminates middlemen who, often unnecessarily, stand in line to collect markups or commissions. Much of today's so-called underground economy involves employed servicepeople moonlighting, which is one kind of enterprise particularly amenable to trade rather than cash. Or if you're moving to another city, you can advertise in that city's paper for a homeowner moving to your town. Then see if you can work out a mutually satisfactory house trade and eliminate two fat commissions to real-estate brokers.

Notice we didn't say that you should use barter to hide income from the government. The IRS hasn't let the burgeoning subeconomy of barter deals slip by unnoticed. They've ruled that exchanging goods and services at fair market value is just another form of income that shouldn't escape their tentacles. Thus you're expected to own up about such exchanges on your income-tax return and pay up if you've realized a profit.

But the IRS can only practice selective enforcement. Individual barter deals interest them less than flamboyant business transactions of real estate or exchange advertising employing TV time blocks. Trading that involves services or privately owned, unregistered goods are very difficult to police. The test, if one of your deals is ever audited, will probably be your "intent" to cut the government out of your private exchanges. Just keep a record of your transactions and agree with your exchange partner beforehand about valuing and reporting your trade.

IMAGINATIVE TRADE-OFFS

Some businesses specialize in arranging barter deals—professional "barter brokers" offer you credits you can trade with any of your fellow members via your Mastercard credit line. But be advised that the IRS has been looking very, very carefully into the records of those companies lately.

If you think hard enough about anything you want, you can probably arrange some kind of barter deal to obtain it on your own. For example:

> When twenty-two-year-old college junior Paul Ferbank discovered that spouses of professors didn't have to pay tuition at Hobart College in Geneva, New York, he knew immediately how he could save $3,400 annually and pass on a tax savings to someone else. His ad in the local newspaper started: "Needy tax-deductible male student seeking marriage contract for tuition purposes."

> One woman who couldn't afford the rent to start an office service borrowed $600 from a bank and opened a serve-yourself office for others who needed space part-time or full-time. Many out-of-towners in need of a city address found the $25-a-day space charge attractive enough to sign contracts guaranteeing them one day a week on a regular basis.

> A judge agreed to waive a one-year prison sentence for a tax evader in Castro Valley, California, if he would agree to lecture to community groups on the perils of income-tax evasion. It was a good barter until the speaker got carried away with his own jokes. ("I sent the IRS 25¢ because I heard I could pay my taxes by the quarter!") When comedy continued to take precedence over taxes, the judge stopped the laughter by reversing the barter and sending the evader to jail, where the former speaker is using his time to study tax law. [1]

You might even be able to trade off your legal fees for pursuing other revenge strategies throughout the book. Whenever you're quoted a price for goods or services, let them know what you have that they might want. (But be careful how you phrase your proposition, especially if people find you sexually attractive.) Just say, "I'm a gardener/party caterer/dentist myself, and I've got a great collection of videotapes (or whatever). Do you think we could work out a barter deal?"

What to Do if a Barterer Reneges on the Deal

Even in the friendly world of trading, people can disappoint you by accepting your goods or services and withholding theirs, or giving you less than you bargained for. To protect yourself, get a simple, signed agreement down on paper (see the Revenge Kit at the end of the chapter). Then if the other party reneges, you can enforce your deal in small-claims court.

If you find you're trading with a dishonest adversary who tricks you and refuses to make good, you can wield the ultimate revenge—reporting that individual to the IRS as a likely tax evader. But wait until after April 15, when you're pretty sure that the exchange has already gone unreported on the scoundrel's income-tax return. And to build up your potential gains, it helps to chat with potential barterers about other trades they've made in the past. Most people love to talk about them, little realizing the motive for your keen interest. Remember that the IRS pays bounties to informants based on a percentage of the unreported taxes they collect from the object of your tattling. In case you're wondering, the IRS keeps its informants' names a closely guarded secret.

Revenge Kit for Barter

SAMPLE BARTER AGREEMENT

  Ashley Wilkes of Twelve Oaks, Atlanta, Georgia , herein called the first party, hereby offers to exchange the following described services with Scarlett O'Hara , of Tara, Atlanta, Georgia , hereinafter called the second party, in exchange for the following services/property described herein.

Terms and Conditions of Exchange:

Ashley Wilkes shall lend to Scarlett O'Hara the estate known as "Twelve Oaks" for two (2) weeks, running from January 5, 198_ for and in consideration of Scarlett O'Hara lending to Ashley Wilkes the estate known as "Tara" for the same two (2) weeks.

The parties agree that if one of the parties incurs any expenses in the enforcement of any of the provisions of this Agreement, the other will be responsible for and pay forthwith any and all expenses thereby incurred, including, but not limited to, reasonable counsel fees, court costs and travel, except that if the initiating party is not upheld in court, then that initiating party will be liabled for the aforesaid expenses.

This Agreement has been entered into in the State of Georgia and shall be construed and interpreted in accordance with the laws of said state.

No amendments or additions to this Agreement shall be binding unless in writing and signed by both parties, except as herein otherwise provided.

IN WITNESS WHEREOF, the parties hereto have executed this Agreement as of the date and year written herein below.

WITNESS:

_____   _____
                                          Ashley Wilkes (Seal)

_____   _____
                                          Scarlett O'Hara (Seal)

Date: _____

Note that the Barter Agreement contains all the elements of a contract—mutual assent through offer and acceptance, definite terms, adequate "consideration" (as opposed to a gift) and capacity (over 21, sound mental health, and sober).

You may wish to add, as we have, the enforcement clause, which guarantees you that a lawyer will take your case at no cost to you—if you're in the right.

This is a *bilateral* contract—a promise exchanged for a promise: Twelve Oaks for Tara. When the contract was formed, there were two rights and two duties legally imposed, with two "promisers" and two "promisees."

But you might prefer a second type, called *unilateral* contract, which offers a promise contingent upon an act by the promisee. This leaves the promisee the opportunity to *not* perform and thereby avoid a contract being formed.

As a barterer, this leaves you the ability to renege as promisee if you've a change of heart. If you were Scarlett, you would have Ashley write this as: "I, Ashley Wilkes, promise to let you stay at Twelve Oaks for six months if you, Scarlett O'Hara, care for my wife, Melanie." Scarlett calls the shots here. At her election, she nurses Melanie and gets a stint at Twelve Oaks.

DEMAND LETTER TO BARTERER WHO RENEGES, BASED ON A UNILATERAL CONTRACT

January 1, 198____

Mr. Ashley Wilkes
Twelve Oaks
Atlanta, Georgia

Dear Mr. Wilkes:

On October 15, 198____, we entered into the attached Barter Agreement. You promised to lend me Twelve Oaks for two weeks if I cared for your wife Melanie for one month. I did so, nursing her for 4.3 weeks. My performance, predicated upon your promise, evidenced by the Barter Agreement, constituted a binding contract.

Your failure to lend Twelve Oaks to me, upon repeated demand, is an actionable breach under the Uniform Commercial Code.

I hereby demand you make Twelve Oaks available for my stay, effective January 5, 198____ at 12:00 P.M. through January 19, 198____ at 12:00 P.M. In the event that you fail to remedy this breach, I will file suit in the district court of Georgia.

I will seek compensatory damages in the sum of $4,000.00. I will also demand $500.00 in consequential damages, for money I spent buying afternoon frocks for barbecues. Further, due to the malice you evidence when you stated I could not stay at Twelve Oaks because I was "no lady," I will ask the court to order punitive damages.

Save yourself the embarrassment of court, attorney's fees, court costs, and damages. Resolve your breach of our agreement immediately.

Yours truly,

Scarlett O'Hara

HOW TO REPORT A RENEGING
BARTERER TO THE IRS

Call your closest IRS Office.

Ask to talk to someone in their Criminal Investigation Unit.

Give the agent your information: "I believe that Ashley Wilkes of Atlanta, Georgia, has concealed income from you in the amount of at least $4,000 and possibly over $20,000 based on barter deals he discussed with me during the month of January, 198_____."

The agent will take the information by phone and relay it to the regional office.

The regional office will review the case and reply to the local office, who will be in future contact with you.

PART IV

People Who
Needle People

12
contractors

Tricks on the Trade

It always sounds like fun to build a dream house exactly to your liking or improve your home with a new kitchen or swimming pool. Unfortunately, that enjoyable phase usually ends after you've sketched your ideas on a cocktail napkin and start calling contractors to execute them. Dealing with contractors can be about as much fun as, to paraphrase gonzo journalist Hunter Thompson's description of traveling with a certain politician, careening downhill in a swaying boxcar with an angry ten-foot rat for company.

Even basically honest contractors—not the outright crooks who "resurface" your driveway with crankcase oil and leave town as soon as they grab your money—have a lot of problems that they're happy to pass along to you, the consumer. Building materials are ridiculously expensive. Good, reliable workers are harder to find than ever. Contractors are often overextended due to taking on more jobs than they can handle. And they generally have to beat down their subcontractors to show a reasonable profit. So expect the same kinds of problems you would when you're buying a new car, multiply that heartburn factor by ten, and you'll have a rough idea of what you're in for. Assume that the job will take longer than you expect—maybe months longer; that you'll be asked to pay more than you intended—possibly 50 percent more, even if you don't change specifications as the work progresses; and that you'll probably find defects in workmanship.

Be prepared to use preemptive first-strike strategies and some real hardball tactics to get your way. You'll need them. Many contractors are used to complaints about their shoddy work. They're also used to being sued. In fact, a lot of them keep their assets in other family members' names, so you can't hope to collect much money even if you win a judgment against them. And they try to wring as much money as possible from you before they do the work, so they're always ahead if you try to outfox them. In short, problem contractors are tough, wily adversaries.

PROTECTING YOURSELF (IF IT'S NOT TOO LATE)

There are precautions you can take beforehand, if you haven't already made arrangements with your contractors:

Ask the local Federal Housing Authority (FHA) office to give you its "DSI" list, which is a running account of contractors whose work the FHA has found unsatisfactory. You should also ask for the local "workmanship ratings." If you're far from an FHA office, write for the DSI list to: HUD Printing Office, 451 7th Street N.W., Washington, D.C. 20410.

Get bids from several different contractors, ask for plenty of references from each one, and check them out. (The problem with this is, of course, that just by the law of averages, every contractor probably has a few undemanding buyers who've been happy with his work.) If you're building a house, make sure the contractor offers the National Association of Home Builders (NAHB) Home Owner's Warranty—a ten-year protection plan against defects in workmanship.

Ask to see the contractor's insurance coverage to make sure it covers all the workers who could injure themselves on the job. And check your own homeowner's insurance policy to see if it covers injuries to individual workers.

Get a contract that *clearly specifies* the materials to be used on the job (by brand name or exact physical description), the completion date, and the contractor's responsibility for cleaning up after himself. If these aren't included, insist on them. You should also agree to pay no more than one-third down to cover material costs, one-third when the job is half-finished, and one-third upon completion. Have the contractor sign this agreement personally, not just as an officer of his corporation, so he will be personally liable if things go wrong.

Obtain the names of all the subcontractors he'll be using and get them to sign "materialman's lien" waivers before you'll let them do the work, so you won't be responsible if the general contractor (GC) doesn't pay them. (In Wisconsin, a GC is supposed to do this for you.)

Most important, find out by calling your state offices whether contractors are supposed to be licensed to do the work you're talking about in your state and whether your contractor is, in fact, licensed. Don't ask the contractor about this; just call the state. As we'll see later, it may actually be to your advantage if the state requires a license but your contractor doesn't have one.

Get a bank loan if possible for home improvements, because the bank will probably have an inspector who will approve the work to protect the bank's interests and yours.

But we'll assume that you haven't taken most of these precautions, and you have problems. One set of frustrations can arise when you're dealing with a real down-and-out crook, and another when you're just working with the garden variety of shoddy, incompetent, or semicrooked problem contractor. We'll look at both here.

HIT-AND-RUN CONTRACTORS

Perhaps you've heard of the roguish clan that run around the country door-to-door stinging homeowners for phony contracting work. Don't give money to anyone who just drops by and offers to do a job for you. This is an invitation to be ripped off. One of their standard ploys is to say they're inspectors who find that you need a job done; or that they're moonlighting on another job and will do yours at a cut rate; or that they've just finished a job in the neighborhood, have some shingles left over, and will do your roof at a bargain price. You should be immediately suspicious.

One way to deal with this kind of drop-in is to say:

HOMEOWNER: (concerned expression) Yes, I guess that driveway could use resurfacing, all right. How long will it take you?

CONTRACTOR: Oh, about three hours.

HOMEOWNER: Well, go ahead and start. I'll just go to the bank, run some errands, and I'll be back by then.

First, leave only if you can have someone in the house to watch it. Then run your errands and stop off at the police station on the way back so you can bring a detective from the fraud division with you. If the contractor is a crook, you'll be a hero for helping catch him. If the contractor is totally honest, you can easily explain that you were only acting as a concerned citizen because you've heard about similar frauds committed in your area. But chances are good that you'll find some defect that will leave him open to a charge of fraud, and you'll place the contractor in a position of just wanting to get away as fast as possible with or without being paid.

If you've already been gulled into giving a phony contractor your money and he's left town, there's not much you can do about it except report it to the police and ask them to notify you if he gets caught somewhere. Then you can prosecute him for your "job," ask the judge and prosecutor to make him pay restitution, and sue the criminal in civil court.

SHODDY OR INCOMPETENT CONTRACTORS

More likely you'll have used your common sense in choosing a contractor and signing an agreement, so if you have a problem, you'll just have to deal with the overextended, inept, or semicrooked kind. Your job is running behind schedule, you don't like the quality, and the costs are running way over estimate. What do you do?

Constructing Your Case. Your first priority is to cover yourself for making a preemptive strike. And the best way to accomplish this is to establish some kind of *criminal* liability on the contractor's part. First, consult an attorney to find out what constitutes such liability in your state. In Maryland, which had adopted model legislation for this purpose, a contractor is guilty of criminal conduct when he or she:

1.   walks off the job without completing it

2.   uses fraud or misrepresentation, such as using materials other than those specified in your contract

3.   participates in financing of the job

4.   conducts business in other than the authorized name with which he or she is licensed

This leaves a houseful of possibilities for establishing a case.

First call your state offices to find out whether the contractor is licensed to work in your state. If he is not licensed, you have a top-shelf negotiating position already—you may not be legally required to pay him a dime. (Check with your attorney to see if this is the case in your state.)

Another excellent possibility for retribution is finding that a contractor has used the wrong materials. Get samples, surreptitiously, of materials the contractor is using. If they don't match the specifications you've agreed to, that's misrepresentation. Also take photographs of work in progress when the crew has gone for the day. Most problem contractors will cheat somewhere. For instance, in building a wall, setting the studs too far apart is standard. Or throwing dirt or gravel in the floor rather than the type of insulation indicated in your agreement. Have documentation of these variances ready.

Suppose you just want the contractor to finish the job correctly or knock something off the bill for work that you don't like or isn't performed on schedule. First check for licensing, then the defective materials. Technically you can't use threat of criminal prosecution to enforce a civil penalty. But you can say something like:

I don't want to get nasty. [No smirking, now.] But I have to protect my interests here and I've found out that you haven't been totally on the level with me. I happen to know you're not licensed to do business in this state/you've used materials other than those specified in our agreement. If you don't take 50% off the job/repair this problem immediately, I'll have to take legal action right now.

"Legal action" is vague enough to mean you'll just sue in civil court. But since you've clearly pointed out criminal liability, he'll assume you're ready to prosecute. This gives you a superb bargaining stance if the contractor wants to continue doing business in your community, avoid fines, and stay out of jail.

The Lockout. But maybe you're so fed up with the contractor that you just want to get rid of her or him and hire somebody else to finish the job correctly.

Most work arrangements involve the contractor's leaving the materials you've already paid for in the house—kitchen cabinets or whatever. So when the contractor has gone for the day, mail the certified letter shown in the Revenge Kit at the end of the chapter, have a locksmith change your lock if the contractor has a key to the existing one, and refuse to let the contractor in the next morning. (You must leave his tools, undamaged, outside for him or *you* could be liable for them.) If you're the type of person who doesn't relish confrontations with angry men who carry hammers, you may want to hire a guard from a local security service (they're listed in your Yellow Pages) and post him outside to send the contractor on his way. If the contractor doesn't leave immediately, he's trespassing and you can call the police to remove him. Then be ready for his call.

CONTRACTOR: What's the story? I couldn't get in your house this morning.

HOMEOWNER: Right. You're off the job, and I've hired another contractor to finish it.

CONTRACTOR: (sputtering) Oh yeah? I'll sue you for not fulfilling our contract.

HOMEOWNER: Go right ahead. I'll show the judge you've used substandard materials/you're not licensed in this state. In fact, I'll call the prosecutor's office in, too. I've got plenty of samples and photographs showing you used substandard materials . . . you threw gravel and dirt inside the flooring for insulation . . .

CONTRACTOR: Listen, you bum, if you think . . .

Hang up on this breach-of-business etiquette. If you have proper documentation, the contractor's in no position to do anything that involves the law, and he knows it.

(One word of warning before getting too tough with a contractor, though. Have your lawyer check him out beforehand to make sure he's not disposed to assault and battery. The building trades attract their share of unsavory characters, and we don't want a mackerel to show up in *your* mailbox, wrapped in a terse note that suggests you'll be sleeping underwater in a car tonight with concrete in your tires.)

After the Horse Is Stolen. But let's assume that the so-called contractor has already done the job, he's cashed your check, and you begin noticing problems that need correction. But when you ask nicely, he refuses to repair them. You still have several options left.

1.   Check for licensing and/or defective materials, and negotiate as discussed.

2.   If there's no clear criminal liability but the job still wasn't done correctly, you can sue in small-claims or regular civil court. A new house, for example, carries an implied *warranty of habitability*. If there are conditions that make the house unlivable or that even reduce the market value of the house substantially, you can sue. You'll need a lawyer's advice before you proceed, but you may be able to negotiate with the contractor when he sees that you're aware of his liability.

3.   If your prospects for suing over home improvements appear too bleak, you can apply for arbitration with the local office of the National Home Improvement Council (NHIC) or the local Better Business Bureau if it offers this service.

If you conclude that your adversary will flick off a lawsuit or complaints to his industry group like so much sawdust, you can resort to the gambit of sending him a copy of the ad you're ready to place in the local paper:

HAVE YOU HAD A PROBLEM WITH THE JACKAL CONSTRUCTION COMPANY? If so, please call me to discuss a class-action suit against the contractor to seek substantial compensation for damages. (Your phone no.)

And appeal to the local media as you would over a problem car dealer (see Chapter 6).

If the contractor advertises in your local Yellow Pages—and many do—you can make a complaint to them. Call your phone company office for the name of the person to contact. The Yellow Pages people will generally investigate complaints that an advertiser isn't entirely scrupulous, and this can put pressure on the contractor to resolve your problem.

But there might be an easier way if the contractor had to put up a cash bond to practice in your state.

The Bonded Edge. Check the records at your State Home Improvement Commission office to see who was responsible for bonding the contractor. Many small contractors don't put up their own bonds and use bonding agencies to do it for them.

Assemble the documentation for your complaint and use the form letter shown in the Revenge Kit to notify the contractor that you'll take your complaint to the bonding agent if you don't get satisfaction. This will make the contractor very edgy indeed, because he needs the bond to do business and he knows the bondholder will drop him if enough customers win judgments against that bond.

So most contractors will work out some kind of settlement when you tap that Achilles heel.

REVENGE KIT FOR CONTRACTORS

TO CONTRACTOR

CERTIFIED MAIL
RETURN RECEIPT REQUESTED

Name:
Address:
Date:

Re: Work Site

Dear Mr./Ms._____:

Reference is made to our contract, dated _____. The work I paid you for is not being done in the agreed manner, and you are in breach of the contract in that you:

1. failed to keep an itemized record of materials used

2. failed to use materials specified in the contract

3. failed to meet time deadlines set out in clause _____ of the contract

4.   failed to perform in a workmanlike manner

As you know, I have given you a chance to cure the various breaches set out herein, but you have refused. In light of the foregoing, this letter will operate as legal notice that I am canceling our contract as of today, and I will sue you for any damages I may sustain as a proximate result of your failure to meet your contractual obligations.

Very truly yours,

REQUEST FOR ARBITRATION

National Home Improvement Council
11 East 44 Street
New York, New York 10017
Date:

Re: (Your Name) vs. (Contractor)
My address: _____
Contractor' address: _____

Gentlemen:

I am having a dispute with my contractor (name), per the enclosed contract. He and I have agreed to submit the matter of his (fill in the claimed breach) to arbitration. We therefore request that you send this letter to your local office in (town) and there convene an appropriate panel to hear our competing arguments. We agree that your decision will be binding with regard to our respective obligations under the contract. Please notify us both at addresses indicated of the time, date, and place of the arbitration hearing.

Thank you for your cooperation.

Very truly yours,

Complaint to Bond Company

Name:
Address:
Date:

Re: (Your Name) v. (Contractor)

Dear Mr./Ms. _____,

I obtained your name from my state Home Improvement Commission office and understand that you are the surety for _____Co. and have agreed as part of your surety bond to cover all losses that result from defective work performed by that company.

I am planning to assert a claim against _____Co. for negligent work and wish to notify you of the pendency of this claim. I hope that you will use your influence to persuade _____Co. to comply with the requisites of our contract and thereby avoid the expense and exposure to both of you that will result from my lawsuit.

Very truly yours,

13
employers
Showing Them Who's Boss

Probably the ultimate employee revenge was wrought by three secretaries in the movie *9 to 5*. They just kidnapped their oppressive boss—a snarling chauvinist of the most porcine variety—strung him up from his bedroom ceiling by a homemade girdle and left him twisting for three weeks while his wife was out of town. Satisfying, to be sure, but not recommended to put you on the fast track in most companies.

However, you can apply some of the techniques you'd normally use against those who try to victimize you in the marketplace to employers who want to take advantage of you in the workplace. What you need to know are some helpful provisions of state and federal laws, plus a few psychological areas in which most employers are particularly vulnerable, and, most of all, some judicious tactics for turning the screws that won't really damage your attractiveness to future employers after you've made off with a bounty from some pin-striped Simon Legree. We'll look at these remedies in three fertile grounds for employer abuse: hiring, exploitation on the job, and firing.

GETTING PAID FOR THE JOB YOU DIDN'T GET

Let's assume that you're not a union employee and you're not looking for a government job. In either of those cases, your employer would be guided by strict union rules or civil-service regulations, so you'd have plenty of guidelines yourself for whistle blowing if he or she tried to flout them. Instead, we'll imagine that you're subject to the whims of corporate employers, the kind who often justify their hiring practices on the grounds of that undefinable "chemistry" between the two of you or whether you'd be a "good fit" with the company. Both criteria are sufficiently vague to hide a rat's nest of individual prejudice or employer paranoia about talented underlings who could too easily outshine their bosses.

We don't think employers should be forced to hire anybody who's legitimately unsuited to a job by reason of temperament or qualification. But if you're a woman or minority-group member who's been passed over for a job you were eminently qualified to perform, there's an opportunity to get even under federal law by revealing discrimination on the employer's part—which isn't as difficult as you might think. Conversely, if you're a nonminority male who's lost out to a less-qualified woman or minority-group member, you can do the same under the principle of reverse discrimination. (We'll tell you right now, though, that your chances of recovering money damages from an employer are better if you fall into the first category.)

The law you'll be applying in either case is called Title VII, a provision of the federal Civil Rights Act of 1964. In plain English, this law sets down two principles any employer with fifteen or more people on staff has to follow:

1.   It's illegal to refuse to hire, fire, or otherwise discriminate against a person—in terms of compensation, conditions, or privileges of employment—on the basis of race, color, religion, sex, or national origin.

2.   An employer can't classify or limit job applicants or employees in any way that would tend to discriminate against individuals on those same bases.

The only exception, which doesn't cover very many jobs, is known as the bona fide occupational requirement. This usually comes up when there's a question of sex discrimination. A woman can't be denied a job as, say, a condor catcher because it's "too dangerous." That's illegal, since it rests on the discriminatory assumption that women are frail, retiring creatures who shouldn't take physical risks. But a woman could be excluded from the list of suppliers to an artificial-insemination clinic, for the obvious reason. Although another possibility hasn't been contested to our knowledge, we suspect that a white actor could legitimately be denied the role of Kunta Kinte in a remake of *Roots*, again for obvious reasons. The point is that you're very unlikely to be seeking a job that falls under the bona fide occupational requirement. And if a prospective employer tries to claim otherwise, you'll probably have the backbone of your case already. For instance:

APPLICANT: Good morning, Mr. Couchon. This is Alice Blackwell.

EMPLOYER: Oh yeah . . . Alice. Right. I'm afraid we couldn't follow up on your application for the sales job, hon. You see, our customers are a swell bunch of guys, but they like to go out with our salesmen and whoop it up a little bit. Know what I mean?

APPLICANT: No, I'm afraid you're being too subtle for me, Mr. Couchon.

EMPLOYER: Well, we sell industrial valves to the guys who build oil tankers, Alice. It's real competitive. I mean our salesmen have to entertain the customers a lot. Take 'em out on the town. Bring 'em to our lodge upstate on weekends. I'm afraid this is one job that just has "sales*man*" written all over it.

APPLICANT: Oh, you mean it falls under the bona fide occupational requirement exception to Title VII?

EMPLOYER: (silence and shuffling of papers) . . . uh, I'll have to get back to you on that one.

APPLICANT: Thank you, Mr. Couchon, I'd appreciate it.

Bear in mind, though, that most employers are familiar with Title VII and will devise more sophisticated arguments to counteract possible charges of discrimination. So you'll have to build a case carefully to enforce your legal rights when they're ignored or sidestepped.

Outfoxing the Evaluation Process. The first hurdle when you're called in for testing or an interview, is to do nothing that would give your prospective employer legitimate cause to deny you a job for which you're qualified. We'll assume, since you're reading this book, that your worldly wisdom includes dressing right and making sure your resumé doesn't look like you took it from the bottom of a birdcage. We'll also assume that your credentials clearly meet the job specifications. (If not, you won't have a case or even a very good reason to be sitting there.)

The first trick a sneaky outfit might try is to give you a test that clearly discriminates against some classes of applicants on criteria that are *not* job related. This is illegal. The case that said so was Gregg *v*. Duke Power Plant, where a written test of knowledge unrelated to job performance was given to all applicants, black and white. The court found, over a long history of test results, that black applicants had more difficulty with the test than white applicants. Thus it was a pretty obvious way to discriminate under the guise of measuring individual abilities.

Let's say Alice ventured in to take a written test for the sales job she wants. If it were a personality-type inventory designed to measure her ability to get along with people or an industry-related test to see how much she knew about valves and oil tankers, she would have to accept the company's refusal to hire her on the basis of a substandard score. But if she thought the purpose of the test was to discriminate, she could invoke the menacing buzz words *Title VII* and *Duke Power Plant*.

INTERVIEWER: (shaking his head sadly) Alice, I'm sorry. You just don't score up there with the other guys . . . er . . . applicants who took our Quick Qualifying Quiz.

ALICE: I'm not too surprised, Mr. Gladhand. Frankly, I don't see why 35 of the 40 questions should cover the batting averages of minor-league baseball players. After all, I'm applying for a job as industrial salesperson.

INTERVIEWER: Well, Alice, a lot of our customers are baseball fans, so we've got to give 'em somebody who can go 'round the bases with 'em, heh, heh. No offense, but I'm afraid you just struck out.

ALICE: Yes, but I'm a very quick study, Mr. Gladhand. Why, just last night I learned all the pertinent facts about Duke.

INTERVIEWER: . . . uh, Snyder?

ALICE: No, Duke Power Plant. As that case related to Title VII.

INTERVIEWER: (sharp intake of breath) I'm afraid I'm not familiar with that case, Miss . . . er . . . Ms. Blackwell.

ALICE: No offense intended on my part either, Mr. Gladhand. But I think you might want to speak to your company's attorney about reevaluating my test results on that basis.

INTERVIEWER: I'll have to get back to you on that one.

The personal interview can also be loaded to meet an interviewer's underlying objective of portraying some woman or minority-group member they don't really want to hire as unfit for the job. But the questions will never be obvious. Instead, they'll probably be the type designed to stress test applicants for very tough positions that require a cool head under continuous fire, or just the wildly open-ended variety that tend to make applicants appear tongue-tied and unable to think clearly.

INTERVIEWER: (cordially) So, Carlos, tell me about yourself. (Impossibly open-ended.)

CARLOS: Uh . . . I don't know quite where to begin.

INTERVIEWER: (smiling even more broadly) Fair enough. Then let's just get one small thing out of the way . . . have you ever been arrested as a juvenile or as an adult? (Stressful. And probably founded on the interviewer's assumption that minority-group members are arrested as juveniles more often than white kids.)

CARLOS: (Thinking about a minor arrest at the age of fourteen for which he wasn't convicted) Uh . . . sort of, but . . .

INTERVIEWER: (frowning) That's like being sort of *pregnant*, isn't it? Our employees have to be *bonded* . . .

And so on through a torture test that would appear to show reasonable cause for turning him down on a nondiscriminatory basis. There's a way of handling both types of questions, though.

INTERVIEWER: Tell me about yourself.

CARLOS: (smiling just as broadly) Sure. Why don't we start with the highlights of my management experience? I've spent five years in a similar position for Allied Sandblast, where I moved up from order clerk to cash manager in two years . . . (Notice the quick focus on establishing his qualifications.)

INTERVIEWER: Yes, I have all that on your resumé. But tell me a little about *yourself*, like (conspiratorial smile) what would you say is your own *worst* trait.

CARLOS: (After two seconds of soul-searching) I guess I'd have to say . . . according to my wife, anyway . . . I'm a workaholic. It's tough to manage the cash function on a nine-to-five basis, since there's always some change that the money markets could effect . . . etc. (Turning an opportunity to commit interview-suicide into a commendable "worst trait," and hopping quickly back on the performance track.)

INTERVIEWER: Carlos, I have to ask this because of the nature of the position: Have you ever been arrested as a juvenile or as an adult?

CARLOS: No, I was always a pretty busy kid, working two jobs after
              school . . . (Since he knows his old juvenile record was
              sealed by the courts or, if not, he took the trouble to have
              it expunged as discussed in Chapter 22.)

INTERVIEWER: What's your favorite "toy" around the house? (Unex-
              pected mind bender designed to throw the interviewee
              completely offbase and say something revealing like "my
              wife's undergarments" or "my gun.")

CARLOS: That's easy. My microcomputer. I like to try out new
              finance programs I can use to enhance the company's
              cash position . . . (And spend even leisure hours advanc-
              ing the company's interests.)

You see the strategy. They can always find something negative in an
outpouring of personal information, but very seldom in a chorus of job love.

What to Do if You're Turned Down Anyway. Even if you've established
yourself as a model applicant, you could still be passed over for someone else.
Of course, any company reserves—and should—a great degree of latitude in
deciding who's right for that firm. But let's say the folks at Universal Sandblast
got together and decided Carlos didn't quite "fit in" with their structure. Even
though he came with the right job credentials from Allied Sandblast and scored
all the right points in the interview, some mean-spirited bigot in the company
just doesn't want a Hispanic person sitting at the cash manager's desk. So they
either leave the job *unfilled* after Carlos has been "considered" or they hire a
WASPy type from Amalgamated Sandblast whose credentials are notably less
impressive than Carlos' but who went to prep school and plays a mean game of
squash. What should Carlos do?

1.   Believing strongly (and rightly so) that he should have been offered the
     job on the merits of his qualifications, he could visit the local Human
     Rights Commission—listed in the White Pages under stage government
     offices—to discuss his situation and, if he is advised that it meets the
     commission's guidelines for "probable cause," file a complaint against
     Universal Sandblast alleging discriminatory hiring practices. (Bear in
     mind that a complaint *must* be filed within 180 days of the violation.
     The commission will take awhile to process the complaint, hear the
     company's response, and try to work out a settlement. But if in the
     meantime Carlos remains out of work or has taken a job for less money
     than the position at Universal paid, he will be building up "actual
     damages" against the company.)

2.   If the state commission grinds away to no avail, he should then take his complaint to a regional office of the federal Equal Employment Opportunity Commission (EEOC) listed at the end of the chapter. They will go through a discovery process of their own to decide if Universal has indeed violated Title VII. And, if so . . .

3.   Carlos can sue in federal court for *actual* damages—the full salary he would have received from Universal from the time he should have legitimately been hired, or the difference between Universal's salary and the reduced compensation he had to accept from another company after Universal turned him down. He can also sue for *punitive* damages and recover the cost of his attorney's fees if he wins.

He can also go to bed with a smile on his face, knowing that the boys at Universal are ready to string one another up with their old school ties for bringing this government intervention, expensive legal liability, and unwanted publicity on themselves.

And the same principles apply, as mentioned earlier, to a woman who has been discriminated against or a nonminority male who received his discrimination with a reverse twist.

But it's important, before charging off to job interviews with an eye toward money damages, to keep one consideration in mind. There should be some reason to believe that the offending company has established a *pattern* of discrimination. If they obviously haven't, your allegation will be harder to prove. As an extreme example, a woman rejected by the staff of *Ms.* magazine for a position as editor will have a hard time proving discrimination. As a more common example, if the suspect company can point to some instances of affirmative hiring, this will also tend to deflate your case. But executives at some companies will turn around with a straight face and answer that they have fourteen white women in secretarial positions and two "minorities" right in the mailroom. This is evidence of discrimination on the job, which brings up another profitable avenue for vindication when you already have a job you hate.

PAYING BACK THE EXPLOITATIVE BOSS

Sounds risky, doesn't it? Business is full of risks, but at least here you'll have the law on your side. That's more than we can say for the price-fixing or illegal campaign contributions the boss may be busy working out with other captains of industry while you stay until midnight laboring over his neglected workload.

There's an important distinction to remember here. It's the fine one between the enthusiastic performance you should at least pretend to show and mulishly bearing an unfair burden for some lazy or sadistic employer. Nobody likes to hear "that's not my job" from an employee, or grumbling about women's lib on the rare occasion when the boss is engaging some client in a critical tête-à-tête and asks if his secretary would mind bringing coffee. Such attitudes undermine the only real carrot of company life. The fact is that most corporate people have convinced themselves that rewards should and will be bestowed on those who accept responsibility graciously. They even mutter reassuring bromides to themselves, like "You're underpaid the first half of your career, overpaid the second."

But we think you'll know when the line's been crossed. It's when you sit down at your desk, observe your work, and beads of blood pop out on your forehead.

Collecting What's Long Overdue. If you're working after dark so often mushrooms are sprouting on your body and have discovered the promised lunch "hour" is a five-minute sprint to the vending machines and back, look up the local Department of Labor in the phone book under state government listings. By law, your employer must allow a minimum time for lunch and coffee breaks. And you must, if you are a full-time employee, be paid time and a half for overtime. Have the Department of Labor or the local office of the federal Department of Labor's Wage and Hours Division send you a copy of these regulations. Attach them to a letter to your boss. Include in your letter a list of grievances, documented with dates and times you worked but were not paid. Submit all of this to her with a bill for compensation. It's not too subtle, but at least you've put her on notice that you intend to enforce your rights. She'll most likely acquiese and avoid the pattern of abuse in the future. When you receive the check for your extra hours, note on it, "Back pay per hours demanded on 1/1/81." Make a copy of your present of documents to your boss and keep everything for your records. If she foolishly tries to ace you out of your deserved pay again, you've evidence for any harsher action deemed necessary.

What if your job description of, say, administrative assistant is so loosely interpreted by your boss as to have you scrubbing washrooms or logging in five hours a day as a shipping clerk? Again, turn to the Department of Labor and follow the same procedure. You're not required to do work outside the normal scope of your job description.

Admittedly, these rather hostile communiqués are not apt to improve the quality of your employer-employee relationship. (Although they will pay your bills and upgrade your duties.) If such aggressive waving of legal rights seems too antagonistic for your career objectives, use a more indirect coercive strategy.

FRAZZLED: Mr. Dithers, I'd like to talk to you. The phones are covered and no one's coming in for an hour.

MR. DITHERS: I don't have time to talk now, Joan. Things are busy around here. Maybe tomorrow.

FRAZZLED: I can appreciate that, sir. And it's exactly what I wanted to discuss. I've been working overtime and going without lunch for the past three months. I've considered asking you for back pay as required by the wage-and-hour regulations, but I'd rather not put it on that kind of basis. Instead, I feel a 25 percent raise would be fair to us both. If you added someone to do all my overtime work, it would cost you much more. Please let me know by Friday or I'll just have to get a second job at night and I won't be able to work after five.

This carries a distinct advantage over the direct-billing approach, since it elevates your status from hourly wage-serf to professional employee whose duties have "expanded." Your employer will have to choose between hiring somebody else to handle your overwork load or paying you the salary increase. (Or firing you, but he'll have a pretty good idea how much trouble this will bring down on his head when you point out why you were discharged to the Department of Labor.) And it's a lot easier for him to talk to the other powers that be about "Let's do something for John" than explaining why he needs another person on staff. Executives who can't get along without adding staff raise the question of replacing the executive instead.

Most corporations aren't structured to give 25-percent raises unless there's a promotion involved. So "doing something for John" will invariably mean giving you a new and better job title that will bump you up to the higher-salaried level. Now you've managed to turn a whining demand for back pay—which suggests little enthusiasm for added responsibility—into a virtually airtight case for being promoted.

Slapping Those Who Practice Sexual Harassment. In most offices, there's a wild and crazy guy who's known for weeks that a "new chick" is being hired. So when the new woman employee arrives, he's prowling around her the first morning in a throat-clutching cloud of Brut, trying to make a date, preferably for a lunchtime tryst, since he's likely to be married.

Now, whatever advances he might make and however unwanted they might be, the female employee doesn't have a solid case for sexual harassment yet. But if he says something to the effect of "You know, I can get you a promotion if you're nice to me/get you fired if you aren't more friendly," there's your opening. Sexual harassment, in the legal sense, occurs when an employer makes dispensing sexual favors a "condition of advancement or employment." That's sex discrimination under Title VII. Now you can make life difficult for the lone wolf. And if that sexual extortionist happens to be your boss, you can virtually rub your hands together in anticipation. (Although there are instances today of female employers who sexually harass their male subordinates, we'll concentrate on the more common relationship. But remember that a male worker would have the same remedies at hand.)

Let's say that Alice finally terrorized Mr. Couchon and Mr. Gladhand into giving her a job with the Macho-Matic Valve Company. She's now a probationary salesperson, responsible for unloading industrial valves on the oil-tanker boys.

By and by, her sales manager, Bob Fairkind, decides he'd like to make Alice his after-hours protégée. Now they're sitting in some hotel bar during a business trip and, inspired by a few bourbon 'n' branches, Fairkind makes his move.

FAIRKIND: Y'know Alice, yer awright. Little inexperienced, but s'okay. How 'bout we go up to my room and discuss your future w' this company?

ALICE: Thanks, Bob, but I'm pretty tired. I think I'll just turn in.

FAIRKIND: Well, lemme come up with you. I'll just stay coupla minutes. Y'see, I'm in a position to help you. Remember, you're comin' up for review in three months . . .

ALICE: And if I say no?

FAIRKIND: Well, les' jus' say I need people around me who don't make waves, y'know?

ALICE: Yes, I think I know what you mean. But I'd rather discuss that with you another time, Bob. I'm very tired now. Good night.

As far as Alice knows, these were just the clumsy slobberings of a lonely pie-eyed male away from home. But who really knows what evil lurks in Fairkind's heart? And why should Alice have to put up with such insulting behavior under any circumstances?

So when she gets back home, she should immediately visit a free-consultation attorney, have the lawyer write up her account of the harassment, and file it away in a bottom drawer. The lawyer will probably be happy to oblige if he or she sees a case building for a Title VII violation. Because, if the lawyer later sues on Alice's behalf and they're successful, the attorney's fees will be paid for by the company. Maybe the lawyer will advise her to file a complaint immediately with the Human Rights Commission. But Fairkind could always plead that it was just friendly banter Alice misconstrued. It would be shrewder on her part to document further abuses.

The very next week Fairkind obliges. Sober as a parson this time, he takes Alice to lunch to "discuss her future."

FAIRKIND: Hey Alice, sorry I got a little bit in my cups back in Foulport.

ALICE: Sure, Bob.

FAIRKIND: (insinuating purr) Because I'd never want a lady to think I was getting *heavy* with her.

ALICE: Of course not.

FAIRKIND: Fact is, I *want* to help you get through your review with the highest goddamn praise I ever gave a salesman . . . er . . . salesperson.

ALICE: I appreciate that, Bob.

FAIRKIND: I just think we should get to know each other a little better. Socially, I mean. Maybe you can come up to the company lodge this weekend; I'll bring a little wine and some Sinatra records, and we'll have a great time.

ALICE: I'm busy this weekend, Bob. And I'd like to keep our relationship on a professional basis. I have somebody I'm seeing now.

FAIRKIND: I just don't think I'm getting through to you, Alice. I can help you out. Or I can make sure you don't stay with Macho-Matic after your three-month review.

ALICE: I see. I'll have to be running along now.

Where Alice should be running is directly to her attorney to write up a second instance of harassment. Now that there's a clear pattern developing, she can complain to top management at the company.

GLADHAND: Hi, Alice. How's our prettiest salesperson these days?

ALICE: Well, I like my work very much, Mr. Gladhand, but I'm afraid there's a problem developing I'd like to bring to your attention.

GLADHAND: Oh?

ALICE: Yes. I'd like to give you a copy of these notes I've taken after two separate conversations with Bob. Each time, he threatened to make my evaluation coming up contingent on our "getting together" socially. I don't think I have to tell you what he had in mind.

So Alice has placed her complaint on record with a top officer of the corporation. The legal effect is that the company itself, once its executives have been notified of a pattern of abuse, is liable for damages under a Title VII violation. Otherwise they could claim, if Bob let her go and she sued afterward, that they didn't know about the problem and she probably conjured up that lawsuit after Bob fired her. Naturally, Alice made a record of the conversation with the corporate official and filed it with her attorney.

Now the company executives might wring their hands worrying about what Alice might do and discipline Bob accordingly. But, just as likely, they'll wink at the whole business and try to solve the problem by getting rid of Alice.

GLADHAND: That Alice was in here the other day with some story about you trying to get her to put out or you'd fire her.

FAIRKIND: Why that little . . . I tell you, Sock, that broad's nothing but trouble.

GLADHAND: Tell me about it. I couldn't even get rid of her with a Quick Qualifying Quiz.

FAIRKIND: Well that's it for her. You just leave everything up to me.

So guess who's discharged after her three-month evaluation.

As soon as Alice knows she's about to get the bad news, she should gather up all her paperwork from the company that would substantiate a record of satisfactory job performance and visit her attorney. Now they will prepare to file a carefully documented complaint with the local Human Rights Commission and/or the EEOC. And they will sue Macho-Matic for:

1.   Sexual harassment as a violation of Title VII's prohibition against sex discrimination, which occurred with the company's full knowledge and implied consent. This would seek actual damages, punitive damages, and attorney's fees, just like Carlos's case.

2.   Intentional infliction of emotional distress—documented by Alice's visits to a doctor—which also involves costly damages.

What's likely to happen, though, is that Macho-Matic will try to buy Alice off by reinstating her or offering her a reasonable cash settlement. Why? Because, the way things are at Macho-Matic, it's a pretty safe bet that there are other women—albeit in clerical positions—who've suffered sexual harassment, too. And if they ever found out what their remedies were, Gladhand and Fairkind might as well stow away on one of their customer's oil tankers before additional lawsuits or even a class action against the company began turning up.

Getting the Boss's Goat. Maybe you just harbor a free-floating dislike of your employer that's not based on some flagrant civil-rights or wage-and-hours abuse. If so, you'd probably like to move on to another company. But you'd also like to get in a few licks beforehand or possibly collect unemployment compensation while you take your time looking for a new job.

Every boss has someone he or she doesn't want to talk to, probably some pain-in-the-neck client or customer. Generally, bosses shift the dirty job of heading off these customers to a secretary. If that's you, you're expected to tell shocking lies on your employer's behalf when they call. Strike back and refuse to be a coconspirator. Politely explain that you cannot compromise your integrity by lying this way. Apply this to other common areas of office deceit, like the check-is-in-the-mail routine or the I-finished-it-yesterday-and-it's-being-typed gambit. If your performance is otherwise up to snuff, your employer will have no legitimate cause to fire you. After all, since when has honesty been anything but the best policy? Without becoming too tiresome, you can even drop a moral chestnut once in a while, like "You don't have to memorize the truth," or "I'm afraid I'm just a bad liar."

If your employer insists that you compromise your integrity anyway, let your loose lips sink costly ships. Naively blow the lies, excuses, and alibis. For example, when the unwelcome client calls and you've recognized his or her voice, immediately say the boss is in but ask who's calling. Then quickly say you're sorry but "Ms. Sharkfin apparently just stepped out of her office." They'll get the message.

When you want to sing out "take this job and shove it," suppress the impulse. Wouldn't it be even more gratifying to let your employer pay, via unemployment benefits, for your leisurely job search?

If there's been tension in your relationship, your boss will likely feel a degree of guilt or discomfort. While he may not feel bad enough to rectify the situation in any meaningful way, he will generally be happy to accommodate you in ways that cost nothing. Use this vulnerability to apply a little coercive pressure. Solicit a glowing reference seemingly unrelated to any employment situation. Tell the boss you want to join a selective club and would appreciate a recommendation for this purpose. Suggest, because your relationship is primarily business, that he address your character and performance in that context. Unless warfare's been openly declared, you're likely to get rave reviews. Armed with this document, get ready for a few skirmishes over the next couple of weeks.

The next time you're mistreated at all, respond with an adamant refusal to take such punishment. Your employers will just not be accustomed to this lack of respect. After a number of these run-ins, you'll probably be given your walking papers. Walk them down to the unemployment line and file for immediate benefits. (Forget your embarrassment. These lines are attracting a better class of people every day.) Explain that you've been fired without cause and produce your month-old recommendation from your ex-boss. He will be hard pressed to deny the virtues so recently committed to writing. Why would he have lied on that document? And if he did lie, isn't there a likelihood he's lying again to try to deny you benefits he should rightfully pay? At the very least, this inconsistency will help the state unemployment people understand why you portray your boss as a schizoid ogre whose firings are sudden and arbitrary.

DRIVING A HARD BARGAIN WHEN YOU'RE FIRED

There are three reasons for being fired. First, you may be fired wrongfully. If so, you should threaten to sue and do it if the company doesn't reinstate you or offer a reasonable settlement. Second, you're fired because the "chemistry" between you and your boss was too volatile or you found yourself on the losing end of some political power game in the office, in which case you stand to gain a heady severance package. And third, you didn't perform your job properly so you got what was coming to you (the least likely possibility).

Wrongful Firing. Here are some of the circumstances in which you can scare a company by threatening suit.

1.   You were discharged in retaliation for a complaint or suit you filed alleging some illegal or discriminatory practice. This might be sexual harassment, as in Alice's case, or a failure to grant you equal pay for equal work or to provide you with the same working conditions as male employees, if you're a woman.

In this case, you should proceed as we've discussed earlier—through a complaint to the state Human Rights Commission and/or the EEOC, preferably with the help of a lawyer who can bring suit for a violation. Now you'll be adding up actual damages in back pay plus lost benefits, damages for the pain you and your family have suffered through the company's illegal and heartless actions, punitive damages against the company for being a nasty—in fact, criminal—corporate citizen, and full compensation for your attorney's fees.

Some companies, reading through this catalog of horrors in your lawyer's brief, will just offer to reinstate you in your old job at the same salary and with the same benefits. The executives might not have much to do with you around the office, but at least you'll have money coming in while your original complaint (remember your original complaint?) is being processed or your first suit drags through the courts. Other companies will try to stonewall and let you sue away. But if you've got a sufficiently powerful case for a lawyer to accept on a contingency basis—meaning no fees until the case is resolved, when the company will pay your attorney if you win—you should pursue it until the bitter end. You could collect up to $100,000 in total damages. And maybe more.

2.   When you feel you've been discriminated against on the basis of age. This is a particular problem for employees over 45, since age discrimination, though it is illegal, may be slippery to prove. Most employers won't accommodate you by saying, "Well, Bill, looks like you just can't cut the mustard around here anymore." What they'll do is give your work to younger workers; or make sure that your skills are not kept current through training, while younger workers' are; or build a case against you by writing up poor performance evaluations over a period of time, then firing you for "cause."

This means you'll have to build a more convincing case against them. Whenever you feel one of these ploys creeping up on you, document it, like Alice did, with an attorney. You must also file a complaint within 180 days after you're discharged with the federal Department of Labor listed under US government offices in your White Pages. This is the agency that enforces the Age Discrimination in the Employment Act of 1967.

3.   When you've come up with some evidence that the company violated its own hard-and-fast policies in firing you. This is your opportunity to be a little more creative. A McGraw-Hill employee, for instance, was fired for reasons he considered arbitrary. So he sued his ex-company for $2 million. He alleged breach of contract because the company hadn't followed the procedures for termination outlined in the employee manual cheerfully titled *McGraw-Hill and You*. Apparently McGraw-Hill and he weren't getting along. At least that's what his supervisor claimed when he fired Weiner for "lack of application." Weiner said his job performance was never discussed, as dictated in the manual. McGraw-Hill's lawyers pointed out that employee manuals haven't been considered employment contracts in past court decisions. But in this case, Weiner had signed a statement, also signed by a company representative, which said that Weiner's employment would be subject to the conditions set down in the company manual.[1]

Just about every company gives you one of those books the first day you arrive on the job. But few people, of course, take the time to dust them off and read them very carefully. Why not be one of the few? Especially if you sign a statement that you'll be bound on those rules and regulations as a condition of your employment. So if you're fired, you can surprise management with a compelling legal brief citing chapter and verse from their own bible and charging a breach of their own policy. Again, this could see you reinstated or put you on the receiving end of a settlement offer. (Or it could just mean you'll spend time in court finding out how good your case is. Before you travel this route, ask your free-consultation lawyer to look up the New York case of Weiner v. McGraw-Hill, which had not been finally resolved at the time of this writing.)

Political firing. The vast majority of people aren't fired because they're victims of discrimination or they didn't perform well. They just didn't get along with their bosses, wound up on the guillotine after some palace intrigue, or couldn't line themselves up quickly enough with a new management group that took over the company.

First of all, don't take it at all personally if you're fired. It's an increasingly acceptable battle scar, even a badge of courage. At least it says you probably had some strength of your convictions, unlike the surviving hypocrites who stoop and genuflect to every new Attila warming the chief executive officer's chair. In fact, let the current crop of CEOs be your model.

Here we find the "professional manager" who'll gut his own company's future growth to show decent short-term earnings, hoping that his wizardry will attract offers from other companies so desperate that they're ready to give him just about anything he requests to show their stockholders some earnings for a change. However, boards of directors can be just as fickle in their own way and often wind up firing the professional-manager CEO six months after he's hired.

But do you think our nomadic CEO accepts two weeks' salary plus a week's severance pay and shuffles out the door? Hardly. He'll cut the best outgoing package deal he can.

And so can you. You'll never find your employer so vulnerable as on the day she calls you in and asks you to shut the door behind you. She knows full well that you were fired for capricious reasons. After all, who was responsible for coming up with them? Now you're no longer perceived as an adversary or a threat but as a victim stripped of livelihood.

Your employer will probably feel more than a little ashamed for placing you both in this awkward position. And, if she is blessed with a modicum of insight, she will no doubt recognize that it's a reflection of her own dubious management skills that your talents couldn't be accommodated in the scheme of things. This is the time to strike.

First, let the tears well up in your eyes if need be to aggravate the guilty employer. Ask for the reasons behind the firing, to help you "see where you were at fault." This will produce a halting explanation that any fool can see holds little objective merit, even your employer.

Then begin scoring off your demands.

> Ex-Employee: Well, I really wasn't expecting this. (Ha) So I guess you'll understand that I'd like to take a few days to myself to think it over.

EMPLOYER: Yes, yes, of course. (She's probably hoping you won't come back at all to cast your grim-reaper presence over the rest of the office.)

EX-EMPLOYEE: I'd also appreciate it if you could extend my medical benefits for a couple of months. I don't think I've told you this, but my wife/husband has been taken very ill recently.

EMPLOYER: (feeling even guiltier) Why no, I'm sorry. I'm positive that can be arranged.

EX-EMPLOYEE: Do you have any idea what I have in terms of severance?

EMPLOYER: (finding the papers) Well, Personnel sent something over this morning. It looks like two weeks' salary plus two weeks' severance.

EX-EMPLOYEE: (virtually gagging) Ohmigod. I've got a balloon payment on my mortgage coming up. That could mean I'll lose my house. Is there any way I could work just a couple of extra weeks to get a month's total salary plus the severance check?

EMPLOYER: (fidgeting, because—again—the last thing she wants is to have the corporate equivalent of a recently deceased corpse lingering around the office, so others will be constantly reminded of their own mortality) Well, let me talk with Personnel about that. Frankly, I'm sure I can work out a couple of extra weeks, seeing you've been here for over five years. But since I'd prefer to have you thinking about a new position someplace, I wouldn't ask you to come in those extra weeks.

EX-EMPLOYEE: Thanks. I appreciate your consideration. I hadn't really thought about getting a new *position*. This is all so *sudden*. Do you know if the company does anything in terms of outplacement? (This means helping you sharpen your job-seeking skills and finding a new position at the company's expense.)

EMPLOYER: (Plucking you from the chair and steering you out of her office before you have a nausea attack on her carpet.) I'll recommend that something along those lines be arranged. Just let me go down to Personnel right now and see. Er, naturally, I'll give you a fine reference.

Now you can hotfoot it back to your office and get all of those promises down on paper, which you'll enumerate in a letter that starts:

Dear _____,

Thank you for extending the additional severance benefits we discussed . . .

This will go to top management, too, of course.

Then you might want to book a quick trip to Acapulco to polish up your resumé in more comfortable surroundings.

The best revenge, of course, is squeezing all you can out of a company that doesn't appreciate your talents *before* you're fired. We don't mean stealing erasers, either, but meaningful things like:

1. Use all the company's paid educational benefits to get an MBA, law degree, or whatever else you can argue will enhance your job performance while you're on the company's payroll. You can also take out a federally guaranteed student loan of up to $2500 a year for going to graduate school part-time, which you can pay back slowly and cheaply. As soon as you get your degree, of course, it may be time to move on to another firm. You can't usually earn significant salary increases with the same company. You'll have to hop around every two years or so just to keep ahead of inflation.

2. Use the company's in-house public relations department to get you publicity. Offer to co-author articles with somebody who can write well in the PR group. Thoughtful articles on your particular specialty, which the PR people will then place in the magazines of your trade, is how headhunters find you, identify you as hot stuff, and call you about lucrative new positions when they come up.

3. Use, like our more ambitious federal government employees do, company time and resources to set up your own business. Your company probably has computers to answer your questions, Xerox machines, IBM Selectrics, QWIP copiers, and other high-tech equipment that could get you going as an outside consultant or in another information-related field. You can usually get company lawyers to give you free advice, too, if you couch your questions as company-related matters. The same goes

for your corporate research people. What more gratifying retribution can you enjoy than using the company you hate to set up and finance one you love? Your very own.

REVENGE KIT FOR EMPLOYEES

SAMPLE COMPLAINT FORM
FROM STATE HUMAN RIGHTS COMMISSION

```
COMMUNITY RELATIONS
       COMMISSION

   on the complaint of

NAME          Complainant,              COMPLAINT NO.

         against

NAME          Respondent,
```

I, _____, Telephone: _____
residing at _____
charge _____
whose address is _____
with an unlawful discriminatory practice relating to:
    EMPLOYMENT   PUBLIC ACCOMMODATION
    EDUCATION   HEALTH & WELFARE
on or about the _____ day of _____, 19__,
because of my:
    RACE RELIGION COLOR NATIONAL ORIGIN ANCESTRY

(Complaint)

_____, being duly sworn, deposes and says: that __he is the Complainant herein; that __he has read the foregoing complaint and knows the contents thereof; that the same is true of h__ own knowledge, except as to the matters therein stated on information and belief; and that as to these matters _he believes the same to be true.

Subscribed and sworn to on this
_____ day of _____, 19__.   _____

SAMPLE DEMAND LETTER TO EMPLOYER AFTER EQUAL EMPLOYMENT OPPORTUNITY COMMISSION INVESTIGATION

To: Scrooge & Company, Inc.
Address:
Date:

Re: Equal Employment Opportunity
Commission Case #

Dear Mr. Scrooge,

On _____(date), the above-referenced case was determined in my favor. The result was the EEOC finding that there was reasonable cause to believe your organization had engaged in unlawful employment practices under Title VII of the Civil Rights Act of 1964, as amended. You were invited to participate in conciliation discussions pursuant to Section 706(b) of the Act, as amended. You failed as requested to participate, or to note your intent to do so with the commission within seven days.

I will be filing suit against you within two weeks to recover my job and back pay. In the event you do wish, upon the EEOC's finding, to avoid protracted litigation, please advise.

Very truly yours,

Certified Letter

SAMPLE COMPLAINT AGAINST AN
EMPLOYER IN DISTRICT COURT

UNITED STATES DISTRICT COURT
DISTRICT OF _____

EMPLOYEE'S NAME ADDRESS	CIVIL ACTION NO. ___
Plaintiff,	
vs.	
EMPLOYER'S NAME ADDRESS	

COMPLAINT

1. This action is brought by the plaintiff to enforce the provisions of Title VII of the Civil Rights Act of 1964, 42 U.S.C. §2000e-et seq., as amended by the Equal Employment Opportunity Act of 1972. Injunctive and other appropriate equitable relief, including reinstatement and back pay, are sought. Jurisdiction is conferred upon this Court by Section 706(f) of the Civil Rights Act of 1964, 42 U.S.C. §2000e-5(f).

2. Plaintiff is a female who is a resident of the State of _____.

3. Defendant, _____Company, Inc., is a body corporate doing business in the State of _____. It employs more than twenty-five (25) persons and is engaged in an industry affecting interstate commerce.

4. Plaintiff was employed as a Sales Representative by the _____Company, Inc., on (date) Plaintiff was terminated on (date) The termination was because of her sex.

5. The employment practice described in Paragraph 4 is a violation of Section 703(a)(1) of the Civil Rights Act of 1964, 42 U.S.C. §2000e-2(a)(1).

6. Plaintiff is suffering irreparable injury by virtue of the practice described in Paragraph 4 hereof. She is without an adequate remedy at law.

7. Plaintiff filed timely charges of discrimination based upon her sex against the Defendant with the Equal Employment Opportunity Commission (hereinafter the EEOC) pursuant to Section 706(c) of the Civil Rights Act of 1964, 42 U.S.C. §2000e-5(c). On March 25, 198_, Plaintiff received from Equal Employment Opportunity Commission pursuant to Section 706(f)(1) a Notice of Right to Sue Within 90 Days, which is attached hereto.

WHEREFORE, the Plaintiff prays that this honorable Court

a. Issue a permanent injunction enjoining the Defendants, Employer, their agents, successors, employees, attorneys, and those acting in concert with them from engaging in the unlawful practices shown to be in violation of applicable law;

b. Grant such other and further relief as may be just and proper, including reinstatement and back pay to the Plaintiff;

c. Award the Plaintiff the costs of this action;

d. Award the Plaintiff's attorney fees in this action.

_____
Name
Plaintiff

14
landlords and neighbors

Vengeance Begins at Home

With all the skirmishes a day can bring, retreating to your own home should offer you refuge and solace—your personal oasis of sanity in a troubled world. But how do you feel when your apartment's bracing chill seems reminiscent of Yukon King? Or your next-door neighbor demonstrates that the *1812 Overture*, complete with cannons, can blast right through your wall? Do you just throw on two more sweaters and soundproof earmuffs? You can do better. Every day the law grows increasingly mindful of your rights against stingy landlords and oppressive neighbors. And if legal remedies don't do the job, some guerrilla tactics can.

OVERCOMING BARONIAL LANDLORDS

In medieval times, English landlords gave their serfs (in addition to the occasional taste of a sword) a symbolic clod of dirt to commemorate their tenancy. This pretty much set the tone for landlord-tenant relations today. Traditionally the landlord held all the rights to your castle, protected by strict property law borrowed from the system of King Arthur. If tenants didn't like it, they could always move. But recently, our courts have moved away from property-law axioms to grant you a consumer's brand of protection. In New Jersey and Washington, D.C., for instance, there's Truth-in-Renting legislation. This forces landlords to disclose your rights as a tenant before you sign a lease. It also prevents them from writing clauses into leases which would eliminate these prerogatives. If landlords fail to comply, they can be subject not just to the usual civil remedies but to criminal penalties as well. Most states haven't gone so far in their pro-tenant enthusiasm, but a great many have set down punchy rights and warrantees you can throw at a bullying landlord.

In the Black Trunks, the Baron. Your landlord still holds considerable advantage over you when you sign a lease. The landlord is represented by a lawyer who has drawn up favorable terms for his or her client, unfavorable for you, in arch legalese. Most tenants can't decipher this pre–Magna Carta document, so they accept it for what the landlord claims it is. And with living space at a premium today, tenants often sign hastily on a take-it-or-leave-it basis. Even if most tenants were engineers, they couldn't go knocking down walls to check out the insulation and wiring or figure out if the upstairs neighbor's bath water trickles down every time he or she turns on the water. So tenants usually see only the most superficial characteristics of the apartment they're renting.

You also have to remember that the landlord is conducting a business and dealing with you in hard-nosed terms of return on investment. Since the decision to take your living space is made partly on emotional issues—you want to be happy there, you want to raise children in the neighborhood (if your landlord will let you), or it's a place to entertain relatives and friends—the average tenant is looking for a parcel of very personal and subjective benefits over and above the cost per room.

In the White Trunks, the Tenant. Today tenants enjoy protection that varies from state to state. Basically your legal rights can include:

1. A Warranty of Habitability. This is a consumer-law provision gaining great acceptance, despite the loud protests of landlord lobbies. As its name implies, your apartment must be offered and maintained by your landlord in "habitable" condition (just as an appliance must be "merchantable," or fit for its intended use). An apartment must be fit to live in, and even though what constitutes habitable premises may be a subject of philosophical debate between you and your landlord, generally you can assume that the law covers whatever your state or city housing authority (listed in the White Pages under the appropriate government offices) would tell the landlord to fix as a violation.

    If winter temperatures in your apartment fall below the minimum level set by your authority or you're paying for broken or ineffective air conditioning on hot summer days when inside temperatures soar to incubator levels, that's not living. Similarly, a supply of hot water, even at 8 A.M. when all the other tenants are taking showers, is a hallmark of civilized apartment life. If you have to share your apartment with vermin or cockroaches because the landlord won't pay for regular exterminator's visits, this would be considered a health violation by most housing authorities. So is garbage piled in your common hallway if it's there because your landlord won't provide proper refuse disposal or collection.

    Elevators are supposed to work most of the time. So are the kitchen and bathroom appliances your landlord probably bought at discount prices. And if you're paying rents considered high in your community for a "luxury" apartment, the courts are likely to hold your landlord accountable for providing more amenities—including those advertised in the newspaper or the colorful brochure you were given when you came to look at the place. (But don't get carried away and think your apartment has to look like the artist's rendering in the brochure. It seems that landlords are allowed sufficient flights of puffery to depict any pile of bricks as the palace of their fantasies.

2.   Reasonable Security. Your landlord-baron doesn't have to build you an impregnable fortress but does have to make sure your building won't become a sanctuary for burglars and muggers. If the lock on your outer door is broken and remains unrepaired despite your written notice, you can hold the landlord liable for what happens due to his or her negligence, including a burglarized apartment or a tenant being attacked in the hallway. The key legal test here is whether your landlord *increases* your risk of crime by failing to take reasonable precautions or not making timely repairs when notified that a condition affects tenant safety. Sometimes a breach of security falls under the habitability law. But where that remedy isn't available, you still have grounds to threaten or file a suit for damages based on the landlord's negligence.

3.   Quiet Enjoyment. This does not mean that enjoyment of your apartment must be confined to tiptoes and whispers. Quite to the contrary. Quiet enjoyment is a legal doctrine that says, in effect, that your landlord has given you the equivalent of an "estate in land," and you have the right to enjoy it unfettered so long as you don't damage the premises. This means your landlord can't drop by at all hours, without adequate notice, to find out if you're a model tenant. Your lease will probably include some clause that says your landlord can barge in anytime there's an emergency. But that should only be taken to mean a serious threat to the building or other tenants, such as your bathtub leaking or an electrical fire. Otherwise, your landlord can only demand access during normal hours (between 8 A.M. to 9 P.M.), after giving you *reasonable* notice, to make repairs or show the apartment to prospective tenants, not to see what's for dinner or whom you wake up with in the morning.
      It also means you're free to hang pictures and otherwise make your estate livable as you see fit, just so you don't damage its "structural integrity." If you put up shelves that can be taken down when you leave without damaging the walls, this would generally be okay. What's not okay is a major "improvement" such as removing a wall.

When a landlord breaches any of your rights—again depending on state law—you can usually respond by (1) terminating the lease, (2) suing for damages, (3) withholding rent and asking for a "retroactive abatement," or (4) sometimes, all three. This is true even if a clause in your lease seems to give your landlord an ironclad defense against such actions.

The Lease: Preemptive Bargaining

We can't stress strongly enough that you should *read* and *know* your lease. Landlords and their attorneys have come up with a host of sneaky lease clauses over the years that can make life hellish for you. If you come across any or all of them, you have two options. You can try to negotiate them out, or you can recognize that the landlord who uses them is stacking the deck so hopelessly against you that you're likely to encounter more strife later on. Think about that when you weigh all your emotional decisions.

The Nonlease or Oral Promise. Unless you're nomadic by nature, we'd strongly advise against entering into an oral lease. Here you're counting almost totally on your landlord's goodwill. And what's to prevent her from dispossessing you at the slightest whim? True, your rent receipts offer evidence of tenancy. But your landlord can also evict you on thirty days' notice in most states or raise your rent as much as her conscience will bear on the same notice. Oral agreements also gain you little support from judges, who like contracts they can peer over themselves.

Be especially wary of the landlord who offers an oral lease on "good-natured" pretenses.

LANDLORD: Lease? You've got it. Hey, a handshake was good enough for my father, and it's good enough for me.

PROSPECTIVE
TENANT: Well, maybe if we just put it down as a simple letter of agreement . . .

LANDLORD: C'mon, it's too much hassle. We trust each other, don't we?

PROSPECTIVE
TENANT: Sure. But my brother's a lawyer and he advised me . . .

LANDLORD: You didn't say anything about your brother being a lawyer.

PROSPECTIVE
TENANT: You never asked.

LANDLORD: Well, I don't rent to troublemakers.

An oral promise about repairs, sublet rights, or any other issue that isn't dealt with in the written lease affords you the same protection (the kind usually extended to illegal immigrants). If you can't get the landlord to put something in writing, assume that it will only be honored in the breach.

Signing Away Your Rights. None of the tricky clauses listed here may be technically illegal in your state. But an overview of the usual wording reveals what they do to your tenants rights—"surrender," "abate," "release," "disclaim"—you get the idea. And you can't expect to declare a lease void just because they snuck one blatantly illegal item in and you happen to catch it. Watch out for:

Exculpatory Clauses. These protect the landlord from his own negligence. Like "Landlord will not be held liable for any loss of property or injury to tenant resulting from theft or other criminal activity." Make sure you can bring suit in your state for negligence anyway by calling on a free-consultation lawyer, your local housing authority, or the civil-court clerk.

Waiver of Jury Trial. Juries are the scourge of landlords. Thus your lease might say ". . . the respective parties hereto shall waive trial by jury in any action or counterclaim brought by either party . . ." This evenhanded wording isn't much of a concession on their part, since they'd have a tough time packing the jury with landlords. Again, check to see if your state recognizes such a dubious waiver.

Waiver of Right to Privacy. This gives the landlord ". . . access to enter at any time and for any reason . . ." etc. Negotiate this one and ask to insert a clause saying, for instance, "Landlord has the right to enter the demised premises from _____ A.M. to _____ P.M. after giving reasonable notice of at least 24 hours."

Waiver of Right to Legal Notice. This gives the landlord free rein to lock you out, raise your rent, or anything else such a kind heart might desire, without notice. But this is illegal in most states and should be deleted from the lease before you sign it. Point out that it "violates your right to due process" and say you'll take it up with an attorney before signing.

Waiver of Right to Sublet. Here the lease may say something as inoffensive as ". . . the demised premises shall be occupied only by the tenant and the members of the immediate family of the tenant . . ." with no further clause to discuss the matter of subletting. Demand a clause that covers the possibility that you'll want to sublet someday, preferably one that says, ". . . The landlord will not unreasonably withhold the right to sublet, and such sublease will be granted on an *assignment* basis." This protects you in two compelling ways. If a landlord can't unreasonably withhold the right to let you choose your own subtenant, this gives you considerable freedom of selection. In fact, the landlord may be committing a form of slander by alleging that your subtenant would not be a "fit tenant." Also, an *assignment* of your lease lets you share your risk with the subtenant if he or she doesn't pay the rent as agreed.

"Escalator" or "Pass-Through" Clauses. This permits the landlord to raise your rent before the end of the lease, which defeats the basic purpose of getting a written lease, namely, to contract for the longest term possible so you'll benefit from inflation. No matter how exorbitant the current rent may seem, it will look more like your garage rent two years into a three-year lease. So delete this clause or don't sign if you want a fixed rent.

Late Fee Charge Clause. Here you can be assessed a penalty that might be $25 or more every time you pay your rent after the first. So ask your housing authority if this isn't an "illegal liquidated damage penalty" in your state.

Distraint Clause. Pore over your lease carefully for this medieval-dungeon clause. It means the landlord can lock you out of your apartment and take your furniture or personal belongings as compensation for any unpaid rent. Chances are that it's illegal in your state and should be deleted. We wouldn't advise signing a lease that includes this charming tactic where a landlord can use it legally.

Integration Clause. Most leases include a final dismissal of your rights stating, in effect, that the lease is ". . . the entire agreement among the parties, and oral or collateral agreements shall have no force or effect " Now you can see just how binding the landlord intends to make those unwritten promises. Your answer should be to have the landlord attach a series of *addenda* or a *rider* that clearly spells out his intentions to make repairs, let you sublet, or whatever else you may demand as a condition of signing the lease.

After you go to all this trouble, the landlord might tell you it will take "a few days" to make the deletions and addenda, so you can't expect your signed lease until you've already moved in. Well, don't expect it to say what you thought it would, either. This is another clue to the Baron's true intentions. Point out that, since your moving at all is a condition of the right lease terms, you aren't about to fulfill that condition until you have the signed document clutched in hand.

TROUBLE IN YOUR ESTATE? RETALIATE.

Now you've settled into your estate in land and have your self-protective lease to enforce your rights. Or maybe you've already signed a lease that gives you the same protection the Man with the Hoe enjoyed from his feudal master. Either way, you can apply a number of the legal and coercive remedies your state law permits when problems arise.

Temperatures Rising. Many of us in the Cold Belt find our landlords more zealous about saving energy than anyone requests or requires.

If your teeth are chattering and your landlord hasn't responded to your complaints, get to the phone and call the people at your local housing authority. Tell them the temperature in your apartment has been below the statutory minimum (find out what that is first) and point out that you've been suffering most of the winter. Ask them to send an inspector over as soon as possible. Unless your landlord is paying off someone at the housing authority, he won't be notified until after the inspection. By and by, someone will arrive from the authority, walk around your apartment holding a thermometer up in the air at key locations, and take notes. If your landlord is found to be in violation for not providing enough heat, he'll hear about it. But maybe he won't do anything about it.

In that case, what you want to establish is a pattern of violation, preferably by calling the authority several times after the first inspection and placing your chronic complaints on record. If you're getting influenza every month courtesy of your landlord, keep your doctors' visits and medication expenses documented, as well as your time off from work.

Now you can either visit an inexpensive lawyer—to write a letter on your behalf to the landlord—or you can take matters into your own icy hands and send the landlord one yourself. (See sample letter in the Revenge Kit.) You'll undoubtedly hear back or receive a personal visit.

COLDLORD: This is Mr. Gruel. Can I come in?

TENANT: Sure. Nice tan.

COLDLORD: Thanks. Just got back from vacation and saw your letter. It doesn't feel very cold in here.

TENANT: Well, I can't afford the fur coat you're wearing. I think it's freezing. And the housing authority agrees with me. In fact, I'm home from work today with the flu, and my doctor tells me it's from living in the cold. My lawyer calls it a breach of the warrant of habitability.

COLDLORD: Sure, sure. I know a little about the habitability thing, too. So I'll turn up your heat, fair enough?

TENANT: That's fine for starters, but let's discuss my long, cold winter. I've been talking with some of the other tenants, and . . .

COLDLORD: What other tenants?

TENANT: I've been advised not to discuss other members of the committee at this time.

COLDLORD: Don't tell me you're trying to start some kind of tenants' committee. Good luck.

TENANT: I didn't have to try very hard. We'll be meeting with my lawyer next week.

COLDLORD: (sigh) Look, I've got one problem with you, but you're going to a lot of expense and trouble when you don't have to. If you'd just called me, I would have worked things out.

TENANT: I did. Several times.

COLDLORD: So I was away. Just what is it you want?

Note the buildup of (1) your problem, (2) the more general warrant of habitability, and (3) the assembling crowd of "other tenants," who can remain nameless since there might not be any. Now it's becoming a building problem for the landlord rather than just one unhappy tenant, and the point of diminishing returns from ignoring one individual's woes becomes evident. The cheapest way he can handle it now, unless he thinks you're bluffing more than you seem to be, is to buy your docility and avoid a palace revolution.

This same strategy also works for other violations of the warrant of habitability and security.

Garbage in the hallway? Get busy with your camera and photograph it at regular times over a period of several days—as long as it's left there. File a written complaint with the authority (see the Revenge Kit), with copies of the photos attached for documentation. If you don't have adequate water, photograph the faucets turned to the "on" position full blast, with the tiny trickle barely visible. If there are repairs needed because of water damage, poor maintenance, or whatever, photograph the situation as your evidence. Always notify the landlord first and give a reasonable time—like five to ten working days—to respond.

If there's a breach of building security, you'll want to capture the evidence in photographs, too. Then send the letter in the Revenge Kit putting the landlord on notice. The longer she delays, the more likely that someone will be victimized by criminals. If you're victimized, launch a hefty suit against the landlord to recover those damages due to documented negligence.

But if you're still sitting there in the cold and the housing authority can't get an inspector out until late May, here's a guerrilla tactic that can be easily applied in many apartment buildings.

After the cost of fuel made landlords conservationists, they had to do something about the individually controlled thermostats that still exist in many apartments. So many of them put glass cages, similar to the goalie's mask in a hockey game, over those thermostats to keep your hands off them. You can outsmart the self-regulating thermostat under the goalie mask by making it think the room temperature is even colder than it really is. Much colder. All you need is an ice bag, which you can easily make by scraping the frost off your dining table and dumping it into a plastic bag. Then put the bag on top of the goalie mask, which will force the thermostat to send more warmth up to the polar ice cap above. Your landlord's heating bill may go up a notch, but he won't know why you stopped complaining.

Acting Alone. As we said, there are many actions you can take alone to get even with your landlord. If you happen to live in the right state (and, again, you should check with a legal clinic, the housing authority, or the civil-court clerk), you can:

> Repair and Deduct. If you can't get a landlord to make needed repairs, hire a plumber, electrician, or whatever and have the problem fixed yourself. Keep your receipts for services rendered. Then deduct the cost from your next month's rent check. Attach a copy of the bill to substantiate your deduction, plus a copy of your original complaint letter(s) to support the landlord's inaction.

> Withhold Rent. If you're suffering from a violation of the warranty of habitability, you can give the landlord notice and, when she fails to respond, withhold all or part of your rent until the problem is resolved

to your satisfaction. You can also demand a retroactive rent abatement for the months the problem went neglected. The legal obligation you have to fulfill is to put your withheld rent in an *escrow account* for the purpose. Talk to a lawyer first, or the local court clerk, to determine what you have to do to have your escrow fund approved by the court. Otherwise, of course, your landlord will sue for withholding rent and try to evict you.

But the trouble with going on such crusades by yourself is the loneliness of it all. There you are tweaking your landlord, who has infinitely greater resources at his disposal, all of which revolve around removing you from your home or making you miserable as long as you stay. He can serve you with a dispossess notice for nonpayment of rent, which essentially tells you to pay up or get out. He can harass you in any number of imaginative ways, from declaring the need for emergency repairs at odd hours of the night to making anonymous phone calls.

He can even bide his time for a while and practice "landlord's revenge," which is legally known as the *retaliatory eviction*. This is an eviction that comes about because you lodge legitimate complaints. And it's illegal, so most landlords aren't doltish enough to serve you with some trumped-up charges on a *petition to evict* the day after your complaint arrives. They'll wait a couple of months, then strike with the same trumped-up charges, which will now be harder to dismiss as retaliatory.

Forming a Tenants' Committee. Remember that the struggle is for your estate, not waged in the back office of some distant credit card company that's studying your disputed bill for a clock radio. So we would advise you to frighten your landlord by organizing a tenants' committee of other dissatisfied renters and attacking as a disciplined army. We know what you're thinking: You hated the Boy Scouts or the Brownies. You're barely up to joining a committee of anything, let alone trying to organize one in your building.

The first chore of organizing a tenants' committee is drawing up the document that spells out purpose, rules, and by-laws. We've provided for that in the Revenge Kit. So you can offer to assume that crushing responsibility (which will amount to copying the model and filling in the blanks) if other people will handle administration duties.

You'll see the value when you can descend on the landlord en masse and threaten a *rent strike*. (See Revenge Kit for sample material.) This is absolutely the last development any landlord wants to see, because it cuts off not just a few dollars from one disgruntled tenant but most of the building's cash flow.

The more people you have with you, the better your case will look to a judge. One angry tenant can be dismissed as a crank, two or three as a conspiracy. But 80 percent . . . 50 percent . . . even 30 percent of a building's rent roll organized against a landlord tells any court that there's something very wrong at the Baron's buildings. And landlords know this. Which means that unless your demands are so outrageous it would be worth a few months' lost cash flow to fight them, most landlords will surrender at the out-of-court settlement stage and give in to their tenants' reasonable needs, particularly when the case against them involves documented breaches of habitability or security. The landlord knows that he could only be shot down in flames by some judge after months of costly battle.

However, you might expect most landlords to put up an Oscar-winning show of hurt feelings and indignation to try to diffuse any such organized revolt from the outset. The usual tactic is to divide and conquer. He'll take old Mrs. McGallicuddy aside and threaten her with eviction, or tell the young couple down the hall they can have a new dishwasher if they just listen to reason. If you're one of the principle rousers of this rabble, he'll come to you first with a peace offering that would make you happy.

But remember, once you've been bought off, everybody in the building will know it, and you'll probably ruin the prospect of a tenants' association or rent strike forever. And the landlord can go right back to his old loathsome ways. So stick with it. If every rent strike we've witnessed offers any indication, you'll come out ahead. And there's no landlord-stunning blow more satisfying than the grudging acceptance and ultimate fulfillment of your group demands.

Breaking Your Lease. There may come a time when you're dissatisfied with your landlord's shabby premises and just want to get out of your lease. Particularly if you have a long term to go and you never negotiated a sublet clause, if you walk out without a by-your-leave or depart in stealth some night, your landlord can and undoubtedly will sue you for money lost in rent until another tenant can be moved in. The landlord can also claim expenses for phony "cleaning fees" or "repairs" because the apartment was damaged and other assorted charges that mount up to a whopping total. Because a tenant who breaks a lease and steals away with no shrewd planning is not likely to show up in court, the landlord will probably obtain an easy *default judgment* for that bloated sum and pursue the ex-tenant to collect via a city marshal. And marshals can be highly motivated to track down judgment debtors, since they're often paid a percentage of what they collect from the hunted.

A more gracious and rewarding tactic is known as *constructive eviction*. The legal theory behind this move dictates that a landlord cannot take action or (more frequently) launch a program of inaction that deprives you of the "beneficial use" of your rental property. If the landlord does shirk her responsibility in this fashion, she has in a sense evicted you already. If that is the case, you're free to walk off in a huff, owing nothing.

The usual grounds for a constructive eviction involve a landlord letting the premises slide into such disrepair that they're not habitable or allowing some threat to a tenant's safety to go unabated. In either case, no self-respecting tenant would want to remain in squalid conditions.

If you have a series of violations on record at the housing authority, you're already on your way. If you can also substantiate safety violations, you've got legal walking papers. In most older buildings, these aren't too difficult to find. A call to the local fire department for an inspector's visit will undoubtedly turn up conclusive evidence of neglect.

Then visit a low-cost lawyer or legal clinic for a letter notifying your landlord that a constructive eviction has taken place. If the attorney agrees that you have a reasonable case, the twenty-five dollars or so for the letter will be well worth it, since your landlord probably won't risk going to court, especially if the case casts her in the role of Slumlord.

Security Regained. In order to collect your security deposit, no matter how you happened to wind up your lease, a few straightforward procedures can ensure that you get your due.

Before you leave, take photographs of the apartment establishing your good care of the premises. (If you left the place in a shambles, you'd better write your deposit off.) Then see the letter in the Revenge Kit that demands your deposit back including interest in full or an itemized accounting of any deductions.

If you feel you're being ignored, go to your local small-claims court and fill out the form you need to file a suit. For "reason," write: "Failure to return apartment security deposit of $_____ or accounting of deductions within statutory time limit." Ask the clerk what the time limit is. You should also add money damages for time off from work or any other inconveniences. Then send a packet with *copies* of your original demand letter, the court paper ready to file, and your supporting photographs. In your cover letter write: "Please remit $_____ within 48 hours or suit will be filed."

If they don't get the message, file suit. The judge will order the landlord to pay if your claim is valid, and you will be able to use a marshal to collect it, if need be. It may be of interest to the particularly devoted revenge fan to hear this story: A law student was once stonewalled by a landlord when he demanded his security deposit. He was awarded the money in court, but the landlord never paid. So the student proceeded through higher court levels, earning successively greater damages, until he received the final punitive award—his landlord's building.

NEIGHBORLY RETRIBUTION

We'll begin this section with the killjoy observation that most sparring with neighbors just isn't worth the effort. Even victories usually fail to satisfy over the long run. First of all, practicing retribution around the neighborhood tends to create vendettas that can see you wasting many of your leisure hours. Then there's the fact that neighbors, unlike some landlords, aren't trying to gouge you. They're most often relatively nice people who happen to have dogs that romp through your trash, or the occasional sociopathic child, or just a taste level that isn't quite up to the neighborhood standard, as demonstrated by the rusted '65 Chevy sitting on blocks in their driveway.

But let's assume that some of those good folks have grown intractable on an issue that directly affects your sanity. You've spoken to them politely more than once, but they obviously have little respect for your own needs when it comes to tying up the dog/disciplining the child/moving the old Chevy into their living room. Now you feel your good-neighbor resources are spent, and you have to deal with them as you would any other selfish, inconsiderate adversary.

The Noise Next Door. So we come back to the audiophile neighbor with her *1812 Overture.* If you live in an apartment, you can always get to your noisy neighbor through your landlord. Every lease has a clause that says something like:

> No tenant shall make or permit any disturbing noises . . . nor permit anything that will interfere on the rights, comforts or convenience of other tenants. No tenant shall play upon any musical instrument or operate a phonograph, radio, television set or similar instrument that shall disturb or annoy any occupant of the same building.

But, as specific and authoritative as that sounds, enforcement depends totally on the landlord and the resolve of the tenant who complains. Some complainants get dismissed as cranks. They're ignored by the landlord and left to sit and suffer the throbbing migraine of base speakers pounding through the cranium. Some of them shoot their neighbors or their neighbors' speakers, but there's a less drastic, more effective solution.

Courts have upheld the concept that your landlord's failure to silence noisy neighbors constitutes a breach of the warranty of habitability or the quiet enjoyment clause. Try the landlord letter in the Revenge Kit for breach of this warranty, and threaten to sue for money damages. If you can't get satisfaction from your landlord, use some revenge creativity.

Allan and Lynn were apartment dwellers next door to whom moved a couple named Harv and Breezy. The wall separating them happened to offer all the soundproofing value of cheesecloth. So Allan and Lynn, who were sociable but quiet people, began suffering evenings of torture at the hands of Harv and Breezy. The new neighbors had their loud friends over frequently for off-key singing to music played at outdoor concert level, joke telling only the riotously drunk could appreciate, and raucous laughter into the early morning. Worst of all was Breezy's screeching cackle, which sounded like somebody strangling a gerbil in the next room.

After two weeks of this punishment, Allan and Lynn were becoming unglued. They complained to the landlord, but he shrugged. When the police were called at one point, Harv and Breezy turned them away with a wink, quieted down for a few minutes, then picked up the same level of pandemonium within a half-hour. When Lynn confronted Breezy at her door during a party, the response was predictable.

BREEZY: Well, honey, why don't you just come on in and join us? (Making Allan and Lynn out as spoilsports if they refused.)

LYNN: We're busy tonight, but we'd appreciate your turning the music down. We can barely hear our own stereo.

BREEZY: We'll do what we can, but you know how people are when they're having a good time. (screech)

So Allan and Lynn just gritted their teeth until the party dissolved hours later.

But the next day they decided to apply a guerrilla tactic designed to force even Neanderthals like Harv and Breezy to show some consideration for their neighbors—or move.

During the next party, Allan and Lynn attached the sensitive microphone on their own cassette recorder to the kitchen air duct, where the din from Harv and Breezy's came in most clearly, and recorded the goings-on next door. Then they waited until 9 A.M. one Saturday morning after a party that had just broken up two hours before. Placing their powerful stereo speakers directly against the wall of their neighbor's bedroom, they turned the set up to impressive volume and treated Harv and Breezy to an all-day reprise of their own party, right up to the 10 P.M. curfew for record playing stipulated in the lease.

Then Allan went next door to visit a groggy Harv and spell out their terms. Every night that Harv and Breezy had a loud party all night, they'd get it right back the next day. No exceptions. If they didn't like it, they could move to another apartment. Faced with the prospect of being allowed no fun at all by the people next door, Harv and Breezy took another apartment at a distant corner of the building.

If you live in a house next door to an unusually boisterous type, you can't very well complain to a landlord or even follow a strict adaptation of the Allan and Lynn scenario, since the rest of the neighborhood would probably gang up to silence the two of you.

But there's a variation for the truly dedicated sufferer who's exhausted every other remedy. The law in most states permits you to light up your property all night long for security purposes. We don't know how your property's laid out, but we suppose you'd want to flood some areas with the kind of superintense lights used to illuminate night baseball games—just to be on the safe side. And if one of the hot spots happened to be around your noisy neighbor's bedroom window, we suspect that would put you in a better bargaining position to discuss your need for peace and quiet.

Misbehaving Dogs and Kids. W. C. Fields aside, these neighborhood nuisances are considered together for a good reason. The adults responsible for both usually believe that you should put up with the nasty habits of their loved ones. If you protest, they will make you feel guilty for complaining about them. With the disbelieving attitude reserved for social ogres, they explain patiently, "Bruno/Butchie is just a dog/child. You can't blame *him* if he barks all night/ rides his Bigwheel through your flower garden." The law recognizes that you can't hold dogs or small children responsible for their actions. That's why the courts place the burden of responsibility where it belongs—with the owner or parent.

Let's take dogs, surely the most guileless of all creatures. It's not right to help a dog out of your garbage with a hobnailed boot. But it's certainly cricket to call the owner and tell him you've had to clean up after his dog twice and you don't intend to make a routine of it.

DOG OWNER: Yes, but dogs will be dogs (chuckle).

NEIGHBOR: I know. That's why I'm taking it up with you and not him. I had to buy a new set of refuse containers with a special twist-off lid to prevent your dog from getting into them and dragging the garbage across my lawn. I'm sure that, under the circumstances, you wouldn't mind taking care of the bill for them.

DOG OWNER: I certainly will not. I can't buy new garbage cans for everybody in the neighborhood!

NEIGHBOR: Oh, then other people have complained too?

DOG OWNER: Just one or two.

NEIGHBOR: Then you've already been notified that your dog is committing a nuisance, and I'll just have to obtain a restraining order from the court.

DOG OWNER: A what?

NEIGHBOR: Ask your lawyer about it. Your dog has to be *leashed* by local ordinance. And you're responsible for damages he causes to other people's property if you're negligent in keeping him restrained. I'll overlook the first couple of times this happened if you send me a check today for the new containers. Otherwise, I'll have to have him restrained by the court and assess you for the same cost plus all my cleanup expenses.

DOG OWNER: Well, I think there's something wrong with people who hate dogs, but you don't have to make a big deal out of it. How much were the garbage cans?

There are other times you'll use the same strategy, but much more forcefully. The courts, to be honest, aren't in total agreement that dog owners should have to pay for a neighbor's garbage cans. But you can almost always count on their fierce support of your rights against dog owners who let their pets bark all night and disturb you. In that case, you can use the appropriate letter in the Revenge Kit. And if you've been bitten or terrorized by a dog or some other pet, you can certainly go for money damages, on one condition: A legal cliché has it that a pet is entitled to "one free bite" before you can sue or threaten to sue the owner. What this means is that a dog owner needs to have some prior knowledge that her pet is dangerous before the courts will listen to your plea to restrain it or assess damages.

But if you believe that a dog is dangerous, you can establish this prior knowledge by sending the letter of notification in the Revenge Kit. When a German shepherd bares his fangs at you and growls in a mean fashion, we'd say that's frightening enough in itself to warrant a letter. But if you're menaced by a toy poodle yapping and prancing around your children, you might have to watch for that one free nip (or attempted nip) before writing to the owner.

Then there's the neighbor who keeps an "exotic" pet around the house. If it's a cockatiel that never leaves its cage, no problem. But when some neighborhood Tarzan has an ocelot or chimpanzee loping about the yard with little or no restraint, that's a situation the courts presume to be dangerous. In this case, you can send the letter shown in the Revenge Kit and notify the owner before the pet tries to or actually does hurt somebody. It's been our experience that many people who keep wild pets are making some personal statement other than animal love, and their charges often don't get the special care they need to survive. So you could be doing the animal a favor by having it taken away from a curiously motivated eccentric and turned over to the nearest zoo.

So much for dogs and other pets. What about neighborhood kids who damage your property or your own children? Basically, the courts feel the same way about dangerous children and their parents as they do about dangerous dogs and their owners. Parents can be held responsible for their children's actions if they're notified beforehand that their children are menacing your property or offspring. They can also be sued in civil court, although the extent of their liability may be limited in some states to five thousand dollars or so.

Your ability to sue for damages rests on proving that a parent was negligent in failing to supervise a wayward child. This means you'll have to send a variation of the letter for this purpose in the Revenge Kit, putting the parents on notice that you're waiting for the child to run amok one more time so you can pounce on the negligent parents.

One addition to this letter will be particularly unsettling, even to the neighborhood bully's thickheaded parent. This refers to the "age of liability" in your state—usually six or seven—after which kids can be held responsible for criminal actions. So if a miniature Raging Bull over the age of liability starts pummeling away at your child, don't be afraid to visit your local police station and bring criminal-assault charges against the little rotter.

But let's say a child damages your property before you've had a chance to notify the parents of their kid's predisposition. Fortunately, virtually all states recognize the possibility and offer *vandalism* laws covering willful destructive acts to let you seek retribution against the perpetrator and proud parents. The catch here is that the law varies considerably from state to state as to how much you can sue for—from a paltry $100 in Minnesota to a generous $10,000 in Kentucky. But this may be adequate to cover most of your vandalism problems.

For example, maybe you wake up one night to the sound of adolescent giggling from the direction of your suburban carport. You sneak outside and manage to seize one fifteen-year-old vandal by the carotid artery just as he's pouring a bag of sugar into your car's gas tank. His friends have run away with usual teenage daring, but you have the important culprit. Now you have to take a few simple steps:

1. Call the police and tell them you want to prosecute your captive. Have them come over right away and get him out of your house. No doubt he'll implore you not to do anything, whining that he'll pay you back out of his allowance or whatever. Don't listen. You have to protect your own interests or you'll wind up paying to get your car back in shape yourself.

2. Call your local civil court clerk the following day and ask what the maximum liability is in your state under the vandalism law. Also find out that statute number.

3. Send the kid's parent the demand letter shown in the Revenge Kit. If the parent won't settle with you, go to court. You can almost always settle a vandalism case in small-claims court. Since the child is already being processed in the juvenile-court system and was caught red-handed, you'll undoubtedly receive your award for damages.

Many times, of course, you don't catch a destructive kid red-handed. But if you recognize him or her fleeing from the scene, you can call the police and prosecute anyway. Now as the complainant, you can leave the burden of fact-finding up to the juvenile-court system. Just step in with your civil suit when the child vandal is adjudicated.

Unattractive Nuisances. You've probably heard about the legal doctrine of the *attractive nuisance.* This is a condition existing on some neighbor's property that might "attract" children and threaten life and limb. A next-door swimming pool with no fence around it is a common example. But here we'll use the concept more creatively.

Let's assume that some neighbors have created a kind of "Sanford and Son" environment around their house that drives other people in the neighborhood crazy, including you. Not only do they feature the requisite rusted-out car with no front hood up on blocks in the driveway, but there's the top half of an RV trailer sitting on the front lawn, also choked with rust, a collection of abandoned parts from outboard motors and power lawn mowers, and other fauna that tend to give your whole block a seedy image.

The courts won't do much for you on the basis that your neighbor's place is an eyesore. "One person's vulgarity," as they say, "is another's lyric." Except for the wildest obscenities, a judge won't rule on matters of personal taste.

But if your young kids or other small children in the neighborhood might get hurt by wandering into that mine field of rusted and broken parts, you could very easily ask a judge to rule that the condition is an attractive nuisance. If a neighbor's mess upsets you, it probably annoys some other people on the block, too. So you can count on enlisting plenty of help for your cause. First write a demand letter as shown in the Revenge Kit, which will ask the human dumpsters to clean up their property or build a fence around it (that will effectively seal their bit of Tobacco Road off from civilized eyes, anyway). Then go to court if they don't oblige you by getting rid of the junk, which they'll probably elect to do since it's cheaper than building a fence.

Should you ask them politely to do something about their property first? If you like, but we don't think it will do much good. If they were all that sensitive, they would have noticed a slight difference between the appearance of their place and the rest of the neighborhood before and tried to do something to bring theirs up to standard.

Combat Zoning. Then there are other little whistle-blowing tactics you can bring to bear on any troublesome neighbors that reflect your strict adherence to local *zoning ordinances.* Look over your neighbor's property with a critical eye and see if there are potential violations. For example:

> Did the neighbor build an outdoor greenhouse or Jacuzzi that might have required a zoning variance? Chances are they didn't apply for one, and if the local building code authorities were notified, those violations might have to be torn down.

Do the neighbors run an *unauthorized business* of some kind? If they're babysitting for more than three children a day, they're running a de facto day-care center in some states. (You can also assume that they're taking in unreported cash, so an anonymous report to the IRS may be in order.) If there are a few cannibalized automobiles outside, they might be running an unlicensed "repair shop."

You get the idea. But remember about people in glass houses. Better get your own Jacuzzi approved first if you're blowing the whistle on your neighbors.

REVENGE KIT FOR LANDLORDS AND NEIGHBORS

LETTER DEMANDING RENT ABATEMENT

To: Landlord
Address:
Date:

Re: Notification of Breach of
Warranty of Habitability*
(Building Address & Apartment Number)

Dear Mr./Ms. _____,

This is to notify you that since you have failed to abate the defective conditions (and/or) housing authority code violations described in my letter of (date) attached, I have been advised that these conditions constitute a breach of the implied warranty of habitability.

Thus I will place all future rent payments in a court escrow fund until those conditions are abated. It is also my intention to bring an affirmative-damage action against you for this breach and to ask the court to remit to me all rent payments made while said conditions exist.

Please call me within five (5) business days to resolve this matter, or I will commence legal action.

Very truly yours,

Certified Letter

* Check state law as indicated in this chapter.

COMPLAINT TO HOUSING AUTHORITY

To: Housing Authority
Address:
Date:
      Re: (Building Address and Apartment Number)

I am a tenant of (Landlord) and have rented the above-captioned apartment since (date).

Please note that the following conditions exist in this unit that I believe violate the housing authority code:

(List your problems—for example, lack of heat or chipped lead-based paint.)

I herein request that you investigate these conditions to determine whether they are in violation of the code and, if so, notify the landlord to abate them within the statutory period.

I wish the record of my complaint to reflect that I have notified the landlord of these conditions (please see letter attached) and that he/she has failed to take appropriate action since my notice of (date).

Please notify me as to when you will be making your inspection.

Thank you for your cooperation.

                    Very truly yours,

Certified Letter

LETTER THREATENING LANDLORD OVER
BUILDING SECURITY

To: Landlord
Address:
Date:
  Re: Liability for Breach of Building Security (Building
    Address and Apartment Number)

Dear Mr./Ms. _____,

This is to advise you that since the breach of building
security described in my letter of (date) attached has not
been abated after appropriate legal notice, you are enhanc-
ing the risk of criminal activity in the building and may be
held liable for any and all damages arising as a proximate
result of your negligence. I strongly suggest that you
contact your attorney to discuss the full extent of your
liability.

I am also notifying you that I will place all future rent
payments in a court escrow fund until the same condition is
abated, and will advise other tenants to do the same until
the condition is fully abated.

I will expect to hear from you within five (5) business days
before commencing legal action.

       Very truly yours,

Certified Letter

REPAIR-AND-DEDUCT NOTICE

To: Landlord
Address:
Date:
  Re: Notification of Repair-and-Deduct Liability*
    (Building Address and Apartment Number)

Dear Mr./Ms. _____,

Be advised that unless the condition described in my letter
of (date) attached is abated within five (5) business days, I

---

*Check state law as indicated in this chapter.

will hire (Name) contractors to repair the defective condition and will deduct that cost from my next rent payment(s) pursuant to state law.

This remedy, however, will not preclude the possibility of a lawsuit I may bring for any losses sustained as a result of this breach of the warranty of habitability.

Very truly yours,

Certified Letter

LETTER DEMANDING RETURN OF SECURITY DEPOSIT

To: Landlord
Address:
Date:

Re: Liability for Failure to Return
Security Deposit (Building Address
and Apartment Number)

Dear Mr./Ms. _____,

Following the termination of my lease on (date), it is your statutory duty to return my security deposit of (amount) with simple interest at the rate of (%) within 30 days.

If that amount is not returned to me within five (5) business days, I will bring action against you for three (3) times the amount wrongfully withheld plus attorney's fees.*

Very truly yours,

Certified Letter

SAMPLE DOCUMENT TO FORM A TENANTS' COMMITTEE

1.   Name of Organization

_____ Apartments Tenants' Association

* Check with your court clerk to see if treble damages are permitted in your state.

2. Purposes

    To cultivate a tenant-landlord relationship which ensures that rights and responsibilities of both parties are respected and discharged in an equitable and fair manner.

    To provide the means for organized tenant effort in restoring and maintaining luxury apartment house standards with respect to _____Apartments' building upkeep and services.

    To provide a structure through which tenant concerns may be aired and acted upon through appropriate channels.

    To foster a spirit of community within _____Apartments and of cooperation in neighborhood improvement efforts.

3. Membership

    Membership in this association is open to all residents of _____ Apartments upon payment of annual dues.

4. Dues

    Dues shall be twenty-five dollars ($25.00) per apartment for the fiscal year ending June 30, 198____, and thereafter shall be set by the executive board as determined by budgetary needs.

5. Officers

    Officers to be elected by the membership shall be a president, vice-president, secretary, and treasurer. Each shall hold office for a term of two years. In the event of a vacancy the remaining members of the executive board shall appoint a person to fill the vacant office during the interim preceding the next general election.

6. Committees

    Standing Committees shall include the following:

    Apartment Organization: Primary responsibility of committee members, designated as floor captains, is to provide and sustain an open line of two-way communication between residents of their respective floors and the executive board.

Information Services: The function of this committee is to gather and disseminate—through newsletters or bulletins—information on legislation, housing regulations, and other matters of general tenant interest; keep tenants informed of association plans and activities; and may also include contacts with outside news media.

Community Relations: Serve as liaison with legislative representatives, neighborhood organizations and institutions; provide for association representation in appropriate community activities.

Additional standing committees may be established at the discretion of the executive board.

Special committees shall be established by the executive board for specific purposes as need arises and shall remain in existence only until their purposes are fulfilled.

The chairman of each standing committee shall be appointed by the president for a term to run concurrently with that of the president. Chairman of special committees shall be appointed by the president with the advice and consent of the executive board.

The president shall be an ex-officio member of all standing committees. An appropriate member of the executive board shall be an ex-officio member of each special committee.

7. Executive Board

The four elected officers and the chairmen of all standing committees shall constitute the executive board of the Tenants' Association.

The executive board has responsibility and authority for planning the program of the association and directing the implementation of activities required by that program. It is empowered to carry on the business of the association in the interim between membership meetings and to make decisions except those that require amendments to the by-laws or financing in excess of funds acquired through the collection of established membership dues.

The executive board shall meet at least once a month. Four or more present at any meeting shall constitute a quorum. A report of each meeting shall be issued in writing to all members of the association.

Any member of the association may submit to the board, in writing, any matter on which he wishes the board to take action; or a member may be granted opportunity, upon request of the president, to present the matter personally at a meeting of the board.

8.   Membership Meetings

Two regular meetings of all members of the association shall be held each year for the purposes of receiving reports of officers and committees and for any other business that may arise. One such meeting shall be for the additional purpose of electing officers if such election is due.

Notice of each general-membership meeting shall be issued in writing to all members not less than ten days prior to the date of the meeting. Such notice shall include the agenda for the meeting.

Special membership meetings may be called (1) by the executive board when the board deems such meeting necessary; (2) upon written request, accompanied by a statement of purpose, made to the president by a minimum of ten members.

One enrolled member of each membership household is eligible to vote on any matter requiring membership decision.

9.   Method of Amending By-Laws

The by-laws of this association may be amended by two-thirds of the members voting by proxy or in person at any regular membership meeting or at such meeting called for that purpose. A copy of any proposed amendment shall be submitted, in writing, to all members of the association not less than ten days prior to the meeting at which action on the amendment is to be taken.

SAMPLE RENT STRIKE NOTICE

RENT STRIKE!

DO NOT PAY YOUR JANUARY RENT UNTIL YOU READ THIS.

The Tenants' Association, after consultation with the association's attorney, has voted to endorse a general tenant *RENT STRIKE* beginning January 1,

198_____. *PLEASE DO NOT PAY YOUR RENT FOR THE FOL-
LOWING REASONS:*

1. Legal counsel has advised us that the general list of tenant complaints
   about the condition of the building indicates that the "warrant of
   habitability" has been breached, and we are paying for services due but
   not rendered.

2. Specific problems with individual apartments also indicate a similar
   breach.

3. Even if you have no particular problems with *your* apartment, the lack of
   services in the building may represent grounds for a court-enforced rent
   reduction for all tenants if our case is properly presented.

*THE BEST COURSE OF ACTION FOR YOU AND YOUR FELLOW
TENANTS, ACCORDING TO LEGAL COUNSEL, IS AS FOLLOWS:*

1. DO NOT PAY YOUR JANUARY RENT, BUT DELIVER A CHECK
   MADE OUT TO YOURSELF, IN YOUR RENTAL AMOUNT, TO
   MS. MAXINE MAGILLA, APT. #809, FOR DEPOSIT IN THE
   ASSOCIATION'S ESCROW ACCOUNT.

2. A court hearing is scheduled Monday morning, January 15, and should
   any legal action be taken against you for nonpayment in the interim, let
   Maxine know so that it will be included in the Tenants' Association
   class-action suit on that date. IN ADDITION, PLEASE PLAN TO
   ATTEND THIS ACTION SO THAT YOU MAY DEMONSTRATE
   YOUR INTEREST.

3. The court will decide what services need to be provided, set deadlines for
   them, and, when our building is brought to standard, will determine
   what part of the rent withheld is due the landlord. ONLY BY
   WITHHOLDING RENT WILL YOU HAVE A LEVER TO HAVE
   PROBLEMS SOLVED.

This course of action is legal and has been used successfully by other tenant
associations to get results.

*IT IS IMPORTANT NOT TO PAY RENT AND TO FOLLOW THE
OUTLINED PROCEDURE!*

Your dues of $25 per apartment are providing us with proper legal counsel,
who will protect you personally and in court as part of our action.

PLAN TO ATTEND AN ASSOCIATION MEETING FOR ALL TEN-ANTS NEXT THURSDAY NIGHT, JANUARY 4, AT 8:00 P.M. IN THE LOBBY, DURING WHICH OUR ATTORNEY WILL EXPLAIN FULLY OUR ACTION.

IN THE INTERIM, DO NOT PAY YOUR RENT TO THE LANDLORD BUT MAKE OUT CHECKS TO YOURSELF AS DESCRIBED ABOVE.

Tenants' Association
December 28, 198_

LETTER TO NEIGHBOR ABOUT
ANNOYING PET

To: Neighbor
Address:
Date:

Dear Mr./Ms. _____,

Please be advised that since you have not abated the nuisance caused by your pet after my notification, I will be forced to petition the court under city ordinance # _____* to have the animal removed from your premises if you do not (keep the pet indoors/muzzle it) as of this date.

Very truly yours,

Certified Letter

* Call your local court clerk for the appropriate citation.

LETTER ABOUT A TERRIFYING PET

To: Neighbor
Address:
Date:

Dear Mr./Ms. _____,

This is to notify you that you are keeping a dangerous pet on your premises in violation of city ordinance # _____.*
This animal (describe dangerous tendency or point out that the pet is a "wild animal which is, by law, considered inherently dangerous.")

I suggest that you contact your attorney immediately, so that he or she may advise you of your substantial liability for negligence if your pet causes injury.

If you do not (chain your dog/cage your ocelot) as of the date of this notice, I will be forced to petition the court to have it removed from your premises.

Very truly yours,

Certified Letter

LETTER ABOUT A DESTRUCTIVE CHILD

To: Parent
Address:
Date:

Dear Mr./Ms. _____,

This is to notify you that your child, (Name), being over the age of liability, has committed willful and malicious acts as follows: (cite the behavior).

I suggest that you discuss with your attorney the full extent of your liability for any and all damages caused by your child arising from parents' negligent lack of supervision.

*Call your local court clerk for the appropriate citation.

Be advised that if your child commits further malicious acts on my premises, or toward any member of my family, he/she will be arrested on criminal charges and you will be sued in civil court for damages.

                    Very truly yours,

Certified Letter

DEMAND LETTER FOR DAMAGES
CAUSED BY A MINOR

To: Parent
Address:
Date:

Dear Mr./Ms. _____,

Please remit to me within ten (10) days payment in the amount of $_____ in full settlement of damages caused to my personal property by your child (<u>Name</u>), as substantiated in the documents attached.

As you may be aware, a parent is liable in this state for damages caused by a minor child's willful and malicious acts of vandalism.

I trust that you will wish to settle this matter amicably and avoid court action.

                    Very truly yours,

Certified Letter

NOTICE OF UNATTRACTIVE NUISANCE

To: Neighbor
Address:
Date:

Dear Mr./Ms. _____,

Please be advised that certain conditions on your property pose a threat to the safety of young children in this neighborhood.

(List the particulars.)

This type of condition is regarded by the law as an "attractive nuisance," and violates city ordinance # _____.*

We are sure that you will want to remove these hazardous conditions by (building a fence/putting the car parts in the garage) before any child is injured and you are held liable for damages.

Thank you for your cooperation.

Very truly yours,

(Names of several neighbors)

Certified Letter

---

* Call your local court clerk for the appropriate citation.

15
lawyers and doctors
Deflating the Mystique

Whatever happened to Perry Mason and Marcus Welby, anyway? We suspect their fantasy practices were unwittingly closed down by two powerful groups: first, bar associations that conspired to fix prices and kept the law shrouded in mystery-for-profit, and second, the American Medical Association, which lobbied mightily for years to keep the lid on medical incompetence. Simultaneously, another profession grew powerful over the past few years—investigative journalism. These journalists (driven in many cases by their own brand of self-righteousness, to be sure) began airing so many years of accumulated dirty linen that the public was forced to take a more realistic view of their learned professions.

As a result of this investigative reporting, today's clients and patients may be far wiser when it comes to shopping for professional services, but not necessarily when they've been wronged and need vindication. If you fall victim to lazy lawyers, indifferent doctors, or incompetents in either field, professional help is at hand. *

USING LAWYERS FOR FUN AND PROFIT

You may have heard the story about the doctor, lawyer, and accountant who were shipwrecked. Adrift on a raft and surrounded by a school of sharks, they decided to take their chances swimming toward shore. The three jumped overboard. The doctor and accountant were immediately devoured by the sharks. But the sharks interrupted their feeding frenzy to let the lawyer swim through to safety. Professional courtesy.

Throughout this book, we talk about choosing a competent, free-consultation attorney as your ally in avenging missions. But how do you find the right one to begin with and, if you have problems later on, how do you keep your attorney's interests and yours in line?

Choosing a Lawyer. Until 1977, your options for legal aid were severely limited. You could call your local bar association and obtain names through its

---

* So we don't inundate you with a blizzard of his/her references in this chapter, we'll refer evenhandedly to our representative lawyers as male and doctors as female.

lawyer-referral system. Or you could skulk over to your most suspicious neighbors and see if they'd experienced similar trouble. Most likely your woes didn't parallel theirs, and the lawyer they referred you to did not handle your specific problems. You were at the mercy of word of mouth. The brotherhood of lawyers kept their own availability and, especially, their fees secretly clutched close to their breasts, so no fee-cutting attorney could ruin the standardized fee structure many lawyers used to get rich.

Then two young lawyers named Bates and O'Steen avenged the public. They took the position that attorneys had a right, through advertising, to tell people they were available. And the Supreme Court decided that their local bar associations' efforts to muzzle them amounted to tampering with free speech. So now lawyers can advertise, state their specialties and—most important—make their fees public.

The result has been a movement away from traditional law firms. And this has meant lower fees for routine services, more convenient hours, and advertised free consultations. Unless someone comes highly recommended to you, pick up the Yellow Pages and let your fingers walk you to a free consultation. Try a clinic. Do not be overly impressed by the allure of a venerable old name on a firm's door. Most of the time, they're dead anyway.

Beware, however, of legal hucksters. As with any burgeoning movement, opportunists have jumped aboard who are not necessarily prepared to offer a wide range of services. Ask a series of key questions. If the answers to any of them are no, you can probably do better.

Is the office (or offices) listed in the phone book staffed with attorneys on a full-time basis? Some multioffice firms have "shell locations" with lawyers rotating in and out. By listing a number of addresses, it looks like a bigger organization. The problem is apparent. Unless the office has staff attorneys, you may chase all over town trying to locate your lawyer.

Are the fees the same at *every* location? Look out for a new gambit called the downtown office fee. Unscrupulous hustlers can listen to your case and suggest it should go "downtown" for more specialized attention—at higher fees, of course.

Is the firm open evenings?

Will you be seen by a lawyer? Some firms are hiring paralegals for the interview stage. In our view, you might as well stay home. Paralegals, simply put, cannot advise legally.

Avoid legal overkill. Unless you're in a criminal action and your prior convictions read like *The Gangster Chronicles,* there's no need to retain an F. Lee Bailey.

Fee Shopping and Stiffing. Now you should visit a few firms. Most routine cases fall within certain time perimeters, so you can find out up front what you'll be charged—beyond your free consultation, that is. Choose a lawyer who charges a fee based on that time commitment. And watch carefully for "what the traffic will bear" pricing. Too many lawyers try to solicit a pretty clear picture of your financial status prior to quoting a fee so they can adjust it accordingly. Say you're on a tight budget, and don't respond to interrogation about your assets unless you're discussing a will.

Don't be too embarrassed to ask for fee justification. You have a right to know, and the lawyer knows it. Demand an estimate of how much time he expects to put into your case. Relate that to the fee. If it seems like a distant relationship, move on. If the price quoted is not a flat fee but based on hours, request information on the hourly rate for lawyers and paralegals, if any, as well as a guestimate of the hours they'll spend on your case.

And always put your agreement in writing.

But what if you've retained a lawyer and, after quoting you a reasonable fee, the bills are running amok? He's padded his hours, or he's run into mythical "difficulties" that "require" more attention on his part (until you forget the problem that brought you in, buried somewhere under the new ones he's created).

Get a second opinion from another lawyer. Give him a blow-by-blow of what your lawyer's done for and to you. Find out whether he's really performed a fair service at a fair price. If you've been taken advantage of, stiff him. Your stiffing technique is only limited by your creativity. Some guidelines:

1.   The Gary Gilmore Stiff. "Don't bother sending me a bill; I'd die before I'd pay you. You charged me for 100 hours and I happen to know you only started working on my case yesterday. If you want to send a bill, send it to the Grievance Committee of the Bar Association and let them decide whether you earned it."

2.   The Willie Mays Stiff. "I don't understand. You said the bill would be in the ballpark of $1,000. This fee is twice that. I'm going to call station WXYZ and ask their consumer reporter what to do unless we can work this out."

3.   The Jack-the-Ripper Stiff. "Go ahead and sue me for the fee, you incompetent crook. I'll rip your reputation in this town to pieces and spread them to the four winds by the time we're through."

No lawyer would sue you for a fee if you can document irregularities on his part. So get ready to sing loud and clear if he did not competently perform the service he wants you to pay for. *Always* claim malpractice at this stage. Your failure to do so may prevent you from a successful lawsuit against him in the future. Now the question arises of how you build a case against your lawyer for malpractice.

Legalese Spoken Here. Legalese hides a multitude of sins. If you can't understand your lawyer, you can't argue with him. He can explain away needless delays, laziness, incompetence, or breach of ethics while you sit there, mouth agape.

    CLIENT: I don't understand why my divorce is taking so long. (Interpretation: I need money.)

    LAWYER: Well, Ms. Noiles, what we've got here is an *a vinculo matrimoni* with the return date past. Had you come in prior to that, I would have been able to expedite the proceedings. I had to first vacate the DPC, since only subsequently could I obtain a show cause for APL. And we're under the new Marital Property Act. Frankly, your delay created problems. The exigencies of the situation demand a stay until we can depose the complainant, *de bene eso*, and do interrogatories. This all takes time. (Translation: What we've got here is a divorce action that was not answered on time. Guess whose fault that was. But I can probably cover up my incompetence if we have a short hearing, under the new law, to get you some money while your divorce is going on. The real problem was, I've been in Bermuda for two weeks so I didn't work on your case. Now that I'm back, I can try to get some information from your husband. This will cost you a bundle.

    CLIENT: Oh. (Translation: Huh?)

If you ever find yourself coughing through a smoke screen of this nature, force him to be straight with you.

    CLIENT: I don't understand a word you said. I'm not a lawyer, but my brother-in-law is. I'd appreciate that explanation in writing so he can explain it to me. And in the future, please send copies of all pleadings and correspondence to me. By the way, weren't you away for a while? I called for two weeks and you never returned my calls.

Now you've managed, under the guise of innocence, to trap this weasel in a corner of his own making. You've sliced through a mushroom cloud of deceit and obfuscation to identify a number of his vulnerabilities through simple, legitimate requests.

You've forced your lawyer to reduce to writing a nonsensical litany of legalese designed to confuse you. Rest assured the letter will be far more comprehensible and try to provide you with a legitimate explanation.

You've deflected the blame for his lack of diligence and expeditious handling of your case, which he tried to drop in your lap, and bounced it right back to the culprit. This will force him to treat you and your case more respectfully if he wants to get paid for his feeble efforts to date.

You've made him document the progress, or absence of any, in your case. This will put him on notice that he'll have to follow a reasonable timetable. This strategy also includes a crafty legal tactic. You'll now have a duplicate file. This will allow you, if you want, to retain new counsel while stiffing the first one. Otherwise, your first lawyer could claim an "attorney's lien" on your file and refuse to let it go until you've paid him in full. Also, while lawyers are masters of double-talk, they can't afford to be caught lying under their own code of ethics. Especially not in writing.

You've let him know that his work will be reviewed at every stage by another attorney, which will help you put teeth in all of the requests.

You have a case already if your lawyer refuses to clarify his actions in writing or if his performance doesn't match his account of how he's handling your problem.

Lazy-Lawyer Tricks to Watch For. What about the lawyer who never returns your calls? Or the attorney whose secretary routinely says he's in court. These are indications that you're getting the runaround and are abuses you can document to use against him as you choose.

From the date of your first consultation, or suspected abuse, keep a log of dates and hours you call your lawyer. Beside the entry, make a notation about the message you conveyed and whether you said the matter was very important or urgent. Since good lawyers are legitimately busy, it may be a day or two before you get a return call if you don't convey urgency. Conversely, if you plead an emergency, you should reasonably expect a call back that day or the next. (A fair indication that you're being ignored is when you're not told he's out until *after* you've given your name.)

Cross-examine the secretary-receptionist. Ask when you might expect to hear back from your lawyer. Make a note of that. Try to solicit where he's supposed to be. It's a breach of professional standards for a secretary to tell you a lawyer's in court if he's not. But this can be a welcome opportunity for you to bait a trap. There are fairly effortless ways to substantiate the secretary's message. If you've been told for the tenth consecutive day that your lawyer's in court, have a friend call the office immediately after your brush-off. The friend should request a consultation to talk about a million-dollar estate or embezzlement case, depending on the lawyer's specialty. If the secretary puts your friend's call through, you know you've been lied to, and your friend can document the time of the call.

But it's even more gratifying to go for a face-to-face confrontation. Plant yourself in the lobby of his building, camouflaged behind the palms. When you see him come in, call upstairs. If you're told he's in court, politely hang up and present yourself at his office. We guarantee your attorney will look very guilty indeed. Lawyers can't lie, remember?

In both cases, document your findings in a certified letter to your lawyer. Be sure to point out your awareness that he's breached ethical responsibilities. This will prove quite motivational in forcing him to put other cases aside to concentrate on yours and place you in an excellent bargaining position to negotiate new fee arrangements.

Another cute ploy many lawyers like to use is telling you, when you call up for a document you were supposed to receive some time ago, that it's in the mail. Since you might tell your creditors the same thing from time to time, you have a pretty clear idea of the veracity of this statement. This is why so much of your lawyer's correspondence seems to arrive the day after you inquire about it. Check postdates on envelopes carefully, and document the exact time they were postmarked vs. the time you called to ask about them. This matching game, when brought to your attorney's attention in a brisk letter, will add another damning entry to your catalog of abuses.

Up Against the Bar. Most of these coercive strategies presuppose a basic or at least grudging satisfaction with your lawyer. If he's generally performing like Edward Bennett Williams and merely stubs his toe against you once or twice along the way, they will enable you to continue your relationship—with, of course, a better foothold for you. But if you think your lawyer's conduct is actually damaging your case or he's defrauded you, it's time to play a more aggressive game of hardball.

Lawyers are bound by ethical considerations (ECs) and disciplinary rules far more onerous than the statutory law of their jurisdiction. These restrictions are set down by the state's bar association or high court. Your lawyer doesn't have to be skimming off the escrow account you've entrusted to him for weekends in Rio. All he has to do is commit a relatively minor infraction to let you bring him up before the bar association. Check the local bar for a list of their own

ECs. Then decide if your attorney has breached one or more of them and whether you can document all his transgressions. If you convince the bar association that your lawyer doesn't practice law according to Hoyle, he can be censured, suspended, and even disbarred so he can no longer foist his winning ways on unsuspecting clients.

If you wish to pursue this remedy, call the bar and have them direct you to the proper committee for filing a grievance. Obtain a formal complaint form if one is provided. Then, specifically and relentlessly, prepare your grievance by spelling out his breaches of ethical responsibility with times, dates, and supporting documentation attached. Be as comprehensive as possible, since the attorney will have to respond to you point by point. But steer clear of emotional hand wringing, which may suggest Nut City to people who are, after all, your attorney's colleagues and may be looking for a reason to sidestep punishing one of their own.

The attorney you have filed against will be given an opportunity to respond, which generally takes three to four weeks. When the response is forwarded to you, hit him again but harder. Restate your strongest areas of concentration and explain away each of his arguments from your own standpoint. You may have to repeat this scenario a few times before the Grievance Committee rules or chooses to hold a hearing. Be sure to plan well ahead to attend the meeting and put forth your arguments. Lack of interest will definitely be interpreted as a lack of conviction. And as a lay person, you won't be subject to clever courtroom trickery on the part of your adversary. The committee will make sure that you get to present your case as you see it.

If you've been legitimately wronged and play this scene out aggressively and rationally, the committee will be forced to censure the attorney and take appropriate action. But your worst enemy is likely to be your own lack of persistence. Exhausted by the necessary back-and-forth routine, many clients feel their actions are futile. However, firm perseverance should result in a fair ruling.

If your lawyer has actually managed to impair your legal rights and you've suffered damages accordingly, sue for legal malpractice.

While lawyers used to shy away from suing other lawyers, the good-ol'-boy camaraderie of professionals is waning. You should have little difficulty finding a lawyer to sue on a legitimate malpractice suit. Which brings to mind a telling remark overheard by one of the authors. A prospective client had asked a lawyer to sue another lawyer for malpractice. It turns out that the lawyers were neighbors. When that was revealed to the client, she asked whether the lawyer could aggressively handle the suit. To which the lawyer replied, with total sincerity, "Mrs._____, I like your money far more than I like my neighbor."

You shouldn't have to pay an up-front fee for your suit, since malpractice actions are generally handled on a contingency basis. This is your guarantee that you're not falling under the spell of licensed incompetency all over again.

Only a successful recovery for you will mean compensation to your lawyer, and need we say that means a lot when he decides to devote his time and reputation to your case.

Fool's Gold. You've no doubt heard the saying He who represents himself has a fool for a client. Unfortunately, legal bufoonery isn't restricted to self-lawyering. In our litigious society, clients who seem to have more money to spend than common sense can always find greedy lawyers who will file *nonmeritorious* or *harassment* suits on their behalf. Untold hours and dollars later, the defendant may be vindicated in a courtroom (but hardly compensated for the trauma experienced while wading through a swamp of litigation and paying some lawyer handsomely for the privilege).

Most states have little-used statutes that provide for legal action against an attorney who files a frivolous and nonmeritorious suit with substantial punitive damages to you, the wronged client. Remember that if you conclude, after you've cooled off, that an avaricious lawyer took advantage of you when you were carried away by a thirst for vengeance.

HEALING THE PROBLEM PHYSICIAN

It's painful for many of us who were raised on Marcus Welby to accept that some doctors are more concerned with maintaining a healthy ego and bank balance than a healthy clientele. While there may not be a sure way to avenge yourself against a physician's occasional leakage of ego (we know one doctor who believes that astronauts and superstar football players would rather be surgeons), we can tell you how to handle interminable waits in a doctor's office, that surgically misplaced belly button, and charlatans who should be drummed out of the medical corps.

Even a well-intentioned doctor derails occasionally, but psychological pressure correctly applied will have her back on the track in no time. Doctors are as vulnerable as lawyers to righteous whistle blowing and tend to get very pale when they receive a communiqué from your lawyer.

Vengeance Comes to Those Who Sit and Wait. "Waiting room" is an all-too-accurate description for that purgatory where you can waste hours to spend a few minutes with your doctor. One of our greatest satisfactions is overhearing a doctor complaining in an airport about some inconvenience she's suffering from an airline's overbooking policy. How many times have you arrived for a ten o'clock doctor's appointment, only to find yourself missing a twelve o'clock lunch date? Such arrogant lack of consideration is a medical epidemic. But a quick and painful shot to doctor's pocketbook should ensure better service in the future.

We propose three remedies, all of which you can prepare for by following a few simple instructions.

When you call for an appointment, ask for one in the early morning. If you're the first patient of the day, not much should intervene to back the doctor up and keep you waiting. But you'll probably arrive at 9 A.M. to find a waiting room full of people who've also been granted a 9 o'clock audience. When you make the appointment, leave your phone number with the receptionist and ask to be advised by her service of any delay before you leave home at 8:30. Unless the doctor has been called away on an emergency, this courtesy will probably not be extended. But you've begun to establish the basis of your vindication.

At 8:45 on the day of your appointment, pick up the phone and confirm. By all means be prompt. Don't give Doctor a chance to claim that you didn't show up on time.

Unbeknownst to her, she's now playing beat the clock and losing money for every second that ticks by. Naturally she'll keep you waiting despite all your planning. But now, when you pay your bill, you'll be deducting a pro-rata amount equal to your hourly rate.

Send the doctor a certified letter explaining that although you were careful to confirm and be on time and even requested a simple notice of any possible delay, you still lost two hours from your business at an hourly rate of (whatever you decide is fair) through the negligence of her office. If your stay was so extended that you're actually in the red, bill her. We doubt you'll be paid, but we also doubt you'll be sued.

The second option, if you're otherwise fond of your doctor but want to go on record against her overbooking, is a little more cordial. Buy an inexpensive watch (for as little as $3) and mail it to her instead of your check. Point out in a friendly note that time is money for you as well as for her. Unless she's a true megalomaniac, she'll have to admit that your point is well taken, and she'll probably give you better service the next time.

The third option is for those with a decided flair for showmanship. When your bill arrives for services finally rendered after a two-hour wait, arrange for a singing telegram to be delivered *in person* at your doctor's office the following day. (In some cities, there are services like Western Onion that will send a singer to deliver your little chorus dressed as a giant clock or other pertinent symbol.) Instruct the telegram deliverer to stand in the doctor's waiting room and sing very clearly to the assembled patients and receptionist (to the tune of "Deck the Halls with Boughs of Holly"):

> Two whole hours you kept me waiting,
> With my work piled up so far,
> Payment you're anticipating,
> Hardehardehar, harharharhar.

Then have the caroler drop your reduced, pro-rated bill and check on the receptionist's desk and walk out, to the double-take merriment of the captive audience.

If the doctor has a sense of humor, she should respond by taking your message to heart. If not, there's not much she can do. But you shouldn't feel bad about stiffing some inconsiderate tyrant with no sense of humor.

Bringing Doc Holidays to Justice. Here's an interesting question to ponder while you're doing time in the waiting room. What explanation can there be for a physician's charging different prices for identical procedures? And we're not talking here about altruistic reduced rates to the needy, but the kind of discrimination you'll find by checking insurance coverage.

The receptionist first discovers whether you're covered by Blue Cross/Blue Shield (BCBS). If you are, your fee quote may be higher—and sometimes much higher—than the quote for the patient who is not insured. The reason is pretty clear—they can scrape more money from the deeper pockets of a large insurance corporation than an individual. But this practice is unethical if not downright illegal in some jurisdictions. It's a variation of the greedy lawyer's what-the-traffic-will-bear policy, with costs passed on to BCBS holders, and the fee-gouging doctor getting even richer than usual on your increased-premium dollars.

If you see that your doctor engaged in this nasty habit and you want to rock her yacht, file a complaint. Find out where the agency that licenses physicians holds court in your state. The health department can tell you. Then contact them and follow their procedure for filing a complaint. More so than with lawyers, doctors aren't disposed to heal their wayward association members for relatively common fee-gouging practices, so this can be a lengthy and difficult process. Bear in mind, however, that it's even more debilitating for your doctor as the accused party.

Another not uncommon fee-generating practice with an eye toward fat insurance companies involves personal injury stemming from legal actions. For example, the same doctor who will order a half-day's bed rest for a cardiac infarction may see fit to recommend a decade in therapy for cervical sprain— better known as whiplash.

If you find yourself dipping into hydrotherapy more often than the pilgrims at Lourdes but feel in terrific shape, you may be caught in the middle of a medical/legal scam. Doctor Whiplash may order excessive treatments and therapy simply because it will be covered by insurance. If you think you're being duped, get a second opinion. Confirm whether the course of action prescribed for you is warranted. If it's clearly not, report this scenario to the licensing agency, as already described. And if it's not an isolated case, your doctor could be subject to a mail-fraud action by the government.

Performing Surgery on the Incompetent. What about the doctor who makes costly mistakes—the medico who removes female plumbing when a hormone shot would have done as well, or misdiagnoses a patient's chest pain as a pulled muscle and sends him home for a rest—through eternity. If these horror stories become reality, a malpractice suit is an available course of action.

The tragedy here is obvious. Unlike remedies for inept lawyers, there's generally no "right of appeal" from medical incompetence. Too often, negligence results in irreversible problems or death. The legal test for medical malpractice is simple: Did the physician's standard of care and competence fall below the norms of that particular community? If you suspect you've been mistreated, see a lawyer. After some preliminary investigation, he'll be able to determine whether you have a case. While money is precious little compensation for loss of health—or worse—caused by negligence, it's as close as the law comes to rectifying the situation. However, the awards can be staggering and are certainly worth pursuing.

Recently a plastic surgeon replaced a belly button somewhat off the prime meridian during a cosmetic operation, resulting in a six-figure award. All that money for a few inches, but a jury decided that the patient's pain and suffering were worth it.

A word of caution: more and more states, due to the exceptional lobbying powers of the medical and insurance professions, are insulating doctors from direct accountability for their negligent acts through mechanisms called something like the Medical Malpractice Arbitration Board (MMAB) and statutes that say you can't sue a physician for malpractice until you've exhausted your administrative remedies by filing your complaint with the MMAB and allowing them to rule first. (Guess who sits on the hearing panel—not your basic jury of twelve peers, but doctors.) The result has been a backup in litigation that may witness pediatric patients expiring of old age before they ever see their physicians across a counsel table.

One of the major expenses of litigating a malpractice suit is the payment of expert medical witnesses—including, oddly enough, your current physician. The doctors' rationale for fees of $1,000 per day and more is that they are losing money by being away from the office during the trial. Well, who isn't? Of course, your now-treating physician can be compelled to testify for free, but the downside of this suggestion for you can be even more costly. If the testimony that is solicited is not, so to speak, on the money, the case dies with the patient. However, we've developed a little gambit that should secure her expert testimony.

While your treating physician may be presumptuous enough to request a huge payment, she probably won't have the gall to demand it up front. Unless you've actually contracted with her (rather unlikely), don't pay her. You remember—the stiff. She's not entitled and will see the obvious futility of pressing a collection suit. Let her know your integrity is paramount and you wouldn't *dream* of buying testimony. Because that, in effect, is what you're doing.

If It Ducks Like a Quack . . . Consider the billions of dollars poured into nonprofit medical research and the high-profit labs of drug manufacturers every year. No matter what you may believe about conspiracies to suppress breakthrough medical findings, isn't it fairly unlikely that some genius in a walk-up building has concocted, on his hot plate, an elixir that eludes the grasp of well-funded and highly trained researchers?

Medical quacks will usually be found in offshore islands or Mexican border towns, where they can duck supervision and prosecution from medical associations and state laws. But some hold court right in the USA, and if they've been taking advantage of a family member or a friend, they're fair game for your retribution. Their modus is to promise you a miracle cure for your ailment as yet unrecognized—or covered up—by the medical community. They are, out of concern for humankind, ready to part with their secrets—at fees that can stretch far beyond even bloated legitimate medical costs.

Just as charlatans prey on others' fear and gullibility, you can prey on their greed. Once you've decided that a quack is working over a friend or relative, arm yourself with a competent witness. Naively, witness in tow, gush to the witch doctor how thrilled you are with her treatment. Categorize her methodology and her unattainable goals to your witness, under the charlatan's watchful eye. Punctuate every statement with "Isn't that right, doctor?" She will no doubt nod in erudite agreement. Even better, solicit the explanation from her. Introduce your cohort as someone having a sister, brother, or ailing mother with the same problem as your friend or relative. The maverick genius, in the hopes of getting new business, will likely give him the line of prattle reserved for best prospects.

Have your friend observe treatment. It would be fortunate if your accomplice happened to be a photographer who sells to the *National Enquirer* and would offer to do a pictorial testimony. By all means, regardless of his credentials, have him take pictures of patients' "progress." Chances are the befores won't be distinguishable from the afters.

Compile the pictures and attach them to a transcript of the quack's conversation in the form of an affidavit. Have your witness warrant its veracity with his signature, under penalty of perjury. Then contact the appropriate licensing bureau and check on whether the doctor is licensed. If (incredibly enough), she is, have a complaint form mailed to you. Fill it out and attach it to your packet of information and pictures. Send a cover letter with this surprise package to Dr. Strangelove, advising her that unless there is an immediate return of all funds fraudulently obtained from your friend or relative, this grievance will immediately be forwarded to the appropriate medical board. Then, even if you receive a refund, do it anyway.

If the medical board in their discriminating wisdom have refused your "doctor" licensing, you've got her. Visit the local prosecuting attorney and swear out a warrant against her practicing without a license. It won't cost you anything, but the savings in pain and suffering of others can be substantial.

REVENGE KIT FOR LAWYERS AND DOCTORS

SAMPLE LAWYER RETAINER AGREEMENT
FOR A MATRIMONIAL PROBLEM

I, _____, hereby retain (Name of Firm) to represent me in all matters growing out of my domestic difficulties with my spouse, _____.

In consideration of their representation and legal advice, I AGREE to pay (Name of Firm) or its authorized representatives the sum of $_____ for an UNCONTESTED case.

Should any matter concerning this case become CONTESTED, then, and in that event, I AGREE that the MINIMUM FEE of $_____ shall be paid plus $_____ for each hour or fraction thereof over eight (8) hours. In this regard, I understand that (Name of Firm) shall maintain a time record of the hours expended in pursuing my case to a conclusion, and shall account to me for the time spent in a contested case. I AGREE to make payments as they shall become due for the time expended in my behalf.

In addition, I AGREE to pay all court costs, MASTER-EXAMINER fees or other costs as and when they shall become due.

I AGREE to pay $_____ down and $_____ per week/month until the fee and all costs shall have been paid in full.

_____   _____
Date   Signature

SAMPLE LETTER TO BAR ASSOCIATION
GRIEVANCE COMMITTEE

To: (Locality) Bar Association Grievance Committee
Address:
Date:

Re: Application for fee arbitration

Dear Sirs:

On November 19, 198____, I retained the firm of Robb &
Cheate to handle what I believed to be the preparation of an
uncontested Separation Agreement. As you can see from the
retainer agreement (attached hereto), the fee for same was
to be $250.00. You will also note it was paid on the same
date, in full.

My lawyer now claims that the matter has become contested. In fact, my spouse and I are in complete agreement
as to the contents of the document. My only purpose in
obtaining counsel was to have our agreement reduced to
writing in proper legal form.

I wish to submit this case to your panel for fee arbitration.
Please forward to me any forms necessary to process my
case.

I would appreciate your contacting me as soon as possible,
since I feel that I have been damaged both financially and
emotionally by the attorney's behavior:

(Your Address)
(Your Phone Number)

Thank you for your cooperation.

Very truly yours,

SAMPLE BAR ASSOCIATION
COMPLAINT FORM

Date _____

1. Your Name   Mr. ☐   Mrs. ☐   Ms. ☐

_____
(First)   (Middle)   (Last)

_____
(State)

_____
(City)   (County)   (State)   (Zip Code)

Telephone Number(s): Business: Home:

2. Attorney Against Whom You Wish to File a Complaint
   (see Note below, after No. 8):

_____
(First)   (Middle)   (Last)

_____
(Street)

_____
(City)   (County)   (State)   (Zip Code)

3. Did you employ the attorney? Yes ☐ No ☐ If yes, give
   the approximate date you employed him or them and the
   amount, if any, paid to him or them: Date: _____
   Amount: _____

4. If your answer to No. 3 above is "No," what is your
   connection with the Attorney? Explain briefly: _____

   _____

   _____

   _____

5. Write out *on a separate piece of paper* and send with this
   form a statement of what the attorney did or did not do
   that you are complaining about. Please state the facts as
   you understand them. Do not include opinions or arguments. If you employed the attorney, state what you

employed him to do. Sign and date such separate piece of paper. Further information may be requested.

6. If your complaint is about a lawsuit, answer the following, if known:

   A. Name of Court or Agency (for example, District or Circuit Court, in what county): _____

   _____

   B. Title of Suit (for example, Smith against Jones): _____

   _____

   C. Number of Suit: _____

   D. Approximate Date the Suit was Filed: _____

   E. If you are not a Party to this Suit, explain your connection with it briefly:

   _____

   _____

   _____

7. If you have made a Complaint about this same matter to any Official or Agency, state its (their) name(s), and the approximate date you reported it: _____

8. If you are or have been represented by any other attorney with regard to this matter, state the name and address of the other attorney: _____

   NOTE: If you are complaining about more than one attorney, write out the information about each in answer to Questions 2, 3, 4, and 5 above on separate sheets if necessary.

   Signature:

SAMPLE LETTER TO HEALTH DEPARTMENT
COMPLAINING ABOUT A DOCTOR

To: Physician Licensing Authority
(Address)
(Date)

      Re: Complaint Against Licensed Physician
            (Doctor's Name)

Gentlemen,

I wish to file a complaint with your department, or by your referral to the appropriate licensing agency, against the above-captioned physician.

(List your allegations of illegal or unethical behavior. For example:

On July 12, I was asked by the Doctor's receptionist whether I had Blue Cross/Blue Shield insurance. When she determined that I was covered, my bill was presented in the amount of $335. I have since determined that another patient who received identical treatment but was not covered by insurance received a bill for only $95. The physician has refused to explain this difference to my satisfaction.)

Please advise me as to whether this complaint will be processed by your department or, if it is referred to another agency, whom I may contact for further action.

                  Very truly yours,

SAMPLE LETTER TO CONGRESSIONAL REPRESENTATIVE PROTESTING MALPRACTICE ARBITRATION FOR DOCTORS

To: Senator or Representative
Washington, D.C.
(Date)

Dear Senator/Representative _____,

I am a constituent of yours, residing in the _____th Congressional District. I recently became aware of pending legislation which would prohibit a patient from filing a suit directly against a malpracticing doctor.

It is my feeling that this law is unconstitutional in that it robs me of due process. I would like to go on record, strenuously, as requesting that you vote against this proposed statute. Please advise as to your position.

Very truly yours,

PART V

Climbing on the Bureaucrats' Backs

16
government
Punishing Uncivil Servants

Did you ever wonder why there are signs in post offices that warn, "It is a federal offense to assault a postal employee"? It might be because government bureaucrats have taken a well-deserved beating from just about everyone lately: their one-time media friends; the voters who pay their salaries; and newest on the horizon, an administration that would like to do away with half the government payroll.

Many people—ambitious people—are drawn to working for the government, especially for agencies charged with upholding our legal rights. And any consumer will be fortunate to have one of those aggressive watchdogs on his or her side. We want to deal with the special problem of the "Stubbornly Obstructive Bureaucrat," whom we'll refer to for simplicity's sake as the S.O.B. He or she may be found working for the federal, state, or municipal government. The distinguishing characteristics are (1) a lack of desire or ability to work at all, in the private-sector sense of the word, and (2) a tendency to direct whatever flow of energy he or she might control to avoiding, misplacing, or tying up your problem indefinitely rather than attempting to solve it.

If you already know about the S.O.B. and have made it your business never to involve the government in your life, you may wonder why such strategies should interest you.

First of all, you won't be able to enjoy your arm's-length relationship forever. Someday you'll receive a little note from an IRS auditor who, by disallowing your medical deductions, seeks to make up those revenues lost from oil millionaires through the depletion allowance. Or you might be involved in a small business that's forced to comply with the same regulatory paperwork requirements as ITT.

Second, you might want to use government in your revenge missions to help sort out some problem with a marketer, employer, landlord, or whomever. The worst evil that can befall you in that case will be to find your original problem fading by comparison with the treatment you're getting at the agency. This can become as frustrating as trying to crawl out from the interior of a Chinese box.

So be ever vigilant to artful-dodging behavior in government offices. You won't be disappointed. And be ready to apply some coercive strategies, if need be, to blow the whistle on a boondoggling Consumer Cop.

STALKING THE S.O.B. ON GOVERNMENT TURF

What's the worst damage you could ever inflict on obstructive bureaucrats? Get them fired? Let's dwell on that option for a moment. All career government workers fall into some kind of civil-service classification. It's tough to get fired. In the federal government, for instance, they have to fit employment categories set by the US Civil Service Commission, then pass tests administered by the Bureau of Recruiting and Examining, and finally compete against two other top contenders chosen from a vast supply of applicants for the same job. You might ponder why anyone would go to all that trouble.

The answer, of course, is that it's even tougher to get fired. Once lodged in a government cubicle, a civil-service worker can't be dislodged for very many offenses less serious than appearing at work every day on LSD or dropping great quantities of it in a District of Columbia reservoir. The specific grounds that can terminate a US government worker, other than lying on the job application, are:

1.   immoral conduct

2.   excessive use of alcohol or drugs

3.   disloyalty to the American form of government

Unless you have a great deal of free time to devote to personal vendettas, we don't think you'll find much to work with there. But you might discover more fruitful opportunities in a general policy that employees can be discharged for "such reasons that will promote the efficiency of the service." This is highly discretionary and, we hear, only invoked for practical purposes when an employee makes huge waves in a department, like leaking whatever today's equivalent of the Pentagon Papers might be to the *New York Times*. However, you can still wield this ultimate stick (lacking a carrot in most dealings with government folk) against a troublesome employee. You probably won't see the person fired but, if you substantiate his or her inefficiency with the kind of obsessive documentation all civil servants admire, you can reasonably fantasize the person writhing on the carpet before a very displeased supervisor.

Building a Dossier of Dereliction. One factor that will operate in your favor is that many government workers, attuned to lackadaisical performance as a way of life, will routinely make statements that can advance your case. For instance, one of the authors recently phoned a state department trying to reach an elusive employee we'll call O'Leary.

APRIL 2, 11:00 A.M.

TAXPAYER: Mr. O'Leary, please.

EMPLOYEE: He's on his break now. You can try later.

TAXPAYER: Well, I'll be busy most of the day. Tell him I'll call back at about a quarter to five.

EMPLOYEE: Better make that 4:15. We get ready to pack it in around here about 4:30.

TAXPAYER: I see. Whom am I speaking to, please?

EMPLOYEE: Ms. Demaris.

Now the statutory workday for that office happens to be 9 to 5, approximating normal business hours. So you can begin to see how, by calling at the right time over a period of days and documenting your messages, you can establish an impressive pattern of dereliction.

APRIL 3, 1:15 P.M.

TAXPAYER: Mr. O'Leary, please.

EMPLOYEE: He's not back from lunch yet.

TAXPAYER: Well, tell him I'll call late this afternoon. Could I have your name, please?

EMPLOYEE: Mr. Caldwell.

APRIL 3, 3:15 P.M.

TAXPAYER: Mr. O'Leary, please.

EMPLOYEE: He's on break.

TAXPAYER: And you're . . . ?

EMPLOYEE: Ms. Ormsby.

APRIL 4, 9:05 A.M.

TAXPAYER: Is Mr. O'Leary in?

EMPLOYEE: I don't think so. Let me check. (Five minutes later) Somebody said he was here, but I can't find him.

TAXPAYER: Thank you, Mr. . . . ?

EMPLOYEE: Johnson.

APRIL 5, 4:40 P.M.

TAXPAYER: Mr. O'Leary, if he's there.

EMPLOYEE: No, he's gone for the day.

TAXPAYER: Thanks, Ms. Demaris.

EMPLOYEE: Sure thing. Can I have him call you?

TAXPAYER: (sigh) No thanks, I have to go out of town. I'll just try to reach him when I get back.

Let's say that this bureau happens to have its own policy similar to the federal clause, "promoting the efficiency of the service." When you add this catalog of documented sloth to the original problem with the S.O.B., you'll have a very tidy package to present to your adversary's supervisor. Marshal all your evidence and enumerate it coldly, objectively, in crushing detail. Name names, give dates, and at the bottom of your list of particulars, point out that:

> I am sure you will conclude, as I have, that I have made every conceivable effort to reach this individual and resolve my problem with his original handling of the important matter I brought to your department. Frankly, I believe that this employee's nonavailability— during all hours at which he is supposed to be handling matters such as my own—does not meet reasonable standards for public service and, in fact, does not promote the efficiency of your department.

A couple of things will probably happen when this unexpected dossier arrives at the supervisor's office. First, your adversary will be notified of the charges you've made against him. Faced with these charges, most government employees, accustomed to brushing off taxpayers with minimal effort and a few second thoughts, will be as close to terror as a protected civil servant could ever come, particularly for a fairly new employee still on his or her probationary period or for an employee with any other complaints floating around in his or her employee file. And you may rest assured that under the circumstances, he or she will not risk mounting a countervengeance offensive against you. Next your matter will undoubtedly be placed in the hands of another employee, who will apply a much greater furor to resolving your original problem—which was all you wanted from this department, anyway.

The Job-Description Gambit. If you can't quite muster the venom to enter a scourging document in some government worker's file, there's a more creative remedy that offers the same embarrassment value without the obvious malice on your part. And it works for virtually any government staffer, including those who hold lofty titles.

A friend of ours, whom we'll call Lisa, moved last year into an expensive condominium development that was touted as a model of urban living. In fact, the federal and local governments had raised most of the construction money by floating bond issues. The city itself was in charge of overseeing most aspects of the project, including community relations. So a "project coordinator" was hired by the city to ensure that residents weren't inconvenienced by the messy construction activities that would continue for some time as each new phase of the development progressed.

Lisa happened to live in a completed area next to a new-construction site. And the road to her garage was littered with the usual construction debris, which included pointy and dangerous objects from nails to irregular piles of broken bricks and rock. This presented a serious obstacle course for Lisa to negotiate in her new car. So after the odd dent or two and one flat tire, she complained several times to the project coordinator. Naturally, he promised to have the road cleared. But, characteristically, it wasn't.

So Lisa made a few inquiries at the municipal housing authority and came up with her S.O.B.'s job description—which is available for all bureaucrats and carefully describes their reason for existence on the public payroll. It read, in essence, that the project coordinator would be responsible for ensuring good relations with the development's existing residents by hastily resolving all reasonable complaints about the ongoing construction.

She also found out the name and address of the coordinator's supervisor, who also happened to be the city executive responsible for hiring him in the first place. And the next day she drafted a letter to that city executive which concluded:

> . . . and, despite the damage to my car and other residents' vehicles as well, no attempt whatsoever has been made to clear the dangerous debris left cluttering our roadway.

Frankly, we would have expected your agency to appoint a person who would be responsible for ensuring better relations with those of us already living in this development and who would resolve significant problems like these immediately, before we are forced to take the legal action I have indicated. We urge you to consider appointing such an individual as soon as possible.

Now when a citizen has to request that someone should be hired to handle the responsibilities outlined in a bureaucrat's job description, you can imagine the aftereffects for that bureaucrat. And you probably won't be too surprised to hear that the road was cleared the following day.

Every S.O.B. has a job description somewhere. And it's yours for the asking. Just use the sources listed in the Revenge Kit to find it. Then compose an irate "suggestion" letter of your own to the responsible agency executive or department head.

The Unkindest Cut of All. But there's an even more insidious attack you can launch on the government's own preserve, one that answers our original question: What's the worst punishment you can inflict on bureaucrats?

You can make them work.

This is as diabolical as it is simple, since it cuts right to the heart of an S.O.B.'s vulnerability. Here are a few profitable suggestions to get you started:

1.   Request extensive information from your S.O.B. under the Freedom of Information Act (FOI). This applies to every US government agency, forcing them to release copies of any nonclassified documents upon demand. (Of course, some of the real goodies, like the secret IRS list of problem income tax preparers, which could clearly show you who *not* to use, are not available because they are potentially damaging to the individuals who appear on them.) There's even been an intriguing book published that's filled with nothing but formerly secret documents its authors obtained under the FOI.

2.   Write to your personal S.O.B. at the Social Security Administration and demand a full accounting of your Social Security payments to date, plus an immediate *refund check* if you've made overpayments to your account. And the odds are about two to one that you have. The way the Social Security system appears to be headed, you might be better off extracting whatever you can right now and reinvesting it in something a little less shaky than that federally mandated pyramid scheme.

3.   Let the S.O.B.s at the IRS do your income tax calculations for you instead of using a storefront preparer. If you're filling out Form 1040 or 1040A and you're not itemizing deductions, you might as well save the

$20 you pay a preparer with two weeks' "professional" training. The IRS people are instructed to follow standard procedures. The storefront preparers can vary wildly according to which office in the same chain you visit, a recent Washington, D.C. investigation concluded. Simple instructions about how to file your return so the IRS can do your work are on the 1040.

At all government levels, you can always plan to attend the *annual budget hearings* for agencies and departments that give you problems. These are occasions at which citizens can get up to testify, which we're sure you'll want to do after you've been bruised by the S.O.B.s within. Do your homework first, though. Make them give you all the information you need to prepare a well-documented case against them.

USING ELECTED OFFICIALS

Sometimes you may find it more useful to make an end run around the bureaucrats who have little motivation to help you resolve a problem and appeal to the people who need your vote. This works especially well at the local government level.

True, you might get satisfaction from your US congressperson or senator, too, but we'd hate to see you build your hopes up. Remember that your complaint is arriving among an avalanche of requests for favors and hate mail from other constituents, which is hastily read by assistants while your representative may be off on a fact finding junket to Tahiti, courtesy of the very special interest lobby you're complaining about.

But community, city, and state officials usually see your importance as a lever puller with greater clarity. While they are pressurized by special interests of their own, they also have an interest in keeping you happy with the machinery of government under their control.

Take the example of a sixty-two-year-old woman who was due a check from a local government agency in an eastern city. She exhausted the usual courses of no remedy and finally decided on a heartfelt letter to the mayor, which read in part:

> Because it is your own employees who are responsible for not processing my application for benefits over the past month, I must hold you personally at fault. I am not too proud, and I am even welcoming the opportunity, to go on the (television news show) and eat a can of cat food to show how serious my financial situation really is. But I hope you will see that I get my check this week so I will not have to do so.

Most mayors, including the one she wrote to, are painfully conscious of the backlash such a pitiable spectacle could create with the home voters—especially older citizens, who have an exemplary record of going to the polls and voting *against* particular politicians and issues that arouse their anger.

When you are contacting a public official, always try to couch your difficulty in dramatic human terms. Don't just write a letter about the landlord who's threatening to evict you. Send a photograph of your extended family assembled on the street in front of the house on displaced furniture (not necessarily your own) to give the message poignancy.

TEACHER MALPRACTICE: A LESSON THEY WON'T FORGET

Now we'll consider one government worker who is usually more victim than villain but who can also cheat you like any other inept professional.

Every child in the United States has the right to a free education for at least ten years, depending on state law. But this doesn't say much about, or for, the *quality* of education a child is entitled to.

What's become pretty obvious to any sane observer and has been reported extensively in the media lately is that some teachers can't really teach. In fact, some can barely read and write themselves. We won't speculate on the causes for this fiasco, which experts say range from the influence of TV (not just on kids but on younger teachers who grew up mesmerized by the tube) to a breakdown in family and classroom disciplinary practices.

But we can tell you that the problem is sufficiently widespread that legal remedies are available. Teachers, like any other professionals, are expected to provide a standard of competence roughly equivalent to the norms of your community. So if you have some reason to believe that there's a problem teacher who's not guiding your children toward the skills they should possess at a given grade level, you should quickly speak to other parents and to a lawyer.

We're not talking about those high-school graduates who can't read their own diplomas. That level of tragic comedy reflects a long-standing problem extending over many teachers and probably a whole school system. But if your child is bringing home notes from Teacher that read like fifth-grade scrawlings, or you test your child independently and find no evidence of learning since the year before, there might be good cause to seek a "rebate" of sorts and damages for the teaching services that were never rendered.

Lawsuits for teacher malpractice aren't new. But the traditional suits focused on problems like negligent supervision or excessive force, involving kids who were physically hurt. What's new is the rash of malpractice suits alleging that kids haven't learned the minimum skills required to move on to the next grade level. The legal theory is that teachers are acting as "substitute parents" (in loco parentis) while your kids are in their class. This presumably makes teachers liable for each student's progress under their care. When parents demonstrate that a teacher has been negligent in failing to teach a child the required material, damages can be assessed by a court to compensate the child or, in practice, the parents.

This is an interesting extension of product-liability law, with education as the product. If it's defective, you can "revoke acceptance" and get a refund. If there were actual damages, you can collect them. And the average money damages sought in these suits is around $500,000.

Until the current wave of malpractice actions making their way through appeals courts are settled, it's difficult to conjecture what the chances of getting such a hefty award might be. But we can guess that your school will know they might have a problem beyond the normal PTA squabbles if you slap them with notice of such a suit. It's something you'll want to do through a lawyer, and preferably with other parents involved to show that their own children have suffered, too. Otherwise the school could claim that your child was a special case.

If your child really was a special case, though, you might have another valid argument, for instance, if a child's IQ is very high but he or she wasn't placed with the fast-track students due to a teacher's own negligence. Some insecure teachers don't particularly like the brightest kids and consider them "discipline problems" because they're not as fascinated by Teacher's intellectual prowess as the rest of the second grade.

In this kind of case, it's more important than if you're suing the dry cleaner to sort your objectives out carefully and consider the possible long-range effects for everybody involved. But we believe that any truly negligent teacher should be made accountable for harm done. This evidence of discontent will encourage school boards—and teachers' unions—to weed out their incompetents beforehand.

REVENGE KIT FOR GOVERNMENT

SAMPLE JOB DESCRIPTION LETTER

To: Head of Local City Agency
Address:
Date:

Dear Mr./Ms. _____:

I live at (Address), which, as you know, is a development run by the agency you head.

Over the past several months, it has been my observation and that of my neighbors that we are in desperate need of a project coordinator to look after our interests regarding the cleaning of our roads while the building activity goes on. There have been many nights when the road leading to my house has been unpassable due to heavy construction debris, and my numerous complaints to that effect have gone totally unheeded.

As you undoubtedly know, when we moved into the development, we were expressly promised by your office that someone would operate as a liaison to monitor whatever interference the ongoing construction would cause to the beneficial use of our homes. Why has this not been done?

I, therefore, request that you appoint someone from your office to handle this pressing and important job. My next letter will be to the local paper explaining to the public at large your failure to remedy this situation and your failure to perform as promised.

Please advise.

Very truly yours,

REQUEST UNDER FREEDOM OF INFORMATION ACT

To: Head of Government Agency
Address:
Date:

Re: Your Name:
Address:
Telephone number:
Social Security number:

Dear Mr./Ms. _____,

Please send me within one month from the date hereof a copy of: (e.g., all records and memoranda concerning me held by your agency). This request is made pursuant to and under the authority of the Freedom of Information Act, 5 U.S.C. §552 and the Privacy Act, 5 U.S.C. §552(a).

I will expect your submission to include all documents on file. In the event you believe that some part of my file is exempt, I would ask that you substantiate in writing the basis for any such claim and send to me the balance per this request.

It is my considered opinion that my request is in the "public interest" and, accordingly, I ask that you waive any fee that may be assessed as a result of this request.

Thank you for your prompt cooperation.

Very truly yours,

LETTER REQUESTING
SOCIAL SECURITY REFUND

To: IRS
Address:
Date:

> Re: Social Security number:
> Your Name:
> Address:
> Telephone number:
> Social Security number:

I believe that I have overpaid my Social Security taxes for the period ending (date) in that (e.g., I had two jobs and both employers deducted an amount in excess of maximum). In light of the foregoing, please audit my account and remit to me any such overpayment.

Very truly yours,

17
hospitals

A Taste of Their Own Medicine

> We'd better get this patient out of here
> before we kill him.
> —A staff doctor in the movie *Hospital*

Maybe you're among the one in seven Americans who'll check into a hospital this year. If so, you might want nothing more than some assurance that you'll also check out, but you probably expect a little pampering in return for your few hundred dollars a day, too. Instead, you could be treated by petty tyrants to disagreeable nursing service, malpractice, and a lot of mistakes and unnecessary items on the bill when it's finally presented.

PREVENTIVE MEDICINE FOR HOSPITAL PATIENTS

Although the odds are against malpractice happening to you, there are enough ex-surgery patients who've had the wrong lung removed or now hear funny clanking noises in their stomachs when they go jogging to ignore the possibility completely. And more to the point, hospital costs stagger just about everyone. We suspect the main reason hospitals give you a wheelchair on the way out is that they don't want a pileup of people in shock when they pick up the bill at the cashier's office.

You may well wonder why a single, rather uncomfortable bed in some county hospitals costs as much as a bridal suite at the Waldorf. The obvious reason is that ten bellhops and desk clerks can be hired for the equivalent of one doctor's salary, and a single piece of high-tech lifesaving equipment can cost several hundreds of thousands of dollars.

But there are other explanations for bloated charges, too. A lot of defensive medicine is practiced, in the wake of huge malpractice awards. Doctors tend to cover themselves with redundant tests and referrals to an array of specialists for seemingly simple problems. And many hospitals have more beds than they can fill with sick people (although in certain areas of the country, the exact opposite is true). However, cost control is one area in which you can practice some self-defense of your own before you're even admitted.

If you're totally covered by hospitalization insurance, you probably don't care about saving a few dollars for your insurance company. But if you have a high-deductible policy, that means you'll still be paying considerable amounts for your treatment. And there is the further possibility that certain preexisting conditions are totally excluded. Thus, where nontraumatic, elective visits may be called for, we recommend:

1.   If your doctor says you need surgery, get a second opinion. Maybe you don't need that operation.

2.   For nontraumatic problems, see if you can have the surgery performed outside a hospital. Some experts claim that 30% of all operations do not require hospitalization, and outpatient surgery tends to cost about 50% less. Cosmetic surgery, for instance, is increasingly performed in doctors' offices or clinics. Bear in mind, though, that if some one-in-one-hundred complication develops, you're farther away from the expensive lifesaving machinery in the hospital.

3.   If you do decide you want to be nearer the heavy equipment, telephone different hospitals and get competitive prices (ask for average daily costs), which can vary by as much as $70 per day. The only restrictions are that your doctor has to be affiliated with the hospital (and most doctors are affiliated with several) or that you may need a specific piece of technical equipment that not all hospitals have.

4.   Don't check in, if you can help it, on a Friday night. Many testing facilities usually close down over the weekend, and your doctor won't remove even a hangnail until all your test results are in. Wait, if possible, until a Monday to be admitted.

5.   Determine if "follow-up care" means nothing more than languishing in the hospital for bed rest. (In overcrowded areas, you may never be given this luxury "option.") You can just as easily convalesce at home. Also find out, if you have insurance, whether your doctor's follow-up care can be considered surgery so that it will be covered. ("Surgical procedure" as a term covers a wider universe than you might think: When a dermatologist pops a pimple, it is considered a surgical procedure.)

How to Achieve Most-Favored-Patient Status

If you've ever been in a hospital, you know that the staff can be downright fawning in their attention to some patients, especially if they're related to board members. If you let the hospital know from the outset that you are a person to be reckoned with, you'll improve your chances of receiving the same solicitous attention.

The Attorney Check-In. Especially if your hospitalization is elective, visit a lawyer before you're admitted and have him write a letter that spells out the treatment you expect to receive: It should detail the accommodation you're paying for, with costs clearly stated. Be sure that it describes your understanding about your room, especially what the hospital has told you about "private" and "semi-private" distinctions. We know of some hospitals having entirely different criteria for "semi-private" from wing to wing. All too often, patients complain that they paid for a semi-private room but wound up on an eight-bed ward resembling those field hospitals in old French Foreign Legion films. When you consider what you'll spend on hospital costs, the small fee you'll pay a lawyer for writing such a letter will be worth it. A hospital can't refuse to admit you because you're coming in under the auspices of a lawyer as well as your doctor. You will merely put them on notice that you're well prepared to make trouble when you don't get what you're paying for.

If you have to go to a hospital emergency room (ER), call your doctor and ask her to phone ahead that you're coming—even if the doctor is not affiliated with the hospital. At least, this will prepare them that you are coming and earn you some preferential treatment, provided you are not preceded by an accident or cardiac victim. But even if you are, you should be seen within a reasonable time, and in the case of a dire emergency, this means very quickly. Although the circumstances of the day, time, and location of a hospital may produce heavy traffic into an emergency room, there should be sufficient medical-staff coverage to ensure that you receive treatment within fifteen to thirty minutes of your arrival. Failure to respond within this limit may well be grounds for legal action if, despite repeated attempts to get attention, you are ignored. If all else fails, you're in pain, and nobody listens, *scream.* Someone will come over to you if for no other reason than to quiet you down.

Getting More Room than You Bargained For. Once you check in, you may find that your room has certain M*A*S*H-like qualities that aren't to your liking. Maybe there's a patient next to you who has noisy parties of visitors. You should complain to *your* doctor that it's aggravating your condition, in which case she might transfer you to a private room on "doctor's orders." This may mean that the better room is covered under your hospitalization plan. Check first.

Disciplining Nurse and Doctor. While a nurse's job is to treat you in certain carefully defined medical areas, his or her inclination may be to treat you like a troublesome five-year-old. Say you have a guest who's staying until 8 P.M. or whenever visiting hours are over. But Nurse bustles in at 7:42 in a mop-up operation to clear the ward according to her personal timetable.

NURSE: (to visitor) You'll have to go now. Our patient needs her rest.

PATIENT: No I don't. Besides, visiting hours aren't over for another twenty minutes.

NURSE: (to visitor again, in stage whisper) She's tired but doesn't know it.

Rather than bursting your stitches from the apoplexy this patronizing treatment is likely to cause you, don't bother trying to argue. She's had years of experience dealing with your kind. Just make it your business to document these abuses in your own "Personal Care Log" during your hospital stay. This will give you ammunition to demand better service while you're still inside or to dispute your bill afterward. Or both. Your log can be a regular stationery-store notebook. But be sure to keep it under your pillow if word gets around the grapevine that you're writing up some kind of record of your treatment. Dutifully note, in detail, inconsiderate behavior toward you and your visitors and—particularly—all instances of *neglect*.

Maybe you ring for Nurse but no one sees fit to come by for hours, if at all. Make a note of it. And if there's someone in the bed next to you, develop that patient as a witness. If your roommate hates the shoddy treatment, too, build a case for each other. But if he or she seems apathetic about being on the bottom tier of hospital service, make a little game of it to pass the time. "I'll bet you a quarter the nurse doesn't come when I call. Just watch." Then your witness will probably remember these incidents.

Once you've documented what amounts to a woeful pattern of neglect, bring it to the attention of your physician. Run Doctor through the points in your log or no-show scorecard and point out that since you aren't getting nursing care in any meaningful sense of the word, you'd like the doctor to order a private twenty-four-hour nurse for you, which should be covered by your insurance. Remind Doctor pleasantly that nursing care is expected of hospitals, and your attorney will take note of its absence if you're forced to seek financial redress from the hospital later on. Your doctor probably won't give you a private nurse, but she is very likely to see that you get better attention from the staff.

The other side of this scenario occurs in an underbooked, marketing-oriented hospital. Here nurses are instructed to virtually kill the patient with kindness. They offer to give your wound a new dressing every forty minutes. They bring you snacks and other amenities. They see that you get flowers delivered if you don't seem to have any friends doing so and even offer to buy you a little something from the gift shop. What they're really doing, of course, is churning your bill up . . . and up . . . and up. If your insurance is paying for all these little niceties, you may see landing in a marketing-oriented hospital as a rare blessing. But if you're paying for them yourself, you may wish to speak to your doctor. Ask her to please instruct those nurses to stop playing Santa's helpers and give you only the care your doctor prescribes, unless you request otherwise.

Which brings up the matter of your physician's performance during your stay. What probably worries your doctor more than anything else in life is the white heat of a malpractice suit and its repercussions for her insurance premiums and good professional name. It's very bad form indeed, and not at all canny, to mouth off about this possibility in any but the most serious circumstances. But since she probably harbors some sensitivity—even paranoia—about it anyway, the implications of your lawyer's check-in letter and the log you're keeping will not go unnoticed. If you still feel that your doctor is mistreating or neglecting you, you should be aware of the legal theories underlying malpractice actions.

1.   failure to diagnose properly

2.   failure to give treatment

3.   failure to obtain informed consent for surgery

4.   battery (in the case of unauthorized surgery)

5.   negligence

Gross improprieties should be reported immediately to your attorney: if, for example, your doctor left some tools or sponges inside after surgery, or if, as happened in one case in which the patient was awarded substantive damages from a hospital, you suffer a burn on your body in the shape of a hot-water bottle. But for run-of-the-mill inattention, the most fruitful area is "negligence," which can cover a ward-full of possibilities. In essence, your doctor must offer you a standard of care consistent with what you'd receive from other doctors in your community. And if your physician is a "specialist," this requires a stricter standard than if she were a general practitioner.

DOCTOR: Hi, there. How are you feeling, Mr. . . . uh . . . (looking at chart) Jones.

PATIENT: I barely recognized you. You shaved off your mustache.

DOCTOR: Oh, yes. A couple of weeks ago.

PATIENT: Doctor, I had the feeling I *was going to see more of you* during my stay here.

DOCTOR: Well, I've got other patients too, y'know.

PATIENT: Yes, and I've found that *I have other doctors, too, I never counted on.* That Israeli fellow and the Bolivian lady have been coming around from time to time.

DOCTOR: Oh yes, damn good doctors, both of them.

PATIENT: Well, I have a very difficult time explaining my symptoms to them. I feel there's *a real language problem.* *

DOCTOR: They wouldn't be here if they weren't damn good doctors, both of them.

PATIENT: I'm sure they are, but I was expecting more *continuity in my treatment.* I've noticed that Smith over there, who's in for the same reason I am, *has a doctor in your same specialty who comes to see him everyday.*

DOCTOR: Heh, heh. Every case is different, Mr. Jones.

PATIENT: I'm sure it is, but I'm *feeling rather neglected* just the same. (Notice the careful use of just the prefix *neg-* at this point.)

Now your doctor may well feel compelled to spend some time justifying your treatment, or at least setting your mind at ease about your condition. Once a physician begins wondering whether she might have some liability if anything were to go wrong with you, you can rest assured that you'll be seeing much more of each other during the remainder of your stay.

FINAL PAYMENTS: DISPUTING A HOSPITAL BILL

If you're completely covered by Blue Cross/Blue Shield or a major medical plan—and you'd better be sure you are before you're admitted—you might be inclined to give your bill a cursory glance and let the insurer pay. That's what the hospital hopes you'll do, anyway. The rare insured patient who questions his or her bill will probably hear some version of "Well, you're not paying for it, right?" But of course you *are* paying for it: in higher premiums.

If you think that fighting for adjustments on your bill will never make a difference to the vast brother- and-sisterhood of BC/BS carriers . . . you're right,

---

* Hospitals love to hire and overwork foreign doctors because they'll take much lower pay than USA-grown physicians. But comprehension problems occur. A Chicago hospital once paid Berlitz $30,000 to give its foreign interns a crash course after they flunked the English-competency exam.

of course. We'll be realistic and admit that if every reader of this book beat every hospital bill acquired over a lifetime down to reality, you'd probably see a savings of about thirteen cents on your premiums over the years. So let's concentrate instead on saving your own money. We'll assume you're covered only partially or not at all.

Haggling with a Hospital. When you pick up your bill, it should be itemized down to the last cotton ball. If it's not broken down to your satisfaction, tell them to do so. That's your legal right. When you look over your bill, scrutinize the charges as carefully as you would an overblown check at La Casa de La Maison House. Chances are good that you'll find errors. You might be charged for somebody else's X-rays, bypass operation, or whatever. In keeping your personal log—when you're conscious, anyway—try to keep as accurate a record of what you're getting as possible. Then see if your account jibes with theirs.

If they make a gross error, like charging you for two weeks on a kidney-dialysis machine when you came in to have a broken ankle set, you can bear down even harder on others you suspect. If something appears that's not on your log, challenge it. If you're in one of those great metropolitan hospitals that make you pay before you leave if you're not insured and they tell you to wait around until they substantiate it, you don't have to.

CLERK: Just have a seat over there until Mr. McGurty comes back from lunch, and we'll try to get those records for you.

INVALID: No, I'm not waiting for Mr. McGurty or anyone else. My *doctor* told me to rest in bed for seven days, and that's what I'm going to do.

CLERK: You can't leave until you pay the bill.

INVALID: You know where I live. Send me a copy of the adjusted bill in the mail.

And walk out. If they try to stop you after you've (1) made a good-faith effort to pay, and (2) told them your doctor strictly advised bed rest, you'd probably have the basis for a nifty false-imprisonment suit against them.

But they won't. They'll bill you, and you can contest it from your invalid's couch. By now you'll presumably have all the records they can come up with to work from.

Preemptive Nonpayment. Now let's assume that your stay has been so hellish, so devoid of the milk of human kindness, that you feel a major adjustment of the bill is in order. You have your log to prove it. (And you *must* have something to substantiate your claim of nonexistent services that you have no intention of paying for.)

If you're the type who likes to avoid confrontation, particularly in a weakened condition, you could accept your bill, give them a check and go home. Then stop payment on your check when you find "irregularities" as you go over it later. This means they'll come after you in hot pursuit of their money. You should talk briefly with your lawyer, anyway, before taking such action and make sure you have a case intact. Then issue the hospital a new check marked "payment in full," which reflects your assessment of what you've actually received, with your supporting documentation of no-service. Maybe they'll see that you're in a position to embarrass them, and take the loss. But more likely the billing department will call.

BILL COLLECTOR: You owe us another $380 for nursing services. It's on your bill.

INVALID: Really? Let's look at the record from day one. April 27, 9 A.M.—called for nurse to change uncomfortably itching five-day-old bandage. No response for two hours. April 27, 3 P.M.—refused to accept medication capsule nurse had dropped on floor. No replacement medication until 8:30 P.M.

And go on until the collector hangs up or tells you they'll take you to court. By and by, you'll probably get a letter from their attorney threatening suit for the disputed balance. Or possibly a phone call:

LAWYER: I have your so-called summary of services billed for but not performed here, but I'll tell you right now you can't just refuse to pay for nursing care.

PATIENT: We'll let a jury decide that.

LAWYER: Are you saying you'll bring suit against us? There's no evidence of negligence here.

PATIENT: I'll let you bring the first suit. But I'll ask for a jury. And I'll certainly take my case to the media as well. But what are you calling me for, anyway?

LAWYER: Well, I can see that you fancy yourself an amateur lawyer—

PATIENT: Stop right there, sir. Don't you have my attorney's letter when I was admitted to the hospital in front of you?

LAWYER: (who was too lazy to look through your whole file) Uh . . . I don't know about any such letter.

PATIENT: Well, you had notification on April 25 that I was represented by an attorney. And you know you're not permitted to call me directly when you should be talking with my lawyer. *

LAWYER: What's his name?

PATIENT: *Her* name is . . .

And let the two lawyers talk. What you've established is that you're likely to be a dedicated and formidable adversary in court—the kind who might best be handled by letting the matter drop quietly before you go public and give other prospective patients the same notion.

REVENGE KIT FOR HOSPITALS

LAWYER CHECK-IN LETTER

To: Hospital Administrator
Address:

Re: _____(Your Name)_____
Date of Admission: _____

Dear Mr./Ms. _____,

Please be advised that I have been contacted by _____in regard to his/her admission to your hospital set for _____.

Unless contravened in writing, this letter will operate as a legally binding memorandum of your agreement with my client as to his/her accommodations at the hospital and the cost associated therewith.

It is agreed that my client will have a "semi-private" room, which is defined as a room with no more than one other

---

* A violation of bar-association guidelines. If you're represented by an attorney, the other party's lawyer can't contact you personally. That's taking advantage of a lay person.

patient. He/she will be charged a flat rate of $_____ _____ per day, which sum will totally cover room expenses, food, and all nursing care. In the event optional services are desired, you will explain to him/her the cost therefor and indicate available alternative services before any such optional service is performed. At the end of his/her stay, you will present an itemized bill for all services rendered and document all charges not a part of the flat rate.

Of course, I expect that your staff will give my client the care that is consistent with your legal duty and his/her rights as a patient.

Very truly yours,

SAMPLE ENTRIES FOR
LOG BOOK

<u>Event</u>

4/1/8_   6:30 P.M.   I asked for choice #2 on dinner menu, i.e., the Mexican Fiesta special. I was served Sour Beef & Dumplings, which were cold and inedible.

4/2/8_   7:30 P.M.   Called Dr. _____at 3:00 P.M. His service told me he was making a house call. When he visited me later at 6:45 P.M., the doctor told me he was playing golf at that time. Apparently, he has instructed his staff and service to misrepresent his whereabouts.

LETTER DISPUTING BILL

To: Bill Department
    Hospital
Address:
Date:
          Re: (Your name) _____
          Date: _____

Dear Sir:

Reference is made to the incorrect bill you sent me, dated
_____. I note that I was charged for crutches,
which I find odd in that I was in the hospital for an ear
operation. As well, per your acceptance of the letter of my
lawyer, _____, dated _____, you are under
duty to document all charges in excess of aggregate flat rate.

One final point: I kept an accurate log of the services I
received during my stay, which disclosed that four different
meals were either mixed up or cold and inedible when I
received them. Specific notations are enclosed. Please delete
the cost of those four meals from your flat-rate fee.

                    Very truly yours,

18
insurance companies

Carving a Bigger Piece of the Rock

It seems a lot of you people out there
don't like us very much.

—Headline from a Travelers
Insurance Company ad

Travelers was right. People just don't like insurance companies. And why
should they? Their usual experience is to pay premiums religiously for several
years, send in a claim, and find that the company has shut itself up like a
violated clam when it comes to making good on its promises. All those ads
purring "you're in good hands" or inviting you to "own a piece of the rock"
promise peace of mind: if you're robbed, hospitalized or whatever, you can pull
that dusty policy out of the bottom drawer and claim the "protection" that's
rightfully yours. The reality, however, is that insurance companies apply a
different standard of prompt and full payment to their accounts payable (your
claims) than they do to their accounts receivable (your premiums).

An insurance company won't tolerate your premiums arriving three months
late and would not allow you to invent an arbitrary formula to reduce your
premium payment to half of what you agreed to pay. But that's exactly what
they'll do to you if they're forced to open up their own coffers. For example, if
you're burglarized and file a carefully documented claim for a $7,000 loss, you
won't receive the check for $7,000 by return mail as you'd reasonably expect.
What you're likely to receive instead is an endless stream of correspondence
from the company contesting the value of items you've lost and visits from
adjusters who seem to be in business only to adjust claims downward. Once an
insurance company feels you've been sufficiently humbled, their "final offer"
amounts to a fraction of your actual loss. That is, if they offer to pay anything at
all.

Some companies are clever enough to write *exclusions* into their policies that
effectively insure them against claims. For example, there is the clause in those
"no medical exam required" mail-order policies targeted to older consumers
that excludes "preexisting" conditions. By the time you reach sixty-five or so,

the medical problems that see you hospitalized probably exist to some degree already.

Before you rush to your policy to check its terms, bear in mind that company lawyers have labored hard to conceal their limitations in language few lay people can fathom. Herbert Denenberg, Pennsylvania's State Insurance Commissioner, once measured the readability of insurance contracts on a scale of 1 to 100—the more easily understood, the higher the score. He found that insurance policies earned scores of 10 to −2. For comparison purposes, Einstein's theory of relativity received an 18 on the same scale.

If insurance companies seem to be holding most of the aces in their policymaking bets with you, you still have two hole cards to play. One is directed at your insurance broker, who is the most vulnerable link in the insurance industry's ironclad defenses. The other aims squarely at the company itself, which can find itself liable for heavy damages when it tries to play bureaucratic monolith to stall or squash your legitimate claim.

PREEMPTIVE STRATEGIES: BUYING INSURANCE LIKE AN INDUSTRY EXPERT

Let's see how people who know the twists and turns of this industry protect themselves from paying too much and receiving too little from different types of coverage.

You Bet Your Life. The paradox of life insurance is that you never really want to win this gamble with the insurance company. That would mean dying early enough to make a profit over what you've paid out in premiums. Aware of your ambivalence on this issue, insurance salespeople resort to two selling appeals: (1) forcing you to feel guilty about shortchanging your family in the event of your unexpected demise, or (2) forcing you to save by buying a "cash value" policy that lets you accumulate a nest egg over the years from exorbitant premiums. Since both arguments involve force, you should exert equal strength in turning them down, because both rest on—for most people—premises that only serve the insurance company's interests.

Only about 17 percent of Americans now fall into the traditional one-wage-earner, two-children type of family structure. Most people are single or, if they are married, live in two-income households. If you don't belong in the first category and you're relatively young, we question the need for a $50,000 to $100,000 life insurance policy! If your spouse insists, we suggest you watch the next rerun of *Double Indemnity*. You will probably be better off buying a less expensive policy and investing the money you save.

We strongly advise against a "cash value" life insurance policy. This is a favorite of insurance salespeople, because the premiums are high and they get a commission windfall. Instead, you'll find a better deal in "term" life insurance:

this lets you buy a policy at much lower premiums for a fixed term. Salespeople will pitch a cash-value policy by explaining that it forces you to save, and you'll have a pile of money later on. The catch is that cash-value policies pay about 3 to 5 percent actual return on your accumulated savings. You would earn a bigger return in virtually any kind of investment other than stuffing your mattress. This usually inspires a heroic appeal to your "better" instincts on the salesperson's part.

> SALESPERSON: Ah, yes, you say you'll invest that money somewhere else. *But will you really?* (Knowing grin.) Or will you just throw it away on some new furniture?

To which you should reply:

> FRIVOLOUS: I'd rather sit on new furniture today than on a policy that'll be worth about a quarter of its face value twenty years from now.

This may compel the salesperson to leap to an argument based on the deceitful "net-cost method" of adding up premiums and deducting your cash-value dividends, without taking into account the interest you've lost.

> SALESPERSON: Yes, but here's what you'll pay out in premiums over the years and here's what you'll get back in dividends—look, it comes out the same! Your insurance coverage all those years is actually *free!*

> SAVVY: No it's not. You're assuming I couldn't have been earning a lot more interest on that money somewhere else. Let me see the cost of this policy calculated on an interest-adjusted basis.

> (The more honest method gaining reluctant acceptance in the industry.)

Where you'll find the best buys in term life insurance these days depends on where you live. If you're in New York, Connecticut, or Massachusetts, you can buy Savings Bank Life Insurance (SBLI) at rates well below the standard national insurance companies'. If SBLI is not available write to your state insurance commission for a comparison of costs—calculated on the interest-adjusted method—for the companies doing business in your state.

Healthier Medical Coverage. If your employer doesn't offer you health protection, you should buy your own coverage through the same method a less-stingy employer would—the group plan. There are considerably more groups that will admit you under their umbrella than you think, and a good insurance agent should be able to show you a list of possibilities.

When you buy health insurance, you can save premium costs by turning down unnecessary coverage. Remember that the usual hospital stay is seven or eight days, not the year spent at County General that some policies ask you to pay high premiums for. Look for a policy with a low deductible for the same reason. Some plans try to steer you to a high deductible, which means you'll wind up paying for many of the costs you're likely to incur in the typically short hospital stay. One word of advice—especially for all of you who live in a stressful big-city environment—make sure your policy covers treatment for alcoholism and mental illness. You never know.

We would avoid those mail-order health plans (which are now being feverishly pitched on television) because their premiums are usually high and the exclusions to coverage are legion. Cancer and other catastrophic illness policies are poor risks, too—they're expensive, and they generally duplicate coverage you already have in a regular plan.

Home Policies. Whether you live in a house or an apartment, the odds of your home being burgled are probably greater than those of a fire occurring or your mail carrier breaking an arm in your mailbox while trying to find a Christmas tip. It's important to have adequate coverage for all three possibilities, but concentrate on low-deductible coverage for the theft problem. Bear in mind that a policy should also cover any personal property that is stolen when you're away from home, whether it's from your car, your hotel, or even your wallet on the beach. Make sure you buy a *floater*, that is, additional coverage beyond the basic policy, to protect expensive goods like antiques or valuable paintings. These truly important items are probably excluded from your basic policy, although the language of the policy won't indicate that clearly. If you're not sure, *ask!*

If you live in a neighborhood that has a high crime rate, you may well be turned down for coverage by some public-spirited insurance companies. If that is the case, you can apply for Federal Crime Insurance through your insurance broker.

If you want to save money on home coverage bought from an insurance company, you should write for the results of a comparison study conducted by the Missouri Department of Consumer Affairs, Jefferson City, Missouri 65102. Ask for a free copy of *The Consumer Shopping Guide for Homeowners and Renters Insurance*. It reveals that some companies charge three times as much as others for the same coverage.

Of late, a new problem has been occurring recently when unmarried people who live together want to buy homeowners' or apartment dwellers' coverage. Some insurance agents advise that a policy should be listed in only one person's name to avoid offending the insurance companies' delicate sensibilities about cohabitation. One of the authors followed that sage advice when he and his girl friend shared an apartment. They placed the coverage under his girl friend's name, since she held the lease. That all worked out nicely until the apartment was robbed, and the author documented his own property losses under the clause in her policy that covered the insured's "guests." But insurance companies abide by flexible morality standards. In this case, they said, both parties should have been listed on the policy. And they tried to disallow not only the author's own possessions but an expensive stereo purchased in the author's name. This was only resolved when the author pointed out that the stereo was bought as a gift for his girl friend. The adjuster grudgingly conceded that if the case went to court, the judge would probably agree that the stereo as a gift would have to be covered, but when it came to the question of the author's stolen clothing and sundries, the company steadfastly refused to budge.

This problem was resolved only by retaining the services of a "public adjuster" to sort out the dispute and obtain a better settlement than the insurance company representative would let you think was even remotely possible. If you're not shocked to find out that cash payments made under the table to insurance-company employees often expedite matters, we leave it to your own conscience and desperation to explore that option, too. But we still recommend the public adjuster. Ask your agent for a referral. The public adjuster's usual commission is 10 percent of the final settlement, and as the majority of cases go, we think it's well worth the price.

Based on this experience and a consensus among agents, we suggest purchasing a policy under both unmarried persons' names. If the company balks, find another company that will oblige you. You might want to hire a public adjuster *before* you actually file a claim to guide you through the process of itemizing your losses properly and then negotiating the best settlement.

Whatever your marital status, the most important safeguard you can undertake is to make up a thorough inventory of each item of any value in your home. When you have to stake a claim, you'll need a meticulously well documented record of your losses to impress the company. Find receipts to substantiate your personal property. Then take clear close-up photographs of your possessions, making a comprehensive list with original costs, and obtain appraisals of valuable antiques, jewelry, and artwork. Have the whole packet notarized as a sworn affidavit. Then keep the original documents in a bank safe deposit box, and keep a copy at home. (Some burglars with a nasty sense of humor will steal your records if they find them.) If you later file a claim, always send a *copy* to the insurance company, never the original. (See the Revenge Kit for a sample document.)

If you do suffer a grievous loss through robbery, remember to file a comprehensive list of what you've lost with the police. You usually have a few days to pull this together. Make sure it matches the list you submit to the insurance company. And be sure to include whatever *cash* you have around the home—that little nest egg you might be saving in the cookie jar or whatever loose bills you might have left in your suit jacket. Most claimants, surprisingly, forget about household cash in the agony of the moment, even though the police will remind you more than once to make an accurate cash accounting after they arrive.

Driving a Harder Bargain on Car Insurance. Premiums for auto insurance can vary wildly, depending on where your car is insured, your driving record, and the company that covers you. And there are plenty of ways to knock down costs in each category.

First, use your sophistication in deciding where your car should be garaged and registered, which is often the factor insurance companies apply to find your rate. If you happen to have an apartment in a high-risk-rated city and a weekend or summer place in a low-rated rural area, it doesn't take much imagination to figure out where the car should be insured. But most drivers enjoy only one residence. What can they do to lower their rates? Many people have close relatives in some outlying area register the car in their names. Others rent garages in rural areas because they use the car primarily for leisurely Sunday drives. The car is registered where it's garaged. We're not advising you to make misrepresentations to an insurance company but we do recommend that you assess where your car will be driven most of the time. Insurance rates are often pegged to your driving record and violations. If you've run afoul of some local speed limit or were picked up once with a cocktail or two under your belt, you should refer to our chapter on Driving Violations for a detailed discussion of how to keep your driving record clean and your insurance rates low. But if you were the model of safety-first your instructor held up to the rest of the class in driver's ed, you can qualify for a reduction in premiums from many companies.

This leaves the choice of insurance company. One of the authors owns a Jeep CJ7 (which, if you've read Chapter 7 on Automobiles, you can well imagine is not the insurance actuary's dream car). By shopping carefully, he obtained rate estimates that ranged from over $1000 (Aetna) to less than $400 (Nationwide), and understandably put the man from Nationwide on his side. So get at least ten estimates from different agents by telephone before you sign—it's worth the trouble. Bear in mind, however, that insurance companies can afford to offer lower rates if they routinely stiff customers who put in claims. A recent *Consumer Reports* study compared different companies on the percentage of claims settled to customers' satisfaction and found, for example, that State Farm Insurance Company scored at the highest end and Allstate at the lowest. (Allstate, however, grumbled in reply that their customers tend to live in urban areas and are thus more likely to complain and sue.) To draw your own conclusions, write to the New York State Insurance Department for its latest list of auto insurance companies rated by number of complaints per $1 million in premiums collected. Their address is: 2 World Trade Center, New York, N.Y. 10047.

Putting Teeth in Your Claim
to Force a Better Settlement

As noted earlier, multimillion-dollar companies can wield impressive might in stalling, contesting, and beating down your claim. But there are two vulnerabilities you can turn to your advantage—the broker's self-interest and the insurance company's desire to avoid costly *punitive-damage* lawsuits.

Broker-Squeezing Tactics. Many insurance agents who become aggressive tigers when closing a sale take on the weary resignation of Morris the cat when it comes time to help you press your claim with the company. So your first objective should be to find one who carries some clout with the companies he or she represents. This tends to eliminate single-company *agents*, who may have to get their resumés together if they become too offensive with their employers. Instead, you should find an *independent broker* who will do battle, if sufficiently motivated, to the point of threatening to write no more business with a carrier that won't satisfy his or her customers. And the more business a broker does with the companies he or she keeps, the stronger the impetus will be for a carrier to settle your claim reasonably and avoid losing future customers from that broker.

Thus Rule #1 is to find a well-placed, successful broker who's considered a hero at every company's home office. You can generally find such a broker by calling an insurance company you've chosen for its low rates and responsive claims performance to ask for recommended brokers in your area. Then call them and ask, in the course of outlining your insurance needs, how many different companies they represent and how much business they do with them. The very successful broker will want to brag about it; the less successful will hedge. Go with the biggest braggart in town.

Rule #2 involves using the broker's own solid reputation as your leverage against him. If a broker is making a lot of money, it's generally because he's devoted a lot of time to high-level glad-handing in the community, serving on Lion's Club committees, and other strategies for becoming highly visible and respected. So everyone in town with a bulging ego who thinks he or she needs a million-dollar life-insurance policy will think of that broker first.

With high visibility and a rock-solid reputation as his primary success forces, what might such a broker's Achilles heel be? If you guessed a wave of bad publicity that could severely damage his reputation, we're ready to talk strategy.

Insurance brokers are professionals. They're licensed by the state to give sound advice to people who don't know much about insurance but whose very livelihoods may hinge on a broker's recommendations. You might see the potential for malpractice creeping in here. Brokers certainly see the possibility, and they carry malpractice insurance to cover the unlikely situation in which they'll be sued. We say "unlikely" because (1) there aren't many gross errors of fraud or negligence that can be proven, and (2) people just don't think in terms of suing insurance brokers. But let's say that thought drifted through your mind. On what grounds might a suit be brought?

First of all, a broker could misrepresent the cost or benefits of a policy, perhaps unintentionally, by showing you the wrong *illustrations* in selling you coverage. *Illustration* is the industry term for those custom-tailored charts you are shown to indicate what your particular premiums will be for a specific set of benefits. Some brokers prepare their own, and some have computer service bureaus prepare them. Either way, there's always the possibility for errors in adding up those tiresome numbers. So it will pay to check your broker's representations against another broker's illustration for the exact same coverage.

Then there's an outside chance your broker plays fast and loose with the rules of the insurance game. For example, the majority of people who will buy insurance already have unless they're still in their senior year of high school. So to write new business, brokers often have to see policy holders covered by other companies to make the switch to one of their own companies. They're not supposed to come right out and steal those customers away from the competition. This quandary can inspire some brokers to break the rules and do it anyway. And one improper incentive such brokers might use is to offer an under-the-table *rebate* to the customer who'll cancel existing policies to pick up theirs. One company agent in a recent case offered to rebate the cost of a customer's first-year premiums if the customer would cancel two $250,000 life-insurance policies and place the same coverage with the agent. But his customer, with what degree of naivete we do not know, blew the whistle, and the agent was brought up on industry charges. So keep this in mind and be prepared to write up the facts for future reference if a broker tries too hard to woo you away from a policy you already hold.

Let's assume, however, that your broker is too conscientious and honorable to commit either of these gross errors. There's still the broad realm of possibility for creative litigation, even if you don't take it to court. Stockbrokers, you'll recall, are expected to base their recommendations on sound judgment, taking into consideration your own degree of sophistication about the market. We're sure that most insurance brokers think of themselves as no less professional than stockbrokers. And that's the level of liability we should hold them to.

So you might want to exchange some written correspondence with your broker that establishes your *reliance* on his statements about these key criteria you've set for buying a policy:

1.   That a recommended insurance company's rates are among the industry's lowest for comparable coverage.

2.   That the same company has established an excellent performance record for resolving claims to their customers' satisfaction—in terms of prompt

payment that reflects a carefully substantiated, not arbitrary, assessment of actual losses.

See the Revenge Kit for a sample letter which should elicit a written reply you can put to good use when you're having trouble settling a claim. Say you've been back and forth with the company already and you've asked your broker to jump in and help. He finally calls you back two weeks later.

BROKER: Hey, good news! I went to the mats with the company and got them to commit to $6,000.

POLICYHOLDER: That's still only 60 percent of my loss. My claim was for $10,000.

BROKER: Well, they just couldn't give you the full value you claimed for that collection of 1939 World's Fair ashtrays you lost in the fire. So they cut it in half. And they depreciated those rare cactus plants that burned up 50 percent, too, since they were four years old. But I'd really advise you to take the $6,000. I think it's generous.

POLICYHOLDER: I'm glad you brought that up. Your advice, I mean.

BROKER: How's that?

POLICYHOLDER: Well, I've been doing some research into this company you recommended and discussing what I found with my lawyer. We talked about the company's stalling and the arbitrary way they're knocking down my claim, vis-à-vis the representations in *your* letter about that company's excellent performance in settling promptly and reasonably. We explored the male cactus issue pretty fully.

BROKER: Malpractice? Look . . . I won't be held responsible for the company's . . .

POLICYHOLDER: No, no. The *male cactus* that was worth $1,000. I'll just tell you the facts as I see them. You said the company's rates were substantially the lowest I could get on my coverage. But I got a report from the Missouri State Department of Consumer Affairs that indicates it's one of the more expensive for homeowners' policies. And I talked with two other insurance people recently who indicated that other companies' rates were lower.

BROKER: Well, I don't know what some other guy's going to tell you, but my experience with the company—

POLICYHOLDER: Just hear me out. And I discovered from writing to the New York State Insurance Commission that this company has one of the poorer records for resolving claims in that state. To put it bluntly, I don't think that information and my own lousy experience with the company jibes with the representations you made to me in your letter.

BROKER: I told you that I call 'em as I see 'em. It's my own opinion—

POLICYHOLDER: Yes, your professional judgment, and I relied on it. But just one more point. I also know you're very well thought of as a broker, and I don't want to get into a bitter hassle with you *personally* over this thing. Least of all going to court with you . . .

BROKER: You're barking up the wrong tree if you think—

POLICYHOLDER: *Please* let me finish. All I'm asking right now is that you use your influence with this company, which I know is substantial, to get them to be a little more reasonable. I'll even take $8,000, but $6,000 is just unconscionable.

BROKER: Well, let me see what I can do. But I'm not promising anything.

POLICYHOLDER: I'd appreciate it if you could call me back by this time tomorrow. I'll be seeing my lawyer on another matter, and I'd like to tell him this problem is resolved.

Your insurance broker won't love you for this, but if the money's more important to you, you've given him much to think about. Notice the liberal sprinkling of terms he'll assume you could only have picked up from a lawyer's ominous interest in your dealings with him: "the *representations* in your letter"

. . . "the company's rates were *substantially* the lowest" . . . "your *professional judgment*, and I *relied* on it" . . . and so on. Note, too, your quick reference to his reputation in the community and the specter of a "bitter hassle with you *personally*" in practically the same breath as the word "court."

But you also gave him a clear escape hatch from this mounting gloom—the dollar amount you'd actually settle for, and your awareness of his clout with the company. So it will definitely be to his advantage to go back to the mats with every stranglehold he can muster. For $2,000, which is a lot more to you than to a company that values his business, you've certainly left him a more attractive alternative than a suit that could damage his valuable reputation in the community.

But if all these gentle warnings were to no avail, you should have your lawyer write a variation of the letter in the Revenge Kit setting down your position more forcefully. We think if the insurance company really is giving you less than they should, that he'll get the message.

Motivating the Monolith. Now let's assume that you already have a problem with an insurer and you don't happen to have the world's hottest agent or broker—as you've found out through his or her feeble intervention, which the company seems to whisk aside without fear of reprisals. You can still take on the company directly and intimidate them—strange as that may seem when you compare your relative size and resources—into taking your claim much more seriously.

The law views an insurance company that accepts your premium money but toys with your legitimate claims as a more deserving target for revenge than, say, the department store that won't deliver your new couch on time. The reasons are (1) it's your life and livelihood they're playing with—a much higher expectation for performance than a department store will ever have to worry about, and (2) you're not trying to make any profit from an insurance company but just relying on them to do what they've promised when catastrophe strikes. So when an insurance company's high-handed tactics compel you to sue them, they receive very little sympathy from most judges. And we've already explored the kind of treatment they can expect from a jury of your peers.

We know that most consumer guides tell you to take your case directly to your state insurance commission first. This is the only regulatory agency available to discipline the companies, since their friends in Congress have argued well against federal regulation. Or they tell you to shake the prospect of your filing a complaint before the company's nose so they'll settle up before having to face the wrath of the commissioner.

We don't share this trust in your state insurance commission. In fact, we don't think you can count on the commission to do much of anything but push a few papers at the company and wait for more papers to come back. Some insurance commissions may be firebrands. But many of them are clubfooted bureaucracies that can make your insurance company look sparky. The plain reason is that they're staffed with insurance people—slow-moving people whose friends still run the company you want them to punish. Besides, insurance companies get complaints via the state commission every day. It's not exactly the sort of scare tactic to make an insurance-company executive choke on his danish.

If you want to try anyway, your commission can be found in the White Pages of your phone directory under state offices. But we would advise you to use the Yellow Pages to find an aggressive young lawyer instead, the kind who's itching for combat with a bully over a good case, which we'll assume you have.

The carrot for the attorney—and for you, too—is that he or she will probably try an inexpensive letter first. And if that doesn't work, you may be able to sue the company for *punitive* damages based on the crippling anxiety you may have suffered over their callous indifference to your claim. Your lawyer will probably take a worthwhile case on contingency, because a finding in your favor with a punitive-damage award can be very rewarding. (In one case in which an insurance company caused a claimant a great deal of grief by trying to deny his health-coverage payments due to a "preexisting medical condition"—of the company's own invention—the jury awarded nearly $200,000.) The lawyer's fees are paid by the company if and when you win.

The key questions here are:

Has the company really acted unreasonably in delaying or contesting payment of your claim?

Have you suffered demonstrable mental (or physical) damage as a result of their unreasonable behavior?

If your answers to both are yes, and they are delivered from a psychiatrist's couch to which you've retreated for comfort, you may have a case.

In any event, we think that this prospect waved under the company's arrogant nose will persuade them to settle your claim to your satisfaction faster than any polite letter to the president of the company or complaint to the state commission.

Revenge Kit for Insurance

SAMPLE LETTER TO BROKER
ASKING FOR A RECOMMENDATION
IN WRITING

To: Broker
Address:
Date:

Dear Mr./Ms. ———————,

As I discussed with you over the telephone, I am interested in buying (type of insurance) to cover (extent of protection). Since I'm not familiar with the policies offered in this area or the performance records of companies who provide coverage, please make a recommendation based on (1) the lowest comparable rates for the protection I need, and (2) the record this company has established for timely and reasonable claims settlement.

Thank you for your help. I'm looking forward to working with you.

Very truly yours,

SAMPLE FINAL LETTER TO
BROKER APPLYING PRESSURE
FOR A CLAIMS SETTLEMENT

To: Broker
Address:
Date:

Dear Mr./Ms. ———————,

As you know, I purchased (coverage) from (insurance company) based upon the representation you made in your letter of (date) attached hereto.

I relied solely on your professional judgment in making the decision to buy this policy. You asserted that the company's rates were among the lowest for comparable coverage. I have found the contrary to be true, based on (name and attach documentation such as the Missouri Department of Consumer Affairs Comparison Study cited in the chapter).

But of even greater importance to me in deciding to act upon your professional recommendation, you asserted that this company had established a record of timely and reasonable claim settlements.

The attached document suggests that this company, in fact, has established one of the worst records of complaints per premium dollars collected. (Attach documentation such as the New York State Insurance Department ratings discussed in the chapter.)

I now feel that I have relied on your advice to my detriment, since (detail company's reluctance to pay your reasonable claim, with dates and supporting documents).

Thus I request and urge you to use your influence with this company to honor my claim immediately and in full before I am forced to commence legal action. I must point out that I will consider all my options for recovery in this matter, including possible action based upon my reliance on your recommendation.

Please contact me within five (5) business days so we can resolve this matter amicably.

Very truly yours,

Certified Letter

PART VI

Vengeance on the Move

19
airlines

Enforcing Friendly Skies

Talk about "creative" advertising . . . If airline performance matched the high-altitude bliss sung about in their commercials, who'd ever want to come back to earth? Those fatherly captains discussing the finer points of their craft as if you knew a horizontal stabilizer from a hood ornament. Beaming flight attendants bubbling over with the fun of pouring your champagne and fluffing up your pillow. Luggage handlers pampering your bags with the white-glove treatment usually reserved for the Mona Lisa on tour.

The truth is that most people find a yawning chasm between how airline people perform on camera and off. Air travel today is mass transit: You wait in long lines, luggage disappears, then shows up a week later pummeled beyond recognition; and the flight attendants often look more irritated than you are. To protect themselves from angry consumers, airline lawyers have developed a complicated set of *tariffs*, with the help of the government. These rules supposedly regulate all airline practices but mainly limit their liability in redressing grievances. You can ask to see the tariff books, which must by law be kept at ticket counters. But you'd have to be an airline lawyer to understand them. We'll spell out the ones you can wield like a club here. You'll also meet the Civil Aeronautics Board (CAB), the regulatory agency that advises you of your rights and can sometimes come in handy when you need help pressing a claim.

The Flight: Demanding Preferential Treatment As Your Due

Reserving a More Comfortable Seat. You might have noticed that airline seats seem to be snuggling closer to your knees and squeezing more tightly around your hips. Airlines are just meeting the greater demand for air travel and compensating for higher fuel costs by yanking out the seats from time to time and replacing them with more and smaller ones.

If you're flying coach, you can't specify a wider seat. But you can ensure more legroom by choosing a seat directly behind the divider bulkheads or service areas, which offer more room to stretch. Take advantage of "preseating" by specifying one of those seats when you make your reservation.

Ordering Better Meals. Have you ever sat picking at a miserly, tasteless breast of airline chicken served up on a flight and noticed that your seatmate was enjoying a handsome crab salad? Virtually all airlines will substitute kosher, diet dishes, or seafood if you ask. Just put in your order when you make your reservation. If the reservation clerk pleads ignorance, call the airline's local business office and find out what's available.

Using VIP Lounges. Most airlines maintain lounges with a well-stocked bar, hassle-free check-in, and better company than you'll meet in the spartan waiting rooms and overcrowded airport bars. Contrary to popular belief, you can become a VIP and get in yourself for a moderate fee.

If you travel frequently enough to justify it—and more than three or four flights a year present a convincing case—why not pay the twenty-five to fifty dollars for annual membership and be good to yourself. The better-known clubs are TWA's Ambassador Club, Pan Am's Clipper Club, American's Admiral Club, and United's Red Carpet Club. Call the local business office for details.

Declaring a No-Smoking Area. If you're a nonsmoker who suffers mightily in a clutch of tobacco addicts, the CAB feels for you. They've come up with a little-known regulation giving you the right, if all nonsmoking seats are full, to demand that your immediate surroundings be designated a nonsmoking area. Just tell the check-in clerk or flight attendant and ask him or her to give the bad news to your seatmates.

One word of warning, though: the smokers around you are not likely to sympathize. And it's not their fault you wound up in their section. You might even prompt a noisy confrontation, so this strategy isn't for the timid. On one Eastern Airlines shuttle flight, a nonsmoking lawyer asserted his rights but the smokers around him refused to comply. Their shouting match grew so disruptive that the captain finally told them to knock it off or he would land the plane in Baltimore. They didn't, so he did. The result was a planeload of fuming passengers glaring at the nonsmoker who started it all as they tried to find connections from the wrong airport.

What to Do When Your Flight Is Delayed or Canceled

One of the rules airlines lawyers cleverly wrote into the tariff books states that carriers may postpone or cancel flights without prior notice or great liability for hardships created. The CAB notes that this practice draws the greatest number of passenger complaints, since you might have to miss your next connection, spend hours in a strange airport, or change your vacation plans.

Outsmarting the Creeper. If your flight is delayed, you might fall victim to a trick of the trade known as The Creeper. Here the airline has a problem of its own that doesn't affect other carriers, like something wrong with the "equipment." (Planes are called "equipment," in curious airline jargon.) Knowing that the delay might last hours, the carrier will announce a twenty-minute delay, then another thirty-minute delay, and so on, hoping that you won't immediately switch to another airline's flight. If you feel this ploy creeping up on you and you have a full-fare ticket, check the board to see what other flights are going your way, change your ticket, and leave your first carrier's more trusting passengers behind.

Cancellation Comforts. If your flight is canceled, you're entitled to a guaranteed seat on the next available flight even if that means you go first class and they pick up the cost difference. Point out to the agent that you're aware of this rule.

And if your flight delay or cancellation means you'll have to wait for four hours or more, you can invoke CAB Tariff # 142, Rule 380. This states that the airline must provide you with certain free "amenities" (unless they succeeded in notifying you before you left for the airport). These include:

1.   meals for passengers who would have been given one on the flight

2.   hotel rooms for passengers who don't live in that city, if the delay occurs between 10 P.M. and 6 A.M.

3.   transportation between the airport and your hotel or home.

4.   a long-distance phone call (3-minute maximum)

Sometimes the available staff don't know this rule and what you're entitled to, or they just don't want the annoyance of offering amenities. In this case, ask them to pull out the tariff book, refer to Rule 380, and read them your rights.

HOW TO PROFIT WHEN YOU'RE BUMPED FROM A FLIGHT

If you've ever made an airline reservation and failed to show up for a flight without notifying them, shame on you. That's the reason airlines use to justify a standard practice called overbooking—taking more reservations than they can handle for crowded flights, assuming that a computer-projected number of no-shows will guarantee a full plane. (Actually some reservation agents contribute to the problem by being overly aggressive about taking reservations. Call for fare information, and you're likely to find yourself booked on a flight. Then it's your responsibility to cancel.) At any rate, your reservation may be worthless if you have the misfortune to show up for a busy flight and everyone else did, too.

While the airlines claim that a minuscule percentage of passengers is ever bumped involuntarily from a flight, it could happen to you. It happens to roughly 100,000 passengers every year. And it happened to Ralph Nader, whose lawsuit against Allegheny Airlines prompted a change in the rules for inconvenienced passengers.

Bumping for Dollars. Now you can "volunteer" to be bumped from a flight and receive compensation amounting to:

1.   A seat guaranteed on the next available flight. Before you volunteer, though, find out when the next available flight on which you can be *confirmed* leaves—it could become hairy during holiday periods.

2.   A bonus offered by the carrier, which can be $100 or more. Sometimes you can negotiate for a higher amount if they're having a hard time finding volunteers. Start at $250 and see what happens if this seems to be the case. (One carrier, Eastern Airlines, takes "conditional" reservations on fully booked flights, which they call Leisure Class. If you can't get on, they'll give you a free ticket on the next available flight.)

Bumping for Bigger Dollars. But what if you're involuntarily bumped because the airline couldn't find enough volunteers? In this event, you'll be able to extract Denied Boarding Compensation, which must be paid to you immediately by check:

1.   A bonus payment equal to the cost of the ticket (maximum $200)

2.   A bonus of twice the cost of your ticket (maximum $400) if they can't squeeze you on a flight that will get you there within two hours of your scheduled arrival for domestic flights or four hours for international flights.

In any case, the airline must show you a written statement of your rights if they're about to bump you, and you can decide whether you want to volunteer. How will the airline decide who gets left behind if there aren't enough volunteers? First come, first served is the general policy, so come early if you're worried about arriving at your destination on time.

Say you feel that the CAB's rules wouldn't be adequate compensation for an involuntary bumping that causes you great financial loss or unusual suffering. Bear in mind that the CAB just spells out the *minimum* liabilities for carriers. You can always try to negotiate a healthier settlement by contacting the airline's complaint department. Or, as we'll get to later, you can take them to court. Ralph Nader won $25,000 because his bumping caused him to miss an important lecture. But remember that was, well, Ralph Nader. If you're contemplating suit for more than five hundred dollars or so, consult a lawyer.

Tricky Exceptions. Watch out for these exceptions to the bumping rules, though: When you make a reservation, they normally tell you to check in one hour (or sixty minutes) before flight time. What they don't tell you is that if you don't comply, you can be bumped without compensation. Some airlines require you to be at the gate ten minutes before departure. Ask about their policy. If the flight is delayed or canceled, the rules discussed in the last section apply. If you're left behind because the airline substituted a smaller plane or if (not very likely) government employees have to travel on emergency business, you can be bumped without penalty to the airline. And if you're flying a foreign airline that's technically supposed to honor CAB rulings on overbookings to or from US points, recognize that some take a cavalier attitude toward compliance.

How to Strike Back When They Damage or Lose Your Luggage

Since luggage takes a more hazardous route to your destination than you do, running a gauntlet of mechanical devices, forklifts, and handlers with rough ways and occasional larceny in their hearts, don't become too unglued when a bag gets lost or damaged. You'll be compensated adequately if you plan carefully and follow through.

First of all, plan to take the really valuable items on board yourself in your carryon luggage. Then pay an extra $1.30 to buy extended-liability coverage for $2000 worth of baggage (more if what you've packed is worth more). And most important, keep an impressive file of receipts to back up your claim if anything becomes missing. When you check the luggage in, remember to declare "excess valuation" to buy the additional coverage—the first $750 of coverage is free, and you can purchase additional increments at 10¢ per $100. If you don't declare the excess, the airline liability is limited to $750 per passenger on domestic flights and $400 on international flights.

Whatever else you do, never lose your claim check—your only uncontestable proof that luggage was really checked. The airlines have to deal with a certain amount of fraud and will make things unbelievably torturous if you don't build a proper case.

Making Them Pay for Your Inconvenience. If your luggage doesn't reach your destination with you, maybe it's just delayed. Report the missing bag(s) immediately to an airline rep at the airport, get his or her name, and fill out their form, noting your excess-valuation coverage. Now you're entitled to charge the airline for "reasonable" expenses or damages.

What's reasonable? It depends on how far you are from home and how long it takes to replace your bag. But a friend of ours once arrived in New York from California for an important meeting. He was wearing jeans and tennis shoes on the plane. His bag was delayed, with all his clothes. And, naturally, he couldn't show up dressed as he was for a meeting with potential investors in his company. So he bought a suitable suit ($380 with 12-hour tailoring service), shoes ($120), and accessories ($45) right at the hotel and gave the airline the bills. The airline paid, even though his bag turned up one week later. His claim was "reasonable" because he bought the clothes he needed at the hotel where he was staying, rather than spending the same amount on a shopping spree at far-flung stores. The latter might have been contested. And his purchases weren't out of line for his station in life and the occasion.

When in doubt, never ask the airline whether they'll pay for a specific purchase. Naturally they'll say no. Just buy whatever's reasonable and give them the bill.

AIRLINE REPRESENTATIVE:	What's this? Seventy-five dollars for a bathing suit?
WOMAN PASSENGER:	You're lucky you lost my bag when I was coming to Puerto Rico. If you'd lost it in Montreal, I would have needed a winter coat.
REPRESENTATIVE:	Well, yes, I guess so.
PASSENGER:	And here's the bill for my new evening dress. I couldn't go to the casino in my bathing suit . . .

Once your bag has been officially declared lost, make sure you keep your claim check and ticket. As soon as you get home, put together the documentation of your receipts for what was inside your luggage. (Carriers usually limit their liability to one camera.) File your claim immediately—they give you forty-five days, but the process will be long enough without you slowing it down. Send copies of your receipts, and keep the originals.

Now serious negotiations begin. You might detect a certain suspicious hostility on the airline's part, plus various delaying tactics. Your claim may be shelved for weeks if you don't keep after them. Never sit back and assume they're working on it. Airlines tend to interpret a lack of enthusiasm in pressing your claim as an indication that it's either phony or you're not very serious. When they recognize your claim as serious and heavily documented, they'll make you an offer based on the depreciated value of your goods. Understand that the process of dragging a settlement out of an airline and actually receiving your check takes from six weeks to three months. If you decide it's reasonable, accept it.

If your bag arrives smashed up or torn, the airline will pick up the cost of repair. If it's damaged beyond repair, they'll negotiate a settlement with you, based on its depreciated value. The same goes for clothing or other items inside. But there are two exceptions for which the carrier will balk at paying your claim. One is when goods are damaged inside your bag but there is no external damage: The airline will logically conclude you're trying to make them pay for previous damages. The other is when damage was obviously caused by your carelessness in packing. So don't bother packing an expensive vase you never liked in a suitcase full of cinderblocks; the airline will probably disclaim any responsibility. For damaged goods, follow the same procedure that you would for collecting on a lost bag.

TAKING AN AIRLINE TO SMALL-CLAIMS COURT

If an airline won't give you satisfaction after you've presented a perfectly reasonable case, it's time to put teeth in your demands.

First, send them a demand letter like the one at the end of this chapter, filled in with the relevant details. Then wait a week. If you don't hear from them, call the person you addressed the letter to and ask what's happening. If he or she says anything but "Okay, let's settle this," stroll down to your local small-claims court and have the clerk help you file the necessary papers, correctly filled out, against the airline.

Between the time they receive your summons and the court date, it's likely the airline will find it cheaper to settle with you than to become enmeshed in your crusade for justice and will contact you with a reasonable offer. So decide beforehand the least amount you're willing to settle for.

If you don't hear your minimum figure, weigh these factors: (1) Your small-claims suit is strongest when fairness and justice are obviously on your side; (2) you can appear without a lawyer, but the airline will have to send one or more of theirs, plus any of their staff you'll call as witnesses. This could become very expensive for the carrier and give them additional reason to settle prior to the court date; (3) even if the airline lawyer comes brandishing the tariff rules, the judge can order the carrier to "waive" its tariff and pay the claim; (4) if your claim is *not* actually barred by some tariff, you'll probably stand a greater chance of winning.

In presenting your case, have your ticket, dated copies of any letters sent to the airline, replies, verbatim notes of telephone conversations, sales receipts for lost or damaged goods, and generally as much documentation as you can assemble. Judges are impressed with paperwork, since it tends to make you look like you have much documented "proof" that you're in the right. And a judge will usually try to help a lay person whose cause is fair in deflecting whatever strict legalisms the airline lawyer may dredge up to deny your claim.

WHAT IF YOUR FLIGHT IS "TERMINATED"?

Before you have to seek revenge because your plane went down, take a moment to limit your risk. Make sure the airline you're planning to fly reveals one of the better safety records. But wait a minute. Aren't there only "A" airlines and "A+" airlines when it comes to passenger safety? Hardly, although that's a popular fiction encouraged by the industry.

One reason airlines never mention the concept of safety in advertising reflects an industry-wide concern. Some airlines are much more vulnerable in this area than others, and the kind of facts that might emerge from "comparative" safety claims could prove chilling.

Who's Safest? Domestic airlines flying US routes maintain the best records of miles flown vs. flights "terminated," to use the euphemism of the trade. US-based airlines that fly overseas tend to exhibit the second-best records, since they're subject to controllers with foreign accents, routes traversed by pilots with underdeveloped skills, inadequate landing facilities, and a host of other problems. Then there are the rest of the world's airlines, which have earned records from flawless (Quantas) to terrifying (TAROM). A few have shown improvement. Air France was nicknamed "Air Chance" for many years, reflecting well-publicized difficulties in keeping its flights aloft, but has now been accident free (as of this writing) for several years.

In their eye-opening *Destination Disaster*, a group of London *Times* journalists compiled the most useful comparison chart to date of safety records (see Table 4, p. 283). Use it to select the airline with the best safety performance whenever you have a choice. For instance, if we were flying to Egypt and wanted to reduce our chances of joining the pharaohs, you can bet we'd choose anybody but Egyptair.

Fortunately, the odds are astronomically against it, but what if you have the bad luck to be involved in a plane accident? Well, if you survive intact, you can sue the airline and maybe even the plane manufacturer. Survivors have collected many thousands for the psychological trauma and general shaking up suffered in air disasters, even minor ones.

First, never sign anything shoved in front of you afterward by the airlines or its insurer. Insurance companies, in predatory fashion, may try to reduce their liability by asking you to sign a waiver soon after the accident, including when you're lying, heavily medicated, in a hospital bed. Such a waiver might let them get away with paying just medical expenses.

If you do find yourself in a strange hospital for tests after a crash, you can probably get virtually every short-term need taken care of by the airline just by asking. They'll undoubtedly assign a representative to help you, who will let you charge some new clothes if yours were damaged, place any number of free long-distance calls, fly your family or a close friend to see you gratis (if you still trust the airline with them), and generally try to make you as comfortable as possible. One reason is, of course, that they hope you'll forgive and forget about suing.

Second, never heed any letter you receive from the airline or its insurance underwriter asking you not to hire a lawyer. They'll probably argue that the "intervention" of lawyers will tie your case up in court for years and the only "reasonable" thing to do is settle direct with the insurer.

As you might have guessed by now, we don't recommend dealing direct with insurance companies. You will want to find the best air disaster lawyer you can as quickly as possible. Some law firms, like F. Lee Bailey's, are not at all bashful about running ads in the local paper right after a major air crash. But the best source of referral for a local specialist is the Aviation Consumer Action Project in Washington, D.C., (202) 223-4498.

TABLE 4

HOW SAFE ARE THE AIRLINES?

Roughly speaking, each group has established a safety record approximately twice as good as the group below it.

Group One

1. TAP	6. Trans-Australian	11. National
2. Qantas	7. Japan Air Lines	12. Lufthansa
3. Delta	8. Continental	13. Eastern
4. American	9. United	14. Iran Air
5. SAS	10. Ansett (Australia)	15. Braniff

Group Two

1. Aeromexico	5. Pan Am	9. KLM
2. TWA	6. El Al	10. Hughes Air West
3. New Zealand National	7. Swissair	11. Allegheny
4. Air Canada	8. British Airways	12. Aer Lingus Irish

Group Three

1. Northwest
2. Iberia
3. Alitalia
4. LAN Chile
5. East African
6. SABENA

7. JAT (Yugoslavia)
8. Finnair
9. All Nippon
10. Olympic
11. Mexicana
12. Cathay Pacific

13. South African
14. Ethiopian
15. Canadian Pacific
16. Air France
17. British Caledonia
18. Icelandair

Group Four

1. Cubana
2. Austrian
3. AVIANCA
4. VARIG
5. Pakistan Internat'l

6. Indian Airlines
7. UTA
8. Cruzeiro
9. Air Algerie
10. LOT (Poland)

11. Garuda
12. Aero. Argentinas
13. CSA
14. Philippine
15. Air India

Group Five

1. AVIACO
2. Nigeria

3. Middle East Airlines
4. Turkish Airlines

Group Six

1. TAROM (Rumania)
2. Egyptair

3. VIASA (Venezuela)
4. ALIA-Royal Jordanian

SOURCE: Paul Eddy, Elaine Potter, and Bruce Page, *Destination Disaster* (New York: Quadrangle, 1976).

REVENGE KIT FOR AIRLINES

LETTER TO AIRLINE FOR REIMBURSEMENT OF COSTS FROM LOST LUGGAGE

Name: Director of Customer Service
(obtain name from airline's local office)
Address:
Date:

Dear Mr./Ms. _____,

I was a passenger on (Airline) flight #_____ from Boston to Miami Beach on (date). When I arrived in

Miami for my three-day vacation, my bag was nowhere to be found. I am enclosing copies of my claim check and the receipt indicating that I paid for extended-liability coverage.

As soon as I determined that my bag was missing, I reported this fact to Mr./Ms. _____ at your local office, filled out the requisite form, and went to my hotel to wait for the bag. Since I had nothing to "unpack" at the hotel, I had to replace those items that you lost which were reasonably necessary for me to enjoy my vacation, as I needed them. Thus I am enclosing a bill for ($_____), which I incurred as a direct and proximate result of your negligence. The bill itemizes all purchases made (such as a bathing suit, a lightweight dinner jacket and pants, tennis shoes, and, of course, a camera).

I am also enclosing a list of items that were in the lost luggage, along with my original receipt for each. Those items I was not able to find receipts for I have listed in the separate Notarized Affidavit I have sworn to, including original costs. The aggregate loss amounts to $1,623.00, and demand is hereby made for prompt reimbursement of that sum.

I will wait fifteen working days for you to send me a check or contact me before bringing this matter to the attention of my attorney.

Thank you for your cooperation.

Very truly yours,

FINAL DEMAND LETTER BEFORE GOING TO SMALL-CLAIMS COURT

Customer Service Director
Name:
Address:
Date:

Re: _____ (Your name) v. _____ (Airline)

Dear Mr./Ms. _____,

As you know, I have attempted in good faith to settle my claim with you for three weeks since the date of incurrence of my loss. I am enclosing for the record a copy of my letter dated _____, wherein I explained that you lost my luggage, listed the items that were inside, and included proper and absolute documentation of the value of each lost item. You have failed and refused to resolve my claim despite repeated efforts on my part to engage in meaningful settlement negotiation.

Unless I receive your check in the amount demanded, $_____, within two weeks from the date of this letter, I will file suit against you in (small-claims or district) court and subpoena as witnesses three of your operations people and two of your executive employees to appear and testify as to the facts in this case. I am also considering issuing a subpoena to Mr./Ms. _____, head of your claim adjustment center, to ask questions regarding your official company policy in the handling of these matters.

If you wish to avoid the expense and exposure that will result from suit, you must strictly comply with the terms of this final demand.

Very truly yours,

COMPLAINT ABOUT AN EMPLOYEE

Name: Customer Service Director (obtain name from airline's local office)
Address:
Date:

Re: (Name of Employee)

Dear Mr./Ms. _____,

I was a passenger on (Airline) flight #_____ on (date). The male steward on board, named _____, was offensive to an extreme that has led me to discuss legal action with my attorney.

He dropped a cup of soup in my wife's lap and did not even apologize. He said he was going to get a damp cloth to wipe off her blouse. When he came back (about 10 minutes later), he said he could not find a clean cloth, pulled out his handkerchief, and attempted to wipe off the blouse. My wife could not move from her seat to wash out the blouse herself because the seat-belt sign was on and the steward told her to remain in her seat. She tells me that he whispered to her, "Baby, let Papa do it," when she tried to take the handkerchief herself. Needless to say, this situation resulted in a loud shouting match causing me and my wife great embarrassment.

Please include this letter in Mr. _____'s permanent employment file. And please be advised that unless I receive a suitable apology complete with an indication of what disciplinary action will be taken with respect to Mr. _____, I will instruct my lawyer to file suit against your employee for battery and against you for negligence in hiring him.

Very truly yours,

CAB COMPLAINT

To: Civil Aeronautics Board
Bureau of Consumer Protection
1825 Connecticut Ave., N.W.
Washington, D.C. 20428
(Tel: 202-673-6047)

Date:

Re: _____(Your Name) vs.
_____(Airline)

I would appreciate your help in resolving a dispute I am having with _____Airlines. I am enclosing a copy of my letter, dated _____, to the airline, which summarizes the problem and gives full details as to the underlying set of facts.

I understand that the CAB will contact the carrier involved, then report back to me regarding their disposition toward settlement. I further understand that you will attempt to informally mediate this dispute and work out a satisfactory settlement for me if you believe the facts to be in my favor.

I appreciate your help and look forward to hearing from you once you have discussed this situation with the offending carrier.

Very truly yours,

20
faraway places
Unrolling Your Own Red Carpet

You'd think that Murphy's Law would give you a break on vacation. All you ask is to plop down in a beach chair sheltered by palm fronds and sip a piña colada. But you know, in your heart of hearts, there's no guaranteed peace anywhere on our planet.

There's always the possibility that some overbooked first-class hotel will fail to honor your "confirmed" reservation. So you spend your first night in Paradise sleeping in a rented microcar, with your suitcase for a pillow. And there's a fair chance that your "bargain" charter flight could leave you stranded in a third-world airport for thirty-six hours with a group of proctologists for company, most of whom are talking shop. How do you compensate yourself for such hardship?

Or else you're at a Club Med and some fun-loving *chef du village* pours a pot of cold spaghetti over your head in the madcap spirit of the place. (Yes, it's really happened.) How do you strike back at a tormentor on foreign soil without being written off as an ugly American?

The answer to vacation angst is to take a few precautions before you leave and adopt the relaxed attitude you'll find helpful for the holiday strategies offered here.

USING YOUR TRAVEL AGENT AS GUARANTOR

Travel agencies want you to book every component of your vacation through them. And we agree wholeheartedly that you should, provided you (1) book through a travel agent within 100 miles of your home, and (2) charge the entire package to a major credit card. If you recall the conditions for refusing to pay credit-card charges discussed in Chapter 8, we think you'll see the reasoning behind making your travel agent a full partner in your vacation planning.

If you book a trip abroad piecemeal (i.e., pay the airline for your tickets, the hotel with a check, your rental car with a credit card, and so on) and something goes wrong, you might as well try to collect a refund from the International Monetary Fund as from some foreign traveler marketer. But if you charge the whole business to a travel agency, they're the ones who accept responsibility—to a degree, anyway—for the quality of services you're actually rendered.

We say "to a degree" because a travel agency can always disavow any liability for the charter operator who misrepresents facts about a tour package or the idiosyncrasies of some foreign hotel. But recent court decisions tend to hold travel agencies responsible for what they sell you. As with any other adversary, it makes better sense to keep your money away from an agency until you've received what you paid for. If they act as agents for crooks or unreliable foreign resorts, let them share your liabilities along with their commissions. The important step you should take to build your case beforehand, though, is to make them put their representations of the package you're supposed to get *in writing*. These should include:

> confirmation of the dates, departure times, travel class, and amenities in your airline or cruise plans—with the carrier and ticket price specified

> confirmation of your hotel accommodations, with a full description of what you're entitled to: type of room, bathroom availability, breakfast (European or American plan); a full description of the hotel facilities: golf, tennis, boating, horseback riding, etc.; and free amenities, and finally what's *not* included in the stated price

> confirmation of rental-car reservation with the cost, type of car, and dates you need it specified

> confirmation of any other transportation, tours, and restaurants included in the package and every other item you expect to receive

Once a travel agency provides you with your itinerary and reservations, you have excellent substantiation if and when you have to contest a charge. Once you have your reservations and dockets, these amount to being a written contract, although they may well contain exculpatory waivers limiting the agency's liability. In many states, these waivers aren't binding. Where they are, you still have a strong case for proving *negligence* or *misrepresentation* if any agency threatens to take you to court for withholding payment.

If you return from a problem trip, immediately send a letter, using the letter in the Revenge Kit as your model, to the manager of the travel agency. This will put the agency on notice that you're not paying for some component of the package. The manager will definitely be in touch with you.

MANAGER: What's this about your not paying for 65 percent of your hotel bill in St. Martin? It's not our fault the hotel was still under construction and your room didn't have a roof yet.

They told us you'd get a room and you did. Anyway, you moved into another hotel the next day with no problems.

SUNBURNED: Yes, and that hotel only offered half of what you represented in your agency's letter to me—the one confirming what I was supposed to get on my trip. But the point is that you're negligent if you didn't find out if one of the hotels you represent could provide a roof over our heads.

MANAGER: If you don't pay the whole amount, we'll sue you.

SUNBURNED: Fine. I'd like to show exactly how you breached your contract in front of a *jury*. I have a doctor's note attesting to my pain and suffering from the sunburn I got in my own room that first morning. And do you want to see the beautiful photographs of the sun overhead, shot from the foot of our bed? You can expect a countersuit for damages. In fact, I'm working on an interview on station WXYZ this week to discuss my vacation with their consumer reporter.

MANAGER: I don't believe you.

SUNBURNED: You'd *better* believe I'll go to every media person I can to tell this story. And now that you've refused to accept your responsibility, I've made my good-faith effort to let you resolve the problem. We have nothing more to discuss.

MANAGER: Maybe we could work out some compromise . . .

Faced with an adversary who's obviously itching to go to court *and* go public, the manager will have to consider his next steps carefully. You might get on the evening news and blab the agency's name all over town as a party to your horror story. Or you might go to court and ask for a jury trial. There will probably be other sometime vacationers on the jury, all of whom have suffered their own holiday nightmares and have vicarious revenge in mind. So the chances are good that you'll receive a reasonable settlement before you have to resort to either.

Hotel-Hell Tactics

The decline of quality, or servility if you see it that way, has certainly wormed its way into many of the world's hotels and resorts. Even Europe, that last bastion of fine hostelry, has developed some quirkiness in staff and services. American chains—Hilton, Marriott, and the like—tend to offer "no surprises," as the Holiday Inn ads used to say. But they can fail to offer much in the way of ambiance, too. In a number of Caribbean resorts, you might encounter a certain powder-keg sullenness among staff people that can be discomfiting. The best revenge you can exact on hotels may be to avoid them entirely.

The Barter Option. If your own house or apartment would be a lonely place while you're away, you can always try to work out a barter arrangement with someone in the area you'll be visiting. Granted, it's probably too much to hope that a Pago Pago family would happen to need an apartment in Oklahoma City when you feel like a change of pace, but you can never tell.

(Remember that it's no fair, in representing your house, to rip out a page from *Better Homes and Gardens* and send it in. But you might be able to get away with the wide-angle camera photography they use to broaden a room's vistas in those glamorous decorating magazines.)

The general rules of barter discussed in Chapter 11 apply here. Most people are inclined to treat your house very kindly, in the hope that you'll do the same with theirs. And you'll probably find that your barter partners will go out of their way to provide you with everything you'll need to make you feel comfortable.

The downside risk is that you'll arrive in some distant land and find less than you bargained for. A few barterers have been known to accentuate the positive in describing their own homes, either because they're unrealistically house-proud or because they're trying to trade up on vacation. And we can only guess what such folks would be like as house-sitters. If you do make a barter commitment with foreign partners and they let you down, you can only notify the agency afterward or rush home a day early to confront them and try to work out some settlement if they've damaged your house.

You can't report them to the IRS in case of the possibility that they didn't report income, as you might a barterer in the States. But you could, before you leave the host country, find out if there are local regulations they might have violated, like operating an inn for unrelated guests without a license (although it may be difficult to find a free-consultation lawyer on the Riviera to get that information). Then, safe at home, you can write to that foreign government agency, telling them you stayed at your barterers "inn" and enumerating the problems you had.

But the best preventive course is to see if the house you're swapping for has a history at the agency and ask to contact the last person in the United States who used it.

Making a Hotel Honor Your Reservation. If you do choose to stay at a hotel in a popular vacation area, your holiday's first flush of excitement may occur the moment you step inside. This is when the desk clerk riffles through whatever records they keep and tells you, usually without a hint of the sniveling lie that it is, that they have no record of your reservation. Or you've confirmed for the twenty-seventh, not the twenty-sixth. Or any other lame excuse they can muster to avoid admitting that they overbooked and everybody showed up.

Now you tell them you'll take any room they have available, and you're assured that there are none. This is almost never true. There's probably a room somewhere in the labyrinthine passages of a great hotel that they're holding for someone who may or may not show up—a VIP, the manager's mistress, whomever. All they know is they don't want you to have it. You wave your confirmation from the travel agency, and they stonewall you. Then they might make a feeble attempt to find you a room in some other hotel, but they're all overbooked, too. Sorry, they shrug. You stand there trying to think of an answer to this malignant policy, but nothing occurs.

Don't feel too bad. Shrewd-consumer theorists have wrestled with this one for years. You may have heard about the college professor who, when given this run-around at a hotel late at night, started taking off his clothes and threatened to sleep in the lobby if they didn't find him a room. Which they did, immediately. Well, we applaud his chutzpah, but let's look on the negative side. What if they just stare at you with bemused grins when you start undressing? Are you prepared to strip down to your BVDs? To turn into the Maidenform woman? We think not. If they call your bluff, you're done for. And if they call the police in some banana dictatorship, who knows what could happen. We imagine the police might classify shrewd consumers with drunks who cause a scene and give you the same cell assignment.

There are really only two useful gambits that don't involve taking undue risks.

One is for hotels owned by American chains. Before you leave, find out the telephone number of the chain's headquarters in the states. Call the president's office there and ask for his full name. Then ask for the full name of the company's senior vice-president of operations. Also find out the name of the president's secretary. Write this information down with the telephone number at headquarters, and keep it in your wallet. Memorize them on the flight. When you arrive at the hotel and they run through their lines about no room availabilities, ask to speak to the manager. Tell him or her you want to use the house phone to call the company's headquarters. And give them the office number in the States from memory. Then point out that, when they have headquarters on the phone, you want to speak to "John McPherson" or whatever the v.p. operation's name is.

If the time difference is right, the US office won't be open now. And the local manager can only conjecture how well you might know a key executive in the parent company. Notice you didn't ask to speak to the president of the company. *Everybody* asks to speak to the president. But you did know

McPherson well enough to rattle his name off with his phone number. And he's somebody in the organization the manager probably knows, too. Since they can't reach him by phone to see whether you're an intimate friend, the manager is likely to give you the benefit of the doubt. Even if the time difference dictates that you'll get through to headquarters, the nature of the v.p. operation's job in an international hotel corporation involves much globe-trotting. The chances of finding McPherson out of the office are superb, and the local manager will be forced to conjecture again.

Even if he does happen to be in, he'll probably take a call from someone trying to reach him from the company's hotel in Amsterdam or wherever you are, assuming that you have some legitimate business with him because you knew his name.

> McPHERSON: Yes (crackle) hello . . .
>
> TRAVELER: Hello, Mr. McPherson, I got your name from Ms. Abernathy (the president's secretary) back in the States, in case I had problems here at the Dumpty in Amsterdam. And I'm afraid I have a problem.

If the connection is as bad as usual, McPherson will take away from this message "Ms. Abernathy," which means some familiarity with the president's office and "problem." What you told him was quite true, of course, but he doesn't know you called Ms. Abernathy out of the clear blue sky.

> McPHERSON: What's the problem there?
>
> TRAVELER: My reservation was confirmed, of course, but your Mr. Oomlaut won't honor it.
>
> McPHERSON: Oh. Could I ask you to put Mr. Oomlaut on, then?
>
> MR. OOMLAUT: Hullo, John.
>
> McPHERSON: Hello. Have you got anything to give the man at all?
>
> MR. OOMLAUT: Only number 1100 (an empty executive suite).
>
> McPHERSON: Then please give it to him. I don't know exactly who he is and I don't have time to find out, but I think he knows Henry (the president).

In any event, you're likely to get deferential service as well as a room through such judicious name-dropping.

The other gambit is for hotels that aren't owned by American chains. Usually when you arrive to find you have no room, it's very late at night. Last come, last served is the rule in handling overbooked non-VIP guests. Before you leave, find out from your travel agency the name of the hotel's general manager. He's usually on during the day, leaving a night manager to secure the hotel from guests in his absence.

When you receive the bad news, leave the desk immediately and go to the pay phone. Look up the general manager's name in the local directory and see if he's listed. If so, give him a call.

MANAGER: (awakened) *Sí.*

TRAVELER: (cordially) Hello, Mr. Salmonella. I've just arrived at the hotel and have a confirmed reservation through Hospitality Travel. They gave me your name in case I ran into any problems. Well, I have a problem now getting a room, so I'd appreciate your straightening it out. My name is Smith. I'll call you back in an hour if I still have trouble.

And hang up promptly. Then return to the desk and wait for him to call in, which he probably will since he doesn't want you phoning him again as soon as he gets back to sleep.

If his number is not in the directory, go back to the desk immediately and say you tried to find Mr. Salmonella's number but it was unlisted. Ask the night manager to call him at home. He will probably see waking his superior up at that hour as a greater evil than giving you a room and do his best to find you accommodation somewhere. Remember that he doesn't know how you obtained the boss's name—only that you knew it and were prepared to call him at home on your own, which could give sufficient support to the possibility that you're a VIP yourself so that he might even give you the special rooms he's been saving for a tryst with the chambermaid.

Getting Even for Poor Service. More often than you're treated to some catastrophic problem in your hotel, you're just nibbled to death by little problems. The food's cold once, the pool man sneers at you the first day when you don't tip him enough, room service takes almost two hours one morning, and the bed isn't made when you return at six P.M. to dress for dinner. These small annoyances gnaw away at you, but it's difficult to determine how much you should be compensated for a pattern of reduced services.

But if the hotel is guilty of some gross negligence, now you're ready to wheel and deal. You might have noticed, especially in *mañana* countries, that a hotel seldom if ever gives you important messages. If you were sent a cablegram of extreme urgency while you were at the hotel, and it languished for a full day in your message box, then you'd have something to speak to the manager about. Who knows what money damages you might suffer from failing to receive a cablegram that vitally affects your business interests?

TRAVELER: (to desk clerk) Room 314 please, any mail that's there.

CLERK: Here, *señor*.

TRAVELER: (opening Mailgram) Good God, man! This cablegram's from *yesterday!* Why wasn't I notified?

CLERK: Uh . . .

TRAVELER: Never mind. Let me speak to the manager.

MANAGER: What seems to be the trouble?

TRAVELER: (livid with rage) Look at the date on this cablegram! It's been sitting here since yesterday, with *no* attempt to notify me whatever!

MANAGER: Hmmmnn.

TRAVELER: Now maybe you'd like to hear the message . . . "Opportunity to sell at $300K. Must have your answer by midnight your time." Do you realize what this means? Do you know how much I've lost from your damned negligence.

MANAGER: Perhaps if *señor* would just calm down . . .

TRAVELER: Calm down, hell! Who's your house attorney? I want to speak to him immediately!

MANAGER: This is Saturday, *señor*. He will not be available. But perhaps there is something I can do to make amends.

And perhaps there is, when you "calm down."

And remember when shopping in a hotel's stores to use personal checks or your American Express card in case you discover later on that the merchandise you bought is defective. Personal checks can be stopped, of course. Bear in mind that some large hotel chains have collection services in major US cities.

But usually you'll just get a letter from the hotel after several weeks asking you to "please remit" whatever the amount was. And American Express will, according to a representative, investigate contested charges in foreign countries if you deduct them from your Amex card payment.

Master-complainer Ralph Charell reports a fiendishly clever variation on a guerrilla tactic discussed in Chapter 2, which he once used to bring a resort hotel to its knees. He was grievously upset over the resort's quality in general and a roast-beef dinner in particular. So he requested a safe-deposit box, to which he kept one of the two necessary keys, and surreptitiously left the uneaten portion of his beef inside. Eventually the manager called and asked him to remove whatever was giving the lobby an aura of decay. Charell refused, on the grounds that there was "valuable evidence" inside and any unauthorized tampering with the box would bring severe legal consequences. He finally settled with the manager for an excellent roast-beef dinner and wine for four, on the house.

Overcoming Anti-American Rudeness

Natives of other lands sometimes reveal an undiscriminating hostility toward Americans. Since we've been so obsessed lately with our alleged impotence and the sorry state of the American dollar, we might be surprised to hear that others still consider us too powerful and rich for their liking. If you have a thick skin, it's even reassuring in a way to be treated with that old envious spite. But most Americans are friendly, outgoing travelers who are hurt by instances of rudeness that arise from ancient shibboleths and stereotypes.

Breaking the Language Barrier. To ensure better treatment around the world, we believe the savviest travel investment you can make is a crash course at Berlitz in the language of your host country. Our experience has been that most people respond with infinitely greater humanity when you try to speak their language, even if they speak English themselves. (Naturally, some will let you stammer through a complex question in their language, only to respond in English that they can't help you. But these mean-spirited souls are few and far between.) And more pragmatically, you're in a better position to protect yourself against larcenous cab drivers, short-changing merchants, free-lance "guides" who steal your rented car and all your clothes, and other locals who try to take advantage of unstreetwise foreigners.

But let's get back to the problem of mere rudeness. If somebody hates you for your nationality, there's not much you can do to change her perceptions about Coca-Cola's domination of the world or the fact that someone's mother was abandoned by an American soldier in 1945 or whatever underlies her attitude. All you can do is try not to let her ruin your day and maybe amuse yourself in the bargain. After all, you're on vacation.

The best way to accomplish this is to adopt not J.R. but R.R. as your role model.

Mastering the Reagan Response. Who's the quintessential American nice guy? Right. With a little practice, you can master those pleasant, mellifluous tones and the relaxed toss of the head that serve President Reagan so well, and you will be able to disarm people who try to insult or bait you, too. And this will gnaw at your tormenter much more effectively than if you become loudly indignant or try to outsmart her in her own language.

For example, say that you and a traveling companion sit down at a café on the Champs-Élysées for a glass of wine. You're both feeling mellowed by Paris in the springtime. Then your reverie is threatened by a surly waiter.

AMERICAN: *Bonjour, m'sieur. Je prend un verre de vin blanc, s'il vous plait.*

GARÇON: *Comment?*

AMERICAN: Je prend un . . .

GARÇON: (sigh) Give me in English.

Now, you know you'll probably never get the upper hand trying to discipline this Parisian charmer yourself. Besides, you'll lose your serene mood. But you *can* string him along a bit for your own amusement.

AMERICAN: (Reaganesque cordiality) No, we're not English, m'sieur.

GARÇON: (exasperated) Your *order.* In English.

AMERICAN: Oh. We'll have a carafe of white wine, please.

GARÇON: (writing with a nasty smile) It is easier if you do not try to speak French, yes?

AMERICAN: (uncomprehending look at tablemate, who shrugs and shakes head) Come again?

The Garçon mutters *"trou de queue"* under his breath and goes away.

AMERICAN: (still smiling, beckons maitre d' over) Say, that waiter just called me a *trou de queue.* (good-humored chuckle) My father was here during the war, and he told me once what that means. I wonder if we could have another waiter?

MAITRE D':   M'sieur, there must be some mistake, but you may of course have another waiter if you wish.

The maitre d' will know for sure there was no mistake. And he may even discipline the waiter on your behalf, just because you were so good-natured about it.

The problem with Americans, they say, is that we want to be loved. But if we can't be loved, at least we can be a little smug.

REVENGE KIT FOR TRAVEL

SAMPLE LETTER TO TRAVEL AGENCY REQUESTING ABATEMENT OF CHARGES

To: President
Travel Agency
Address:
Date:

Dear Mr./Ms. _____,

Last month I booked, for two, your ten-day "Sukiyaki Vacation Package" to the Orient. This package was to be all-inclusive from airfare and room and board to all amenities such as tips and a "Howdy Neighbor Cocktail Party" in each of our ports of call.

Let me begin by addressing the accommodations. "Five-star luxury" hotel was a term I requested clarified by you prior to departure. Your written reply was succinct—"the best hotel you can imagine." Personal fantasy aside, I assure you our expectations were in no means met. Single beds bolted to the wall at a distance of 10 feet from the other is not what I imagine in a luxury suite. To say nothing of the fact that the bathroom was down the lengthy hall—contrary to a specific written guarantee from you that our rooms would have private baths. (Please note the enclosed photographs of our accommodations.)

Needless to say, we were never entertained at a "Howdy Neighbor Cocktail Party." My best guess is our tour guide was afraid to bring the disgruntled group together.

Thus I hereby make demand for a $500 abatement of the $1895 total purchase price of the vacation package. Your refusal to comply will result in withholding of any payment to you based on the theories of negligence, misrepresentation, and breach of contract by your agency. I shall also bring legal action against you. If we are forced to a court battle, we will seek not only to recover the full package price but will file for punitive damages based on your wanton disregard of the truth in your letter, to our detriment.

Be assured that we are not unprepared, nor alone. We have compiled a list of aggrieved travelers booked through your agency who are anxious to join our suit.

I will expect to hear from you within ten (10) business days.

Very truly yours,

Certified Letter

HOTEL CHAIN EXECUTIVE OFFICES

Hilton Hotels Corporate Headquarters
Attn: Barron Hilton, chairman
9900 Santa Monica Blvd.
Beverly Hills, California 90212
(213) 277-6203

Howard Johnson's Motor Lodge Office
222 Forbes Road
Braintree, Massachusetts 02184
(617) 848-2350

Mariott Corporation
Mariott Drive
Washington, D.C. 20058
(301) 897-9000

Hyatt Hotel Corporation
9700 W. Bryn Mawr Avenue

Rosemont, Illinois 60018
(312) 860-1234

Holiday Inn Executive Offices
3742 Lamar Avenue
Memphis, Tennessee 38195
(901) 362-4001

Ramada Inns
3838 E. Van Buren
Phoenix, Arizona 85008
(602) 273-4000

Best Western
P.O. Box 10203
Best Western Way
Phoenix, Arizona 85064
1-800-528-1234

21
moving companies
Getting Even for Broken Promises and Damaged Furniture

As of this writing, a noisy battle rages in Congress between those courageous lawmakers who owe favors to moving companies and those who support aggressive federal action to protect consumers against the poor service and larceny rampant in this industry. It seems the Interstate Commerce Commission (ICC), which is charged with regulating movers who cross state lines, became too vigilant a watchdog for the moving companies' liking in 1979. That year the agency filed a staggering 45,000 charges against 45 interstate movers and assessed penalties of $4.5 million.

After years of rolling over consumers with little more than an indulgent wink from the government, the few large companies that dominate the interstate moving business had to wake up their dozing lobbyists. This has resulted in the proposed Household Goods Carriers Act, which is virtually guaranteed passage through Congress. What it will do is curtail your rights to gain redress from movers: The bill will (1) eliminate a regulation that final C.O.D. charges cannot exceed 110 percent of the estimate; (2) restrict civil penalties to cases of "actual harm"; and (3) generally defang the ICC's ability to impose fines on offending movers. What it proposes instead is a system of industry arbitration to resolve your complaints. Good luck.

As you might conclude, this concentrated lobbying effort will dramatically reduce your opportunities for retribution when you've had problems with a mover. And your chances of running into problems are excellent. In the last year of its power, the ICC processed some 32,000 complaints. The most common complaint, by the companies' own admission on the Performance Records they are required to file with the government, is low-balling on estimates. About half of interstate moving jobs run more than 10 percent over estimate. The second most common complaint is loss or damage, which accounts for roughly 49 percent of all the ICC complaints, and finally, delays in delivery, which come in third at approximately 35 percent. All in all, your odds are about fifty-fifty of getting satisfaction from an interstate mover.

There are also the intrastate companies, which aren't regulated by the ICC but usually hold a state license, where required, and are usually regulated by the state's Public Service Commission. These companies vary wildly in professionalism. At the bottom of the industry heap in both pricing and expectations of getting the job done well are the unlicensed "gypsy" movers—students and other unemployed people who rent trucks by the day to get you and yours across town or state.

Unless you feel up to renting your own Ryder van and doing it yourself (which will probably save you 50% or more, depending on how far you're going), we suggest you take a lot of precautions and watch your movers very, very carefully at each stage of the job. If they do cross you at some juncture, and it pays to assume that they will, there are still a few ways to get even.

DEFENSIVE STRATEGY

Before you rush into a move, do some shrewd planning. If you're being transferred or starting a new job and your employer will be picking up your moving tab, they probably have a contract with one company and will command better service for you. If not, use the chart on Performance Ratings shown in Table 4 to help you find a reliable company, and demand their most recent rating. By all means try to schedule your move for any time other than the peak period of June through September. This is when virtually everyone wants to move, in order not to take their children out of school in the middle of a term. So it goes without saying that the likelihood of problems and delays will soar during the peak months, when movers are working around the clock. Also, some carriers raise their rates during that period by 10 to 15 percent. The best times to move are during the spring and late fall, and in the middle of the month rather than at the beginning or end, when apartment leases are up and moving companies are swamped with jobs.

Protecting Yourself Against Overcharging and Damage. Before you let the mover drive off with your precious belongings, cover yourself.

First ask the company for copies of the ICC's *Summary of Information for Shippers of Household Goods* and *Loss and Damage of Household Goods— Prevention and Recovery.* Study these pamphlets carefully, since they explain your rights and smart moving procedure in detail.

When the company representative takes inventory of your possessions, check carefully to see if the pieces that they've described as damaged or "marred and scarred" tally with their actual condition. Most movers will be inclined to overstate existing damage, and some will declare that everything you own is marred and scarred to escape liability. So ask them to decipher all their letter codes on the bill of lading, and make notations where your assessments differ. Have any valuable antiques you own appraised beforehand by an expert, with a written statement of their condition as well as value. It also helps to take close-

Table 5
The Best and Worst Interstate Movers
Based on Performance Records Submitted by the
Moving Companies to the ICC in 1979
(Incidence of problems)

Moving Company	Over-estimated by 10% or more	Under-estimated by 10% or more	Picked up at least 1 day late	Delivered at least 1 day late	With $50 or more loss or damage claim	With claim for expenses caused by delay	Average no. of days to settle a claim	% claims taking 60 days or more to settle	Total Score
AVERAGE - 17 MOVERS LISTED	25.7	25.6	1.9	9.1	17.8	1.3	31	16.0	128.4
Aero Mayflower Transit Co.	32.2	27.0	9.3	7.7	17.3	.6	29	18.0	141.1
Allied Van Lines, Inc.	27.5	26.7	6.3	10.8	19.4	1.5	23	10.4	125.6
American Red Ball Transit Co.	26.8	27.4	3.3	21.8	21.6	2.9	56	39.6	199.4
Andrews Van Lines, Inc.	28.2	29.2	4.7	27.9	17.1	1.1	41	23.2	172.4
Atlas Van Lines, Inc.	29.3	30.6	2.9	20.6	22.3	1.9	25	15.4	148.0
Bekins Van Lines, Co.	32.3	28.0	5.2	11.1	17.3	1.8	29	14.4	139.1
Burnham Van Service, Inc.	28.3	29.2	.0	12.6	18.6	1.1	12	.6	102.4
Fernstrom Storage & Van Co.	11.6	15.8	7.5	15.8	7.0	.3	21	8.6	87.6
Global Van Lines, Inc.	29.3	27.3	9.0	19.7	11.6	.8	30	10.3	138.0
King Van Lines, Inc.	12.7	15.8	2.1	33.8	27.0	1.3	51	33.2	176.9
Lyon Moving & Storage, Inc.	23.1	30.9	1.8	17.2	24.9	1.5	29	.8	129.2
National Van Lines, Inc.	23.0	33.1	8.9	14.2	18.7	2.9	38	25.2	164.0
Neptune World Wide Moving	16.8	25.9	3.5	21.2	16.4	.1	29	8.8	121.7
North American Van Lines, Inc.	22.9	19.9	5.1	8.5	18.2	.9	21	10.8	107.3
United Van Lines, Inc.	31.9	26.1	5.1	14.7	13.5	1.3	23	12.0	127.6
Von Der Ahe Van Lines, Inc.	28.4	22.0	2.5	12.7	19.1	.7	36	13.0	134.4
Wheaton Van Lines, Inc.	32.7	19.8	2.2	12.7	13.1	1.9	38	27.4	147.8

SOURCE: Interstate Commerce Commission, 1980.

up photographs of other valuables, too, for substantiating damage later on. Then make sure that you're covered for loss or breakage beyond the standard 60¢ per pound limitation. Be generous in stating the value of your possessions in anticipation of a future claim. You can buy extra coverage direct from the carrier, and should.

Next, you'll want to avoid being gouged via a trick movers refer to by the cute term of *bumping*. Since you're charged by the pound in interstate moves, they figure out the cost of your move by weighing the truck before and after your goods are loaded inside. But some movers have developed ingenious additions to "bump up" the total weight when your possessions are weighed. So be prepared to exercise your right to stand there, with a witness, and watch both weigh-ins. You might be able to get the goods on your mover if you can prove that they're bumping, which is a criminal offense.

MOVER: Ready to weigh the truck with your goods now, folks.

CUSTOMER: Just a minute. I see three people in the cab of the truck. Only the driver is supposed to be in there.

MOVER: Oh, yeah. Hey, Moose . . . Big Al . . . get the hell outta that truck, will ya? Sorry, lady.

CUSTOMER.   How much gas have you got in the truck now?

MOVER: Couldn't say, ma'am.

CUSTOMER: Well, I saw the driver fill it up between the first weigh-in and this one. That could mean a few hundred pounds more. I want that weight determined and deducted from my total.

MOVER: Jeez, I keep telling those guys not to do that . . . I'll take care of it right now.

CUSTOMER: Mind if I look inside the truck?

MOVER: Uh, not much to see in there but your own stuff.

CUSTOMER: (peering inside) What's that pile of bricks doing over in the corner?

You can't count on this happening, but it's just one possibility to explore in which you might turn up skulduggery.

When the Movers Arrive. Plan to get to your new location before the movers do, which shouldn't be too difficult because they're usually late for one reason or another. (But, again, don't count on it.) If they're days late and you've had to check into a hotel or motel, keep records of those expenses—plus restaurants, clothing, and incidentals you might have to buy—so you can substantiate a claim for *inconvenience*.

When they unload your belongings, check every item carefully against the bill of lading and note the condition it arrived in. You might wonder how they could lose something from a truck that's been sealed from pickup to delivery, but it happens. If they were moving two or three families in the same truck, maybe somebody in Kansas is eating dinner on your heirloom china. Note missing items carefully. Check every piece for breakage and write those items down, too, so you can document your claim for *loss and damage*.

Then there's the thorny problem of payment. By far the smartest way to handle payment is the preemptive-strike option of charging your move to a credit card. Then you can withhold payment when the statement arrives until you sort out your problems, wielding the heavy club of monetary loss over the company. Movers are allowed to take credit cards for payment. But, as you might imagine from their performance records, most of them are extremely reluctant to do so. Like many smart adversaries who expect you'll get mad at them in the course of doing business, interstate movers almost always demand payment in cash, certified check, or traveler's checks before they even unload the truck.

But some licensed local movers will unload before demanding payment. Theoretically, they'll just put everything back on the truck if you refuse to pay them as promised and take it away until you do. However, if you're a nervy person, you could always wait until your goods are inside the house, send the movers outside on some pretext, and lock up the house behind them. Then call the company's representative and tell him why you're not paying them—your actual bill ran way over estimate, you've suffered grievous inconvenience, or you have a houseful of damaged goods. The representative will probably want to come out to investigate, and you should be able to work out an on-the-spot settlement. We definitely wouldn't try this with a couple of unlicensed tough guys who are making the money themselves, but salaried employees of a licensed mover won't have the inclination to break your door down and demand payment. What they'll probably do is just scratch their heads and call the company for instructions. (One bit of good news here—you don't have to tip interstate movers. In fact, it's unlawful to do so, and you can bring that up if they seem to be loitering or pressuring you for one.)

Pressing a Claim. If you're forced to pay up before the truck is unloaded, you'll have to put a claim in later. Add up all your damages for inconvenience, loss, and broken, scratched, or mauled items, and file it immediately with the moving company. Remember that the moving company will depreciate your lost or damaged goods on the basis of age. This is why you protect yourself beforehand (as mentioned earlier) with generous appraisals and high-value coverage. But before you put your claim in, call the ICC—which will have a regional office near you—describe the nature of the problem, and ask them for the best way to process it. The law requires the company to acknowledge your claim within 30 days and to respond to it by paying up or contesting what you've listed within 120 days. (And if you find damages long after you've moved in, you still have nine months after delivery to stake your claim.)

Most claims take about 60 days to process. If they drag their feet or try to beat you down, you have a few options.

If it was an interstate move, you can file a formal complaint with the ICC. But, since the commission may have been cowed by the time you read this through passage of the movers' special-interest legislation, they may not press your claim with the zeal they have in the past few years.

Apply for arbitration with the director of consumer appeals of the American Movers' Conference. (Phone: 703-524-5440.)

If it's a local move, enter your complaint with your state's Public Service Commission, which you'll find listed in your White Pages under State Government.

Check with the Public Service Commission to find out the name of the mover's insurance company and write direct to the chief executive officer of that company. Point out that the mover they've insured has exceeded the statutory time limit for responding to claims or caused you substantial documented damages, which they're trying to avoid paying, and you wish to bring that behavior to the insurer's attention. Insurance companies don't like bad risks, so their own query to the moving company will probably motivate that company to sit up and take greater notice of your intent to collect.

Write a demand letter threatening to sue the moving company. This can be a particularly moving threat in light of a 1976 case called Hubbard vs. Allied Van Lines. In that inspiring action, the Hubbard family was grossly inconvenienced when Allied delivered their goods *months* late because they were using their facilities for higher-priority moves. So the family sued for intentional infliction of emotional distress and sought punitive damages, which they collected.

Samples of all these letters are shown in the Revenge Kit that follows. The best course to follow depends on several factors, not the least of which is the current state of ICC regulations and enforcement powers over interstate movers. Other considerations are the dollar value of your loss, the strength of your documentation, and your chances for obtaining punitive damages in court. If you didn't keep very good records and the amount of your claim is $200 or less, we would opt for arbitration. But if your mover was deceptive and/or negligent, thus causing you a great deal of angst or financial loss, you should talk seriously to a free-consultation attorney.

REVENGE KIT FOR MOVING COMPANIES

SAMPLE CLAIM LETTER

To: Customer Service Executive
Fly-By-Night Moving, Inc.
Address:
March 21, 198____

Re: Claim for Inconvenience and Damages

Dear Mr./Ms. _____,

On March 11, your company's van left our Kansas City, Kansas, home headed for our new home in Kansas City, Missouri. Arrival was scheduled for March 12. On Sunday it became apparent that the furniture was more than a little late. In fact, the van arrived on March 19.

Find enclosed receipts for twenty-one meals for two, seven nights at a hotel, and the obvious incidentals. I am sure you are aware that the law requires you to cover this inconvenience claim for food and lodging.

Find as well an appraisal of the damage you caused to my antique desk from His Majesty's Appraisers, Inc., calculating refinishing and repair costs.

I expect and demand your check for **$2,704.69** in full settlement of both claims within thirty (30) days.

Very truly yours,

Certified Letter

SAMPLE LETTER REJECTING
SETTLEMENT OF CLAIM

To: President
Fly-By-Night Movers, Inc.
Address:
Date:

Dear Mr./Ms. ⸻⸻,

On March 21, 198⸺, I wrote to you, with supporting documentation attached, demanding $2,704.69 for damages and out-of-pocket expenses incurred due to your failure to fulfill your moving contract expediently and with care.

Your $500.00 offer in full settlement is not acceptable.

This is to advise you that you have fifteen (15) business days to issue me a draft for the $2,704.69 demanded. In the event I have not received same, I will be forced to file suit against you.

Be assured that my suit will not be limited to the extent of my losses. I will, of course, seek to recover court costs and attorney's fees. As well, let me caution you that my action will not be limited to contract issues. The loss incurred by your negligence was far greater than a money matter. Based on your breach of the duty to operate within standard codes of conduct in reference to my property, and the consequential damages I suffered, I will be suing you on a tort theory of negligence.

It is clear that you fell below all reasonable standards of care. As a common carrier you are liable for even a *slight* degree of negligence. Bear in mind that I need not prove what happened to my belongings. The doctrine of *res ipsa loquitor* * provides a circumstantial evidenciary basis for my suit.

---

* "The thing speaks for itself."

Thus I urge you to settle this matter amicably by forwarding prompt payment for my claim in full.

Very truly yours,

Certified Letter

COMPLAINT TO INTERSTATE COMMERCE COMMISSION

To: Interstate Commerce Commission
12th & Constitution Ave., NW
Washington, DC 20243

April 30, 198____

Gentlemen,

On March 21, 198____, I wrote Fly-By-Night Moving, Inc., in reference to a claim arising out of their services (see attached).

Last week, after thirty days had passed, their representative called and offered me $500.00 settlement in full. Needless to say, that is unsatisfactory. I do not even consider that responsive.

I believe this company's behavior to be in violation of ICC regulations for the reasons stated in my original letter, and request that you investigate this complaint.

Thank you for your cooperation.

Very truly yours,

Certified Letter

REQUEST FOR ARBITRATION
OF YOUR CLAIM

To: American Movers Conference
1117 Nineteenth Street
Arlington, Va. 22209
Date:

Re: (Your Name vs. Fly-By-Night Movers, Inc.)

Gentlemen:

On March 21, 198____, I wrote the enclosed demand letter to the above encaptioned mover. Their reply was to make an unacceptable offer of $500.00. I understand the AMC is working to develop arbitration mechanisms available.* Please let me know how you would suggest I proceed.

Thank you for your cooperation.

Very truly yours,

SAMPLE LETTER TO
MOVING COMPANY'S INSURANCE CARRIER†

To: Insurance Company
Address:
Date:

Re: (Your Name vs. Fly-By-Night Movers, Inc.)

Gentlemen,

On March 21, 198____, I wrote the enclosed letter to Fly-By-Night Movers in reference to (1) an inconvenience claim

---

* As noted in the chapter, efforts to establish an arbitration mechanism are under way and may be available to you now.
† This should be available as a matter of public record by calling your regional Federal Information Center

and (2) a loss and damage claim arising out of their service.

While my total demand was for $2,704.69, they offered me $500. My feeling is that they are trying to cover this claim out-of-pocket instead of through their insurance company.

Please consider this letter official notice to you of my demands. Please let me hear whether that offer reflects your company's position or was made without your knowledge.

Very truly yours,

Certified Letter

PART VII

Cops and Robbers

22
arrest

Avenging and Burying a Police Record

You don't have to be a real criminal to get arrested. It can happen to innocent people. Aryeh Neier, a former director of the American Civil Liberties Union, points out that:

> Half of all males will be arrested at some time in their lives. If you, dear reader, have not been arrested, chances are your father, brother, or son has been arrested, though they may not have told you about it. The females among your family also have a good chance of having an arrest record. One woman in every eight will acquire an arrest record at some time in her life. . . .
>
> Most people who have been arrested try to conceal their records. Some succeed. Others do not. Public employers and licensing agencies—which control more than 20 percent of all jobs in the United States—generally find out about arrests. So do many private employers, especially those with large work forces. Law enforcement agencies give out this information; credit bureaus collect it and sell it to private employers, insurance companies and creditors.

So if you're ever a victim of false arrest, you should know how to seek retribution for the immediate trauma and how to erase any record of it from the books for good. As one stirring example of retaliation, ponder the case of a New Hampshire couple who tipped the scales of justice over on their own state police and state legislature.

New Hampshire needed a lesson about the meaning of freedom, as this couple discovered when they were pulled off the road and arrested by a state police officer. Their nefarious crime amounted to covering, with a piece of tape, a subtle message the state had emblazoned on their license plates—"Live free or die"—and refusing to remove the tape at the officer's direction. Since New Hampshire's brand of liberty didn't include the right to keep its feisty motto off personal property, our couple brought their case to a federal court, which decided that the state police had violated First Amendment freedoms and ordered New Hampshire to pay the couple $14,000.

But when the state legislature packed up and went home for the year, they somehow forgot to allocate the money. So our heroes, accompanied by a federal marshal, strolled into one of the state-owned liquor stores with a court order to empty the cash register in partial satisfaction of the judgment. The store clerk called the governor's office, which promised that the legislature would take care of its unfinished business. And so it did.

Most police officers and prosecutors are too busy trying to contain the tidal wave of real crime to gratuitously harass civilians. But nobody's perfect. That's why there are laws on the books to offer you recourse against false arrest, false imprisonment, and malicious prosecution. And not just to protect you from the police but from overzealous merchants and unscrupulous or deranged individuals.

TURNING THE TABLES ON YOUR ACCUSERS

The kinds of criminal prosecution most solid citizens might be threatened with usually fall into the following areas:

Bouncing Checks. And who hasn't? When you receive that embarrassing phone call from some merchant holding your errant check, all they usually want is to be reassured that they can resubmit it and collect their money. (If it's really the bank's fault, make an officer give you an explanatory letter as discussed in Chapter 9 to clear your good name.)

But technically, depending on the size of the check and your state laws, writing a check without money in the bank to cover it can be a misdemeanor or a felony. Thus some heavy-handed merchants or individuals may threaten you with criminal prosecution. Now you have to determine whether:

Your state allows a grace period (often ten days) to make the check good.

Your "offense" may be a civil rather than a criminal matter.

A short consultation with the clerk of your local court or a lawyer will tell you if either of these conditions applies. If the payee is threatening criminal prosecution for a civil action, have the lawyer write a letter to that effect, which will buy you more time. In the unlikely event that you're arrested for your unsound money management, you'll undoubtedly be released on your own recognizance so you can make the check good before your case ever reaches the docket. District attorneys aren't too excited about prosecuting nice people who can't balance their checkbooks, unless you make a hobby of it.

But if you did write someone a bad check and wouldn't cover it within a reasonable period of time, don't expect much sympathy if you try to sue the payee for damages. (The better strategy would have been, if you didn't feel that person was entitled to the money, to stop payment on the check as outlined in Chapter 9.)

Shoplifting. Being suspected of committing this offense has produced some exhilarating revenge sagas. It's difficult for a store to prove criminal intent unless you've stuffed records into a pizza box, furtively shoved something into your handbag, or tried to walk out of the store with a full-length Blackglama mink sticking out from under your raincoat. People do careless things with store items that could be misconstrued as shoplifting by employees. But if those employees, including security people, restrict a suspected shoplifter from leaving the store, they're risking lawsuits. And a lot of innocent people have collected heavy damages. Mindful of this fact, most stores won't detain anyone until the person is already outside.

Don't get us wrong—shoplifting is serious, and businesses are increasingly willing to prosecute even rich kids and comfortable matrons who do it for a lark, just to set an example. But if you're innocent and suffer a humiliating escort to the manager's office or actual arrest, you have grounds for retribution.

As in any criminal case, your first move should be to call a lawyer or someone who can call one for you.

Tell your attorney the facts and build your case for what's known as false arrest or false imprisonment—briefly, this means any interference with your freedom of movement, like keeping you inside a store against your will or prosecuting you for theft when you're not guilty. If you're particularly upset by the experience—and arrest tends to be pretty anxiety-provoking for noncriminals—you may consider asking for damages caused by "intentional infliction of emotional distress." This would include visits to a psychiatrist or marriage counselor (if it creates marital problems) and time off from work. It's common in such cases to sue for three times the actual costs involved. So let the circumstances and your lawyer's advice be your guide.

Spiteful Accusations. An outside possibility is that some wrathful or unbalanced individual will conjure up a false criminal accusation against you. Say a neighborhood teenager breaks one of your windows for the second time. So he races home and tells his father. But Dad (and remember that the little fellow had to develop these charming traits from somebody) may figure that he never liked you anyway and decide to have you arrested for assaulting his delicate son. This is known as malicious prosecution—even if the police believe him and you're arrested, you can sue the father in small-claims or civil court once you've established your innocence. Again, you should call a lawyer immediately and begin building your case. Apply the same principles as in the false-arrest or false-imprisonment situation to assess your damages.

Police Error. Or Worse. Sometimes the police make an honest mistake. And oftentimes, the officers who make the mistakes aren't honest about it. If you're arrested by a misguided officer who thinks you're drunk and disorderly, other officers might substantiate his story that you "resisted arrest" to save their brother officer from besmirching his record. If you're a minority-group member, your chances of false arrest increase dramatically. But anyone can be picked up on wrongful charges.

Maybe you attend a small party innocently enough, but the friendly host you've just met turns out to have a hidden cache of illegal drugs at home. Your local police choose this inconvenient time to raid the house, arresting everyone at the party just for being present where drugs were found. Call a lawyer and clear yourself first. Then consider whether you want to pursue a false-arrest suit in either small-claims court (where you can sue police officers up to the state dollar limit) or district court.

Keep well in mind, however, that your chances of winning are much bleaker than if you're suing a private citizen. As we just mentioned, most officers will say anything to protect one another from avenging citizens. It's part of the comradeship that goes with a high-risk job. Police officers are no virgins when it comes to courtroom procedure, so you'd better have plenty of reliable nonpolice witnesses who'll support your view of events.

If you can't get a lawyer to help you, call the local office of the American Civil Liberties Union. You might be able, as the New Hampshire couple did, to take your case to federal court on constitutional grounds.

CLEARING UP YOUR RECORD

If you ever do get arrested, here's what you should know.

Never Plea Bargain if You're Innocent. You may be advised by your lawyer, the prosecutor, the judge, and everyone else concerned to plead guilty or *nolo contendere* to some lesser charge, pay a small fine, and rid yourself of the whole sordid business. Don't. Ask for a jury trial or whatever it takes to prove your innocence. If you accept a lesser charge, you'll have a permanent record of two offenses—the one you were charged with, and the one you plead guilty to. Both the local police and the FBI in Washington will have a copy on file. Anyone who sees it will automatically assume that you were guilty of the more serious charge. That includes: employers, state licensing agencies (if you ever want to open a business), and anyone who wants to make your life truly miserable if, for instance, you ever want to run for the school board.

Always Expunge an Arrest Record As Soon As Possible. Expungement is the legal procedure that lets you remove any record of your arrest from local police and FBI active files. If you weren't convicted, you can do it almost immediately. If you were convicted, you can still expunge it in most cases, but it will take longer. The most important point is that you should realize that whenever you're arrested, the record exists. And it won't go away just because your case has been dismissed or you were found not guilty.

First, use the letter in the Revenge Kit, or call the FBI at (202) 324-3000 if you have questions, to obtain a copy of your arrest record. You'll have to enclose a small fee and a set of your fingerprints. Look in your Yellow Pages for fingerprinting services or ask the local police to do it. Then call the clerk of the court where your case was heard to find out the local procedure for "expunging your record to inactive files." If you were arrested out of state, use the letter to the governor of that state in the Revenge Kit. You can and should accomplish all this without a lawyer. Finally, make sure the local police agency that originally sent the report to the FBI follows up with an order to purge the record from their files as well.

Once your record has been expunged, you're legally entitled to answer no to the question Have you ever been arrested? This is the only correct answer if you want to prevent your one-time brush with the law from haunting you later on.

REVENGE KIT FOR ARREST

LETTER TO FBI FOR
COPY OF YOUR RECORD

To: Federal Bureau of Investigation
9th and Pennsylvania Avenue, N.W.
Washington, D.C. 20537

Attn: Recording Section

Please send me a copy of my own FBI record.

    Name:
    Date of Birth:
    Place of Birth:
    Race:
    Social Security Number:

I am enclosing a fingerprint card with my name and return address on the back, and a certified check/money order* for $5.

Yours truly,

* Even the FBI seems to worry about your bouncing a check on them that they won't be able to collect, which indicates how seriously law-enforcement agencies take bounced checks.

LETTER TO GOVERNOR'S OFFICE
TO BEGIN A PARDON APPLICATION

To: Governor
State:
Address:

Date:

Attn: Legal Affairs Secretary

I am interested in applying for a full pardon for an (arrest/conviction) in this state.

Please advise me as to the correct procedure and the statutory minimum time period after an (arrest/conviction), if any, before I may place this application.

Very truly yours,

NOTE: Usually you will apply by sending a cover letter stating your reasons for pursuing a pardon, a copy of your FBI record (if it shows no other arrests and will support your case), a statement of release from parole or probation, and a number of letters from respectable people attesting to your good character or reformation.

23
driving violations
Keeping Yourself in the Driver's Seat

Whatever kicks we used to get out of driving have been pretty well legislated or priced out of existence today. First the American convertible went the way of the dodo. Then gasoline began to cost about as much as imported beer. Less is more has truly become Detroit's motto, as you'll note from a horrified glance at the sticker prices of those toylike "downsize" models. About the only fun left is having your way with all the folks who torment you on life's highways and byways—wild and crazy drivers, police who ticket and even arrest you wrongfully, and the like.

DEFENSIVE DRIVING AND THE OFFENSIVE DRIVER

Maybe you've been cruising along at 55 mph with the flow of traffic, only to glance in your mirror and spot someone bearing down on you, very fast, from behind. Now this vehicular bully practically locks himself onto your rear bumper, furiously flashing his lights and leaning on his horn. Your speed is creeping up in self-defense. Your blood pressure is soaring because you can't change lanes in the heavy pattern of traffic to shake him off. You're trapped. What to do?

You could slam on your brakes and, once he's rear-ended you, drag the driver and his insurance company through court for the next six months. Unfortunately, the downside of this impulse is evident. The better strategy is to begin by forcing him to back off. If it's daytime, turn on your lights. As your taillights go on, it will appear to your attacker that you have stepped on your brakes. He will intuitively react by applying his own. As he drops back, you can start braking for real and gradually reduce your speed. He will then be forced to continue to slow down to avoid a collision. And no doubt he'll realize he can't move you from his path or induce you to drive as negligently as he does.

Eventually he'll dart from behind you into another lane of traffic. Take this opportunity to teach him an important lesson in driving safety. As he swings by, quickly memorize or—if possible—jot down his license-plate number. Note the color and style of his car—four-door, van, sports car, or whatever. If you're a car buff, you may be lucky enough to recognize the make, model, and year. Make a note of that. Then pull off the road at the next phone booth and call the operator to locate the closest police department. Present yourself at the police station and swear out a warrant for his arrest for assault.

Does this sound farfetched? It isn't. Assault is legally defined as putting one in imminent fear of bodily harm. There's little argument that you would have harmed your body in a car accident. And wasn't that imminent fear you experienced when you thought he was about to run into you? Your good judgment saved the day. You're entitled to protection from this sort of harassment, and enforcing that protection is well within your legal rights. A warrant for assault is based on criminal law. Although the complaint happens to involve a car, your defendant can't weasel out of the charge by claiming that you were driving too slowly. His hearing on assault charges will not examine either party's driving record or even focus on driving rules and regulations. The issue will be narrowly confined to whether or not he committed a criminal act by putting you in imminent fear of bodily harm. Since he did, it should not be hard for the prosecutor to prove.

Don't hesitate to seek this remedy because it seems to be too drastic. Your assailant is a menace to other people, too. You'll be doing everybody a favor by forcing him to see the consequences of his behavior before he actually kills somebody. And don't abandon your cause because of a lack of witnesses, since criminal acts seldom invite standing-room-only crowds. Your sworn statement of facts will start the machinery of justice closing in on your adversary. This costs you nothing but some future morning to attend a hearing. The police will trace the car and driver. The state's attorney will act on behalf of the state, with you as a mere complaining witness, to proceed with the trial. Your attacker will lose far more than a day from work. He will be charged with a crime, forced to bear the expenses of a defense, and possibly be found guilty of assault.

If that taste for blood stimulates you to go on, don't abandon civil remedies. Once your attacker has been found guilty of assault, he has opened the door to civil suit for the emotional damages you suffered. To be convicted in a criminal court, he must be found guilty "beyond a reasonable doubt." This burden of proof is diminished in a civil court. It shifts to a mere "preponderance of the evidence." You might say that to be a criminal, you must be the opposite of Ivory soap—99 $^{44}/_{100}$ percent impure. But to be civilly liable, you only need to be 51 percent in error. Since the heavier burden has already been met, there is every reason to believe that the lesser one will drop on your attacker as well. That leaves you to consider this question to the jury: What amount of money would adequately compensate you for being terrorized by someone who assaults you with his car as if he's in a World War II dogfight?

That may well be the $64,000 question. Talk to your free-consultation lawyer to see if you have a respectable case in your jurisdiction.

Overcoming a Wrongful Summons or Arrest

Police officers, even fresh out of the academy, have heard all the tired little excuses people use for wriggling out of tickets.

OFFICER: May I see your license and registration, please?

DRIVER: Sure. Uh, I wasn't going that fast for very long. I mean, I was just passing another car, so I had to speed up to get around him.

OFFICER: (silent while he studies the driver's license)

DRIVER: Besides, I was going downhill. That's just gravity that makes you go faster. Know what I mean?

OFFICER: (takes out summons book and begins writing)

DRIVER: Anyway, my speedometer's not right. I saw a road test of this car in *Motor Trend* that showed the speedometer clocked three or four miles under the true speed at 65. No kidding. So mine only said I was driving 60 when I was doing 65 . . . er, what I mean is . . .

OFFICER: Look, I didn't see you speeding. I was just giving you a warning for your broken taillight. But if your conscience bothers you that much, here's a summons for doing 65 in a 55 zone, too.

The first rule is to volunteer nothing unless you're asked a direct question. Then, depending on the situation and how guilty you are, maybe you should answer and maybe not. But the best course of action for the two major offenses—speeding and drunk driving—is to take advantage of the limitations of the technical measuring devices that police have to use. And if you can't fault them, save the tired excuses for a judge, who might believe them.

Driving Under the Influence. While we believe that real drunk drivers should be dealt with harshly, we also recognize the frustration of the *non*drunk driver who has been penalized by an imperfect detection system.

It's difficult, maybe impossible, to develop a foolproof instrument to measure whether somebody's too drunk to drive. Some jurisdictions use a fixed percentage of alcohol in your blood as the test. Others consider your total intake of alcohol. But none of them has been able to account for the biological differences among drivers. If you're a 98-pound sylph, your system will just not tolerate as much alcohol as that of a 400-pound sumo wrestler. And there are more subtle physiological differences, too. If you've ever been in the company of an alcoholic, you've probably noticed that he or she might literally keel over before you even realize the person has had a single drink. This tolerance for alcohol and maintenance level is so high that great amounts of liquor may have negligible effect on motor abilities. But a tenth of an alcoholic's intake would have near-teetotalers stumbling into walls if not swinging from chandeliers.

Let's assume that you're headed home from a party where you've had two or three drinks. You're definitely not drunk, but there's no denying you've been drinking, either. Unfortunately, your tire blows out, and the next thing you know, Trooper Rookie is on the scene to find out if he can be of assistance. The police have a chilling effect on most of us; you immediately start worrying about the fact that you've been drinking. You stammer and mumble as you strive to collect yourself. The officer comes closer to hear you, smells alcohol on your breath, and asks to see your license. In your nervousness, you drop your wallet and fifty-four credit cards spill out onto the street. Trooper Rookie now gets it into his head that you're intoxicated and asks whether you've been drinking. You admit honestly to two or three drinks.

That was your first mistake. You're under no legal obligation to offer this type of incriminating information. It will only force him to press the issue, since the drunk who opens his car door and falls out on the highway often owns up to that same two or three.

But having smelled alcohol on your breath and encouraged by your "confession," Trooper Rookie will most likely ask you to take an alcohol test. And you may have a choice, if your state law permits, between a "performance" test and a "percentage of alcohol" count. You'll also have the option to refuse the test. However, this will probably result in an automatic suspension of your license in most states. (Although there's a way to get around losing your license if it finally comes to that, as we'll see later in this chapter.)

If you're not drunk and your senses are not impaired for some other reason, take the *performance* test. Generally this involves a Simon Says routine of touching your nose and walking straight lines. If you can rub your stomach and pat your head at the same time, you're in business. Successful completion may earn you your way out, since Trooper Rookie will be embarrassed at being proven wrong, and you will probably find him as eager to see the last of you as you of him.

Perhaps physical feats are not your forte in the best of circumstances. What about blood tests? Breath analyzers? Take a hint from many defense attorneys. If you have alcohol in your system, these tests will provide hard-and-fast evidence against you. You will be indicting yourself. These procedures are measuring devices used to quantify the presence of alcohol, but they cannot make any conclusions about how this much alcohol affects you individually. If you don't think either test would give you a fighting chance to prove yourself sober, you might refuse to take the test at all and pay what you might hope would be the diminished consequences of your refusal.

One fact you should consider in deciding whether to take the test—and when—is the time it takes alcohol to affect you. You know your metabolism better than anyone else. If you just left the party a few minutes before, the last drink you had may still be sitting in your stomach where it won't affect you yet—booze contained in your stomach will not have you bursting into snatches of "Tiny Bubbles" in front of the cop, so you might choose to take the performance test then and there.

Penalties for failure to comply with testing requirements vary from jurisdiction to jurisdiction. Generally, there's that suspension of driving privileges. But this decision is often handed down in an administrative hearing, and you can present a defense. It provides you with the protection of a day in court. Whatever the outcome of the hearing, it does not result in conviction for drunken driving and the assessment of points on your record. It's merely a forum to chastise you for not being tested. So if you have some mitigating circumstances for not being tested—you had a bad cold and were afraid the officer would conclude that you were drunk, or you just refuse to take such tests on principle because they're coercive—bring them out here. And document your position with doctor's notes or sworn affidavits from passengers in your car that your driving wasn't impaired at all. We would recommend strongly that you see a lawyer for a free consultation first to help you establish a cogent argument.

The Perfect Crime? If you promise to never, ever try it yourself, we'll let you in on a guerrilla legal theory of avoiding arrest for drunken driving. It only applies to husbands and wives who have their car registered jointly in both their names, but here goes.

John and Mary are speeding home, recklessly swaying from one side of the road to the other, rip-roaring and unabashedly drunk. One of them somehow spots a police car in a parking lot, its lights off, hiding behind a dumpster waiting for people like them to flash by. So they quickly round the nearest corner, pull over, and both hop out fast. When the officer reaches them, he sees two obvious drunks propping themselves up on the side of a car.

"Who was driving?" the cop wants to know, so he can proceed with drunk-driving charges. John and Mary refuse to answer. In frustration, the officer drags both down to the police station and charges the two of them with driving while intoxicated.

Neither John nor Mary makes a statement, asserting their rights against self-incrimination. Then their day in court arrives, and one is tried right after the other. In each case, the officer can only testify to having seen a speeding car, following same, and spotting two obnoxious drunks supporting themselves against the same car parked. He simply can't tell who was driving. So he can't prove the state's case.

And both John and Mary refuse to take the stand, again citing the Fifth Amendment against self-incrimination. Each also refuses to testify against his or her spouse, relying on "familial immunity" from indicting your husband or wife. There is no such crime as conspiracy to drink and drive, no crime of accessory to drunk driving. Without a sufficient case against either of them, the judge throws both of them out of court because of a loophole in the law that seems to let drunken drivers squeeze through. But probably anybody who could pull it off is clearheaded enough to take the sobriety test and pass.

Speeding Tickets. Speed kills. No one can argue with that. And until recently, no one argued with radar. Not understanding how that Big Brother device operates, most drivers deferred to its mystical power.

But forget what you've heard in the past. If you've been targeted by radar on your Sunday-morning drive but *know* you were within the speed limit, relax. Ignore the dauntless officer writing out your ticket. Just prepare yourself to go to court armed with enough information to make the judge take notice.

Radar is prejudiced. While it does not sink to discriminating against religion, it is very much partial to size and even, to an extent, your car's color. This is how the procedure works. A police officer, generally camouflaged as some part of the terrain, sets her radar gun in the direction of oncoming traffic. At this point there is no victim in mind. The gun shoots off a beam of microwaves at a specified frequency. This beam travels in a straight line until it strikes an object that makes the microwaves bounce back to the radar system. Receivers pick up this bounced-back signal and determine the speed of the traveling car, which pops up on a meter for the police to read. Simple enough.

However, this very simplicity can make radar waves act simpleminded sometimes. Most laws based on radar reflect the notion that the speed readout the cop is monitoring on her meter gives the speed of the *first* car in the incoming pack. In fact, it's extremely difficult to correlate that readout with a particular car. When the traffic runs heavy, the radar meter can start clicking ahead of itself like a crazed taxi meter.

But radar's major deficiency is that microwaves bounce off some cars more readily than others. (In fact, they can be more partial to natural flora than to cars—a Florida speeding case determined that one radar meter had clocked a swaying tree as a vehicle zooming by at 85 miles per hour.) Only one radar beam is sent out, which is about a quarter-mile wide and travels three or four miles. So the beam is striking more than one object in that wide span, but only one deflection is picked up and recorded—the strongest. What makes a signal strong? Proximity, because the closer the object, the stronger the pulse; and size, since larger objects register stronger pulses. Even design counts—the sleeker the object, the better chance it has of evading the microwaves' tattletale registration.

What all this means is that, generally speaking, the bigger and boxier your car, the more likely it will be to send off a strong signal. This, coupled with the "first car" notion, can produce some odd registrations indeed. A law-abiding Toyota, followed closely by a mad-dog Mack truck, will be picked up as the offender. And some cars go scot-free by design. In a test run conducted by Patrick Bedard, he found the sleek and slippery Corvette to be "darned near invisible to radar." It couldn't be detected further than 520 feet from the transmitter. Compare that to a truck-and-trailer rig, which appeared onscreen from 7650 feet away. So radar isn't so accurate that you can't go to court on the day of your summons and question how the police officer administered it. Ask:

1. When was the meter last *calibrated* before you received the ticket, which should have been less than 15 minutes before your car registered on the gun.

2. How many cars were around, and how did the officer isolate your car.

In some states, you have the right to confront the radar gun when you're stopped to look at the digital readout. If it's been erased, you shouldn't receive a ticket.

You can also raise some of the issues in court that might gain sympathy from a judge, if not the cop who gave you the summons. If you were speeding because of a true emergency, bring substantiation in the form of a doctor's note that your spouse had just been rushed to the hospital or whatever. Most judges will view this as an extenuating circumstance. Or you could take your car to a mechanic and tell him that your speedometer is off, to get a statement that you can bring to court. And you can even fall back on the old standards. Maybe you really were going down a hill and picked up speed before you realized it. Pinpoint the location and go back to photograph the incline. Or argue that you were passing a car, so the speed at which you were clocked didn't represent your true *average* speed. Since you have little to lose and much to gain, you should always go in and plead your case rather than just pay the fine and plead guilty by default.

How to Hold onto Your License. If you've been arrested for an offense that's serious enough to mean suspension of your license—like driving while intoxicated—you could sit back and let the state take your license away without a whimper. But, if you really need your license, you can normally buy months and months of time by exhausting your state's appeals system. You will probably retain your driving privileges for your trouble, as well as prevent a rate hike on your car insurance. Although you'll need legal briefs and the like, you shouldn't need a legal superstar to handle your case. You can probably come out just as well with a newly minted lawyer who'll charge a low hourly rate. Here's what you can do in most states to use the system to your advantage.

1.　Start in *district* court, where your case will be heard first. Go the first time without counsel and ask for a postponement to find a lawyer. Ask your lawyer to try for another postponement or two. You might even ask for a jury trial.

2.　If you're found guilty in district court, keep going with an appeal to *circuit* court. This will buy more time. Now, circuit court just isn't set up for driving offenses. You'll be sitting there in a row of rapists and murderers, against whose truly heinous crimes your infraction will seem pretty trivial. State attorneys as a rule don't like to handle driving violations for this reason and may let you go just to clear your petty matter off the crowded calendar. Also, the process of witness attrition will be working in your behalf. Not even the arresting cop, who has to go to court on her day off, can be relied on to show up every time your case comes back to haunt her. But maybe the circuit court will uphold your conviction anyway.

3.　After months of dragging out your case, you now have another 30 days or so to submit it to the court of appeals. The appeals docket is a busy one, so your case will probably languish here for months. Even if you're still found guilty—and this will be the final judgment—you have some fight left in you.

4.　When you receive a letter from your department of motor vehicles, after the usual administrative delay once they receive the appeals verdict, you can request a hearing. This will come up in another month or so. Show up at the hearing and point out that you need your driver's license to work. A note from your employer to this effect will suffice. Most likely you'll at least be granted limited driving privileges for employment during the period of your suspension.

This should keep you in the driver's seat for the better part of a year, since your license can't be taken away while you exhaust the court system. And your chances of having the case dismissed at some point in the process are, as a practical matter, better than even.

FIGHTING IRKSOME PARKING VIOLATIONS

Most cities have too few parking spaces. And some make a very tiresome game out of figuring out where you can park legally. You see such a gaggle of conflicting signs, you can only assume that they cancel each other out, no cop would be able to figure them out either, and you might as well take a chance. Naturally you rush back from your errand ten minutes later and there's a colorful ticket grinning at you from under your windshield wiper. Or worse, you catch sight of your car rounding the next corner hitched to a municipal tow truck.

If you've been wronged, you shouldn't just pay your fine and forget it or, worse, ignore so many that you're presented with a $400 bill for outstanding tickets when you try to renew your registration. (In New York City, one scofflaw was recently handcuffed and arrested when police trailed him to his beat-up Buick. In a few short years, he had managed to accumulate $47,000 worth of unpaid tickets.) With a little effort, you can contest most tickets and save yourself the fine.

When you get a summons, go to court with some evidence on your behalf. First return to the scene with a camera and photograph (1) signs that contradict each other or are otherwise unintelligible, (2) overhanging trees or other obstructions that could have blocked your view of the sign, and/or (3) painted No Parking designations on curbs that long ago faded into oblivion. If a meter is broken, call the city and demand an investigation. Then get a copy of the report before you go to court or ask for a postponement until it's available to you. And if you get a parking ticket out of state, call your own state department of motor vehicles to see if there's reciprocity—does your state enforce the other's violations? If not, we wouldn't pay.

Or consider the ominous "towing zone." Many jurisdictions require, in addition to No Parking/Tow Zone warnings, a statement on the sign informing you where your car will be towed. The rationale for this ruling is that with the number of car thefts skyrocketing, you might jump to the conclusion that your missing car has been stolen, not towed. Check your local law to see if that's true where you live, and you may well be immune from towing charges. Surprisingly, municipal signs are often deficient in the necessary warning. But once the city realizes their error, they feel it's too expensive to correct and depend on the fact that not many people will know the law.

If you're willing to make a case of it, there's a heartening legal precedent that would turn municipal tow trucks into a mothball fleet forever. A Chicago man's truck was recently towed from an alley and impounded. When he went to pay the city's ransom and claim his vehicle, he was given a parking ticket as well— an all-too-familiar scenario, but this time with a fairy-tale ending. Fed up and frustrated, he sued in federal court, alleging (1) lack of "due process" before they took his property from him, and (2) no finding of guilt prior to his punishment. The US district judge agreed. He ordered not only reimbursement to our hero, but to the other 70,000 to 120,000 similar victims in the Windy City since 1977. We're hoping that kind of legal revenge takes hold. The Constitution says you can't be deprived of your property without due process. But whether similar rulings in other states will put an end to these legalized car thefts remains to be seen.

REVENGE KIT FOR DRIVING VIOLATIONS

LETTER REQUESTING COPY
OF DRIVING RECORD

To: Department of Motor Vehicles
Address:
Date:

Re: (Your Name)
Control Number: _____
(from license)

To Whom It May Concern:

Please send me a copy of my driving record as of the date written above. I'm enclosing my check for $_____ for processing.

Very truly yours,

(Call first to find out the fee. Then when you receive your record, check it carefully for errors.)

STATES IN WHICH YOU
CAN'T USE A RADAR DETECTOR

As of this writing, radar detectors are outlawed only in the following states:

Michigan   Connecticut
Virginia   Washington, DC
Kentucky

If you live elsewhere, we think it's a good investment.

24
burglars, thieves, and muggers

Do Unto Them as They Do Unto You

If anyone can turn a mild taste for revenge into a savage hunger, it's the criminal who burglarizes your home, steals a new cassette deck from your car, or hits you over the head and takes your wristwatch and wallet. This is especially true after the criminal, who has been convicted, strolls home on probation; but you can't even reclaim your property because it's long since been sold to some fence.

How to Avoid Being Sued by Your Burglar

Burglars seem to possess a theatrical flair for righteous indignation, like the clumsy second-story man who fell down an elevator shaft in a warehouse he was looting, then turned around to sue the owner for damages. He collected. So did the sneak thief who robbed a Laundromat's coin machines in Florida, unaware that the owner had rigged a camera to take his candid photograph. When the burglar's photo appeared on the Laundromat bulletin board with the caption THIEF! he sued and recovered damages for the slur on his good character, since he had yet to be convicted.

The law says, in effect, that you have a right to protect your personal property, but your burglar's human rights to life and limb are more important. So if you're a wary type who likes to install spring-loaded rifles and other deadly paraphernalia around the house, you're asking for trouble. Particularly if you dispatch the unarmed fifteen-year-old neighbor's kid who just broke in to steal your Valium (just when you needed it!). And watch what you say about someone who's violated your house or business until after the suspect is convicted. Otherwise that aggrieved party may sue for libel or slander. Fortunately there's a more profitable way to deal with burglars and other criminals who've practiced their skills on you, and it's perfectly legal.

Taking Criminals to Civil Court

Most professional burglars and thieves aren't as destitute as you might think. In fact, many of them are middle-income earners just like you, who have their own cars and stereos if not their own stock portfolios. Muggers tend to be a lot lower in the social strata, but that doesn't mean they don't own personal property.

When a criminal who has victimized you is caught and goes to trial, have a lawyer run a credit check on her or him. If the lawyer turns up some apparent assets such as a regular job, a house, or a car, start by demanding restitution of the prosecutor and judge in the criminal case. That means that as a condition of the usual light or nonexistent sentence, the thief will have to pay you back for what you lost. (Be sure to remember all the cash you had on your person or in your house—most victims shortchange themselves in this accounting under stress.)

But you're not through yet. Now you can sue the convicted criminal for consequential damages in small-claims or civil court. The state has already been vindicated in the criminal process, but you haven't. And you'll have a pretty ironclad case, because your defendant has already been tried according to a stricter standard of evidence in criminal court than you need for an award in the civil arena.

But be sure to assess *all* your damages—medical bills, time off work, lawyer's fees, and whatever else you've suffered as a consequence of the crime.

Many professional criminals who find that you're plunging into their assets for a change will try to play on your sympathy. This is all in a day's work having their lawyer recite a heartrending story of childhood deprivation and pressing family illness designed to sway most middle-class victims to show mercy. So be fair. Grant the criminals as much consideration as they allowed you when they committed the crime. Mercy may be a virtue and therefore its own reward, but revenge is sweeter, at least with criminals.

REVENGE KIT FOR BURGLARS, THIEVES, AND MUGGERS

HOW TO FILE AGAINST YOUR CRIMINAL IN CIVIL COURT

Begin by picking the proper court with jurisdiction over the subject matter. For most revenge purposes, you'll be dealing with small-claims court or district court.

However, a word on "larger" courts—often called circuit courts—is in order. If you decide to go after your personal Son of Sam (or rapist, as singer Connie Francis did) for more than five-thousand dollars, you will want a court that pays redress for grander losses. There are many theories for recovery. Just a few are intentional infliction of emotional distress, trespass, conversion, and invasion of your right to privacy. But you'll need a lawyer to litigate in district court.

In the event that you've elected not to go for broke, a small-claims court (with jurisdiction up to $1,000) or district court (generally up to $5,000) is your forum.

Follow these steps, asking the clerk of your court for additional guidance if necessary.

Pick your court based on the appropriate amount of money you are seeking to recover and the appropriate jurisdiction over the person or property of the defendant.

File your statement of claim. Small-claims courts have printed forms for this purpose. To be on the safe side, fill it out and run it by the clerk for perusal. He or she should be able to let you know if you're on the money, so to speak. Your pleading should include a clear and concise statement of the facts and must contain a demand for a judgment.

(While you're generally entitled to elect a jury trial in cases with over $500 in controversy, we can't recommend you go this route without a lawyer.)

Serve the defendant with a summons, through the court and its sheriff, by registered mail, or by private process server.

Once the defendant is served, you as plaintiff are entitled to "discover" from the defendant any relevant, nonprivileged information to prepare for the pending suit. But in most cases you'll handle on your own, these procedures probably won't be necessary.

The next step is to put your case before the court on the trial date. Be prepared with relevant witnesses and evidence.

But we have a shortcut for you. Remember that the crook you're suing is not John Q. Citizen. This breed prefers to stay out of court and isn't particularly noted for assuming responsibilities graciously.

So when you file in court, there's a good chance your criminal won't even show for trial. Banking on that hope, file a *motion for summary judgment* with your original pleading. This requests the court to rule in your favor, based on the fact that there is no genuine dispute over any material fact in the case and that the law is on your side. Support this position with affidavits and necessary documentation. You may get lucky and convince the judge of your position and get a ruling "summarily," meaning no hearing for your burglar or mugger.

Of course, we've assumed that your criminal is out on probation, as most are. But sometimes, albeit rarely, convicted criminals actually go to county jail or a state prison, depending on the severity of their offenses. This opens up an even more intriguing possibility for you. Now your defendant *has* to show up in court, because you'll file what's known as a writ of habeas corpus ad testificitum to ensure that your defendant will be brought to civil court to testify in your action against him—probably wearing jail garb and handcuffed, too, which tends to influence judges, despite what anyone says.

The nicest bonus in this case is that when you win, you can attach your defendant's assets with little trouble, since he won't be around to hide his car, bank accounts, or other property.

COLLECTING A JUDGMENT

We have yet to witness a judge hand down a judgment in favor of the plaintiff and have the defendant saunter over, shake hands, and gallantly hand over a check murmuring about the better man having won. In fact, you might have to continue your campaign for justice by pursuing supplementary proceedings.

Remember that a judgment usually constitutes a "lien" on real estate of the debtor lying within the county that the order comes from. Assuming failure to pay:

Record the judgment.

File a supplementary proceeding in the same court that ordered the judgment.

Allege the defendant's failure to pay and request "discovery" from the defendant as to his assets, salary, or any other form of legitimate income.

The defendant, upon proper service, will be compelled to provide the information.

Once his information is in hand, levy the assets of your choice through the sheriff by a "writ of attachment." (Go after a far more valuable item than necessary. For example, forego that $200 watch for your $150 lien and attach his $8400 Pontiac Firebird. While you can't keep the balance after his car is sold at auction, you've greatly inconvenienced him and to an extent paid him back for your trouble.)

If the defendant has no assets of any value, but has a job, request a wage lien and have the sheriff "garnishee" his salary through his employer.

Appendix I

Industry Arbitration Sources

If you want to submit a problem for arbitration, call one of these groups listed by industry. We would say that, overall, you have a 50–50 chance of having your way through mediation. Thus we recommend the other tactics discussed in this book as more rewarding but suggest you try mediation when you want redress without too much of a struggle.

Automotive Consumer Action Program (AUTOCAP)
Statewide Panels:

Connecticut	1-800-842-2276
Delaware	302-647-5100
Idaho	208-342-7779
Kentucky	502-583-4555
Louisiana	504-343-8383
Oklahoma	405-239-2603
Oregon	503-233-6044
Texas	512-476-2686
Utah	801-355-7473

Local Panels:

Chevy Chase	301-657-3200
Cleveland	216-241-2880
Denver	303-222-1544
Indianapolis	317-631-6301
Louisville	502-583-0279
New Orleans	504-581-2777
Orlando	305-647-5100
Toledo	419-531-7154
Williamsville	716-634-9611

Direct Mail/Marketing Association
  Mail Order Action Line
  6 E. 43 Street
  New York, N.Y. 10017
  212-689-4977

Direct Selling Association
(door-to-door sales)
  Director of Consumer Affairs
  Suite 610
  1730 M Street N.W.
  Washington, D.C. 20036
  202-293-5760

Electronic Industries Association
  Office of Consumer Affairs
  2001 I Street, N.W.
  Washington, D.C. 10006
  202-457-4900

Furniture Industry Consumer
  Advisory Panel
  P.O. Box 951
  High Point, NC 27261
  919-885-5065

Insurance Consumer Action Panel
  640 Investment Building
  Washington, DC 20005
  202-628-1300

International Fabricare Institute
  (Dry Cleaners)
  12251 Tech Road
  Silver Springs, MD 20904
  301-622-1900

Jewelers Vigilance Committee
  919 Third Avenue
  New York, NY 10022
  212-753-1304

Major Appliance Consumer Action Panel
  20 N. Wacker
  Chicago, IL 60606
  800-621-0477
  312-236-3223

Photo Marketing Association
  Consumer Affairs Department
  603 Lansing Avenue
  Jackson, MI 49202
  517-783-2807

The Dealers and Retreaders Association
  Field Operations Department
  1343 L Street, NW
  Washington, DC 20005
  202-638-6650
  Indiana: 317-631-8124
  Wisconsin: 414-774-6590

Appendix II

Federal Information Centers

To find the right government agency in a hurry, call the Federal Information Center nearest you. (All numbers are local or toll-free.) Describe the complaint you want to file or problem you need to resolve, and the Center will refer you to the appropriate agency immediately.

ALABAMA

Birmingham
205-322-8591
Toll-free tieline to
Atlanta, GA

Mobile
205-438-1421
Toll-free tieline to
New Orleans, LA

ALASKA

Anchorage
907-271-3650
Federal Building and
U.S. Courthouse
701 C St.
99513

ARIZONA

Phoenix
602-261-3313
Federal Building
230 North First Ave.
85025

Tucson
602-622-1511
Toll-free tieline to
Phoenix

ARKANSAS

Little Rock
501-378-6177
Toll-free tieline to
Memphis, TN

CALIFORNIA

Los Angeles
213-688-3800
Federal Building
300 North Los Angeles
St.
90012

Sacramento
916-440-3344
Federal Building and
U.S. Courthouse
650 Capitol Mall
95814

San Diego
714-293-6030
Federal Building
880 Front St.
Room 1S11
92188

San Francisco
415-556-6600
Federal Building and
U.S. Courthouse
450 Golden Gate Ave.
P.O. Box 36082
94102

San Jose
408-275-7422
Toll-free tieline to
San Francisco

Santa Ana
714-836-2386
Toll-free tieline to
Los Angeles

COLORADO

Colorado Springs
303-471-9491
Toll-free tieline to
Denver

Denver
303-837-3602
Federal Building
1961 Stout St.
80294

Pueblo
303-544-9523
Toll-free tieline to
Denver

CONNECTICUT

Hartford
203-527-2617
Toll-free tieline to
New York City

New Haven
203-624-4720
Toll-free tieline to
New York City

**DISTRICT OF
COLUMBIA**

Washington
202-755-8660
Seventh and D Sts.,
SW.
Room 5716
20407

FLORIDA

Fort Lauderdale
305-522-8531
Toll-free tieline to
Miami

Jacksonville
904 354 4756
Toll-free tieline to
St. Petersburg

Miami
305-350-4155
Federal Building
51 Southwest
First Ave.
33130

Orlando
305-422-1800
Toll-free tieline to
St. Petersburg

St. Petersburg
813-893-3495
William C. Cramer
Federal Building
144 First Ave., South
33701

Tampa
813-229-7911
Toll-free tieline to
St. Petersburg

West Palm Beach
305-833-7566
Toll-free tieline to
Miami

Northern Florida
(Sarasota, Manatee,
Polk, Osceola, Orange,
Seminole, and Volusia
counties and north)
800-282-8556
Toll-free line to
St. Petersburg

Southern Florida
(Charlotte, De Soto,
Hardee, Highlands,
Okeechobee, Indian
River, and Brevard
counties and south)
800-432-6668
Toll-free line to Miami

GEORGIA

Atlanta
404-221-6891
Federal Building and
U.S. Courthouse
75 Spring St., SW.
30303

HAWAII

Honolulu
808-546-8620
Federal Building
300 Ala Moana Blvd.
P.O. Box 50091
96850

ILLINOIS

Chicago
312-353-4242
Everett McKinley
Dirksen Building
219 South Dearborn St.
Room 250
60604

INDIANA

Gary/Hammond
219 883 4110
Toll-free tieline to
Indianapolis

Indianapolis
317-269-7373
Federal Building
575 North Pennsylvania
46204

IOWA

Des Moines
515-284-4448
Federal Building
210 Walnut Street
50309

Other Iowa locations:
Toll-free line to
Des Moines
800-532-1556

KANSAS

Topeka
913-295-2866
Federal Building and
U.S. Courthouse
444 SE Quincy
66683

Other Kansas locations:
800-432-2934
Toll-free line to Topeka

KENTUCKY

Louisville
502-582-6261
Federal Building
600 Federal Place
40202

LOUISIANA

New Orleans
504-589-6696
U.S. Postal Service
Building
701 Loyola Ave.
Room 1210
70113

MARYLAND

Baltimore
301-962-4980
Federal Building
31 Hopkins Plaza
21201

MASSACHUSETTS

Boston
617-223-7121
J.F.K. Federal Building
Cambridge St.
Room E-130
02203

MICHIGAN

Detroit
313-226-7016
McNamara Federal
Building
477 Michigan Ave.
Room 103
48226

Grand Rapids
616-451-2628
Toll-free tieline to
Detroit

MINNESOTA

Minneapolis
612-725-2073
Federal Building and
U.S. Courthouse
110 South 4th St.
55401

MISSOURI

Kansas City
816-374-2466
Federal Building
601 East Twelfth St.
64106

St. Louis
314-425-4106
Federal Building
1520 Market St.
63103

Other Missouri
locations within area
code 314:
800-392-7711
Toll-free line to
St. Louis

Other Missouri
locations within area
codes 816 and 417:
800-892-5808
Toll-free line to
Kansas City

NEBRASKA

Omaha
402-221-3353
U.S. Post Office and
Courthouse
215 North 17th St.
68102

**Other Nebraska
locations:**
800-642-8383
Toll-free line to
Omaha

NEW JERSEY

Newark
201-645-3600
Federal Building
970 Broad St.
07102

Paterson/Passaic
201-523-0717
Toll-free tieline to
Newark

Trenton
609-396-4400
Toll-free tieline to
Newark

NEW MEXICO

Albuquerque
505-766-3091
Federal Building and
U.S. Courthouse
500 Gold Ave., SW.
87102

Santa Fe
505-983-7743
Toll-free tieline to
Albuquerque

NEW YORK

Albany
518-463-4421
Toll-free tieline to
New York City

Buffalo
716-846-4010
Federal Building
111 West Huron
14202

New York
212-264-4464
Federal Building
26 Federal Plaza
Room 1-114
10278

Rochester
716-546-5075
Toll-free tieline to
Buffalo

Syracuse
315-476-8545
Toll-free tieline to
Buffalo

NORTH CAROLINA

Charlotte
704-376-3600
Toll-free tieline to
Atlanta, GA

OHIO

Akron
216-375-5638
Toll-free tieline to
Cleveland

Cincinnati
513-684-2801
Federal Building
550 Main St.
45202

Cleveland
216-522-4040
Federal Building
1240 East Ninth St.
44199

Columbus
614-221-1014
Toll-free tieline to
Cincinnati

Dayton
513-223-7377
Toll-free tieline to
Cincinnati

Toledo
419-241-3223
Toll-free tieline to
Cleveland

OKLAHOMA

Oklahoma City
405-231-4868
U.S. Post Office and
Courthouse
201 Northwest 3rd St.
73102

Tulsa
918-584-4193
Toll-free tieline to
Oklahoma City

OREGON

Portland
503-221-2222
Federal Building
1220 Southwest Third
Ave.
Room 109
97204

PENNSYLVANIA

Allentown/Bethlehem
215-821-7785
Toll-free tieline to
Philadelphia

Philadelphia
215-597-7042
Federal Building
600 Arch St.
19106

Pittsburgh
412-644-3456
Federal Building
1000 Liberty Ave.
15222

Scranton
717-346-7081
Toll-free tieline to
Philadelphia

RHODE ISLAND

Providence
401-331-5565
Toll-free tieline to
Boston, MA

TENNESSEE

Chattanooga
615-265-8231
Toll-free tieline to
Memphis

Memphis
901-521-3285
Clifford Davis Federal
Building
167 North Main St.
38103

Nashville
615-242-5056
Toll-free tieline to
Memphis

TEXAS

Austin
512-472-5494
Toll-free tieline to
Houston

Dallas
214-767-8585
Toll-free tieline to
Fort Worth

Fort Worth
817-334-3624
Lanham Federal
Building
819 Taylor St.
76102

Houston
713-226-5711
Federal Building and
U.S. Courthouse
515 Rusk Ave.
77208

San Antonio
512-224-4471
Toll-free tieline to
Houston

UTAH

Ogden
801-399-1347
Toll-free tieline to
Salt Lake City

Salt Lake City
801-524-5353
Federal Building
125 South State St.
Room 1205
84138

VIRGINIA

Newport News
804-244-0480
Toll-free tieline to
Norfolk

Norfolk
804-441-3101
Federal Building
200 Granby Mall
Room 120
23510

Richmond
804-643-4928
Toll-free tieline to
Norfolk

Roanoke
703-982-8591
Toll-free tieline to
Norfolk

WASHINGTON

Seattle
206-442-0570
Federal Building
915 Second Ave.
98174

Tacoma
206-383-5230
Toll-free tieline to
Seattle

WISCONSIN

Milwaukee
414-271-2273
Toll-free tieline to
Chicago, IL

Index